A SHORT HISTORY OF
RECONSTRUCTION,
1863–1877

A SHORT HISTORY OF
RECONSTRUCTION

1863–1877

ERIC FONER

Illustrated

UPDATED EDITION

HARPER**PERENNIAL** ● MODERN**CLASSICS**

NEW YORK ● LONDON ● TORONTO ● SYDNEY ● NEW DELHI ● AUCKLAND

HARPER**PERENNIAL** ● MODERN**CLASSICS**

The map "Major Physical and Cash Crop Regions of the South" on page 57 is adapted from Sam Hilliard, *The Atlas of Antebellum Southern Agriculture,* by permission of Louisiana State University Press. Copyright © 1984 by Louisiana State University Press.

HarperCollins books may be purchased for educational, business, or sales promotional use. For information, please email the Special Sales Department at SPsales@harpercollins.com.

FIRST HARPER PERENNIAL EDITION PUBLISHED 1990.

FIRST HARPER PERENNIAL MODERN CLASSICS EDITION PUBLISHED 2015.

Library of Congress Cataloguing-in-Publication Data

Foner, Eric.
　　[Reconstruction]
　　A short history of Reconstruction, 1863–1877 / Eric Foner.
—1ˢᵗ ed.
　　　　p.　cm.
　　Abridged ed. of: Reconstruction. c1988.
　　Bibliography: p.
　　Includes index.
ISBN 0-06-055182-8 — ISBN 0-06-096431-6 (pbk.)
ISBN 978-0-06-096431-3 (pbk.)
1. Reconstruction.　2. United States—Politics and
government—1863–1877.
3. African Americans—History—1863–1877.　I. Title.
E668.F662　1990
973.8—dc20　　　89-45347

ISBN 978-0-06-237086-0 (updated edition)

22 23 24 25 26　LBC　17 16 15 14 13

For Daria

Contents

Illustrations

Following page 48

"Emancipated Negroes Celebrating the Emancipation Proclamation of President Lincoln"
Unidentified Civil War Sergeant
Robert G. Fitzgerald in His Navy Uniform
Black Refugees Crossing the Rappahannock River
"Secret Meeting of Southern Unionists"
"The Riots in New York"
Richmond Ruins
Laura M. Towne and Pupils
"Prayer Meeting"
Unidentified Black Family
"The Freedmen's Bureau"
Democratic Broadside
"Rice Cultivation on the Ogeechee"
"The Sugar Harvest in Louisiana"
Cotton Pickers
An Upcountry Family
Andrew Johnson
Thaddeus Stevens
Lyman Trumbull
Charles Sumner

Following page 144

"The First Vote"
"Electioneering at the South"
Benjamin Turner
P. B. S. Pinchback
Blanche K. Bruce
Robert Smalls
Robert B. Elliott
James L. Alcorn
William G. Brownlow
Henry C. Warmoth
Albion W. Tourgée
Adelbert Ames
Democratic Campaign Badge
Zebulon Vance
John B. Gordon
Wade Hampton

William H. Trescot
Klan Warning
"Two Members of the Ku-Klux Klan in Their Disguises"
Klansmen Firing into a Home
Victoria Woodhull
Jay Gould
Roscoe Conkling
Crazy Horse
Susan B. Anthony
Railroad Workers
"Capital and Labor"
The Corliss Engine
Ruins of the Pittsburgh Round House
"And Not This Man?"
"This is a White Man's Government"
"Colored Rule in a Reconstructed (?) State"

Maps

Preface

Revising interpretations of the past is intrinsic to the study of history. But no period of the American experience has, in the last twenty-five years, seen a broadly accepted point of view so completely overturned as Reconstruction—the dramatic, controversial era that followed the Civil War. Since the early 1960s, a profound alteration of the place of blacks within American society, newly uncovered evidence, and changing definitions of history itself have combined to transform our understanding of Reconstruction.

The scholarly study of Reconstruction began early in this century with the work of William A. Dunning, John W. Burgess, and their students. The interpretation elaborated by the Dunning school may be briefly summarized as follows: When the Civil War ended, the white South accepted the reality of military defeat, stood ready to do justice to the emancipated slaves, and desired above all a quick reintegration into the fabric of national life. Before his death, Abraham Lincoln had embarked on a course of sectional reconciliation, and during Presidential Reconstruction (1865–67) his successor, Andrew Johnson, attempted to carry out Lincoln's magnanimous policies. Johnson's efforts were opposed and eventually thwarted by the Radical Republicans in Congress. Motivated by an irrational hatred of Southern "rebels" and the desire to consolidate their party's national ascendancy, the Radicals in 1867 swept aside the Southern governments Johnson had established and fastened black suffrage on the defeated South. There followed the sordid period of Congressional or Radical Reconstruction (1867–77), an era of corruption presided over by unscrupulous "carpetbaggers" from the North, unprincipled Southern white "scalawags," and ignorant blacks unprepared for freedom and incapable of properly exercising the political rights Northerners had thrust upon them. After much needless suffering, the South's white community banded together to overthrow these governments and restore "home rule" (a euphemism for white supremacy). All told, Reconstruction was the darkest page in the saga of American history.

During the 1920s and 1930s, new studies of Johnson's career and new investigations of the economic wellsprings of Republican policy reinforced the prevailing disdain for Reconstruction. Johnson's biographers portrayed him as a courageous defender of constitutional liberty whose actions stood above reproach. Simultaneously, historians of the Progressive School, who viewed political ideologies as little more than masks for crass economic ends, further undermined the Radicals' reputation by portraying them as agents of Northern capitalism who cynically used the issue of black rights to foster Northern economic domination of the South.

From the first appearance of the Dunning School, dissenting voices had been raised, initially by a handful of survivors of the Reconstruction era and the small fraternity of black historians. In 1935, the black activist and scholar W. E. B. Du Bois published *Black Reconstruction in America*, a monumental study that portrayed Reconstruction as an idealistic effort to construct a democratic, interracial political order from the ashes of slavery, as well as a phase in a prolonged struggle between capital and labor for control of the South's economic resources. His book closed with an indictment of a profession whose writings had ignored the testimony of the principal actor in the drama of Reconstruction—the emancipated slave—and sacrificed scholarly objectivity on the altar of racial bias. "One fact and one alone," Du Bois wrote, "explains the attitude of most recent writers toward Reconstruction; they cannot conceive of Negroes as men." In many ways, *Black Reconstruction* anticipated the findings of modern scholarship. At the time, however, it was largely ignored.

Despite its remarkable longevity and powerful hold on the popular imagination, the demise of the traditional interpretation was inevitable. Its fundamental underpinning was the conviction, to quote one member of the Dunning School, of "negro incapacity." Once objective scholarship and modern experience rendered its

racist assumptions untenable, familiar evidence read very differently, new questions suddenly came into prominence, and the
entire edifice had to fall.

It required, however, not simply the evolution of scholarship but
a profound change in the nation's politics and racial attitudes to deal
the final blow to the Dunning School. If the traditional interpretation reflected, and helped to legitimize, the racial order of a society
in which blacks were disenfranchised and subjected to discrimination in every aspect of their lives, Reconstruction revisionism bore
the mark of the modern civil rights movement. In the 1960s, the
revisionist wave broke over the field, destroying, in rapid succession, every assumption of the traditional viewpoint. First, scholars
presented a drastically revised account of national politics. New
works portrayed Andrew Johnson as a stubborn, racist politician
incapable of responding to the unprecedented situation that confronted him as President, and acquitted the Radicals—reborn as
idealistic reformers genuinely committed to black rights—of vindictive motives and the charge of being the stalking-horses of Northern
capitalism. Moreover, Reconstruction legislation was shown to be
not simply the product of a Radical cabal, but a program that
enjoyed broad support in both Congress and the North at large.

Even more startling was the revised portrait of Republican rule in
the South. So ingrained was the old racist version of Reconstruction
that it took an entire decade of scholarship to prove the essentially
negative contentions that "Negro rule" was a myth and that Reconstruction represented more than "the blackout of honest government." The establishment of public school systems, the granting of
equal citizenship to blacks, and the effort to revitalize the devastated
Southern economy refuted the traditional description of the period as
a "tragic era" of rampant misgovernment. Revisionists pointed out as
well that corruption in the Reconstruction South paled before that of
the Tweed Ring, Crédit Mobilier scandal, and Whiskey Rings in the
post–Civil War North. By the end of the 1960s, Reconstruction was
seen as a time of extraordinary social and political progress for blacks.
If the era was "tragic," it was because change did not go far enough,
especially in the area of Southern land reform.

Even when revisionism was at its height, however, its more
optimistic findings were challenged, as influential historians portrayed change in the post–Civil War years as fundamentally "superficial." Persistent racism, these postrevisionist scholars argued, had

negated efforts to extend justice to blacks, and the failure to distribute land prevented the freedmen from achieving true autonomy and made their civil and political rights all but meaningless. In the 1970s and 1980s, a new generation of scholars, black and white, extended this skeptical view to virtually every aspect of the period. Recent studies of Reconstruction politics and ideology have stressed the "conservatism" of Republican policymakers, even at the height of Radical influence, and the continued hold of racism and federalism despite the extension of citizenship rights to blacks and the enhanced scope of national authority. Studies of federal policy in the South portrayed the army and the Freedmen's Bureau as working hand in glove with former slaveholders to thwart the freedmen's aspirations and force them to return to plantation labor. At the same time, investigations of Southern social history emphasized the survival of the old planter class and the continuities between the Old South and the New. The postrevisionist interpretation represented a striking departure from nearly all previous accounts of the period, for whatever their differences, traditional and revisionist historians at least agreed that Reconstruction was a time of radical change. Summing up a decade of writing, C. Vann Woodward observed in 1979 that historians now understood "how essentially nonrevolutionary and conservative Reconstruction really was."

In emphasizing that Reconstruction was part of the ongoing evolution of Southern society rather than a passing phenomenon, the postrevisionists made a salutary contribution to the study of the period. The description of Reconstruction as "conservative," however, did not seem altogether persuasive when one reflected that it took the nation fully a century to implement its most basic demands, while others are yet to be fulfilled. Nor did the theme of continuity yield a fully convincing portrait of an era that contemporaries all agreed was both turbulent and wrenching in its social and political change. Over a half-century ago, Charles and Mary Beard coined the term "the Second American Revolution" to describe a transfer in power, wrought by the Civil War, from the South's "planting aristocracy" to "Northern capitalists and free farmers." And in the latest shift in interpretive premises, attention to changes in the relative power of social classes has again become a central concern of historical writing. Unlike the Beards, however, who all but ignored the black experience, modern scholars tend to view emancipation itself as among the most revolutionary aspects of the period.

This book is an abridgment of my *Reconstruction: America's Unfinished Revolution, 1863–1877*, a comprehensive modern account of the period. The larger work necessarily touched on a multitude of issues, but certain broad themes unified the narrative and remain crucial in this shorter version. The first is the centrality of the black experience. Rather than passive victims of the actions of others or simply a "problem" confronting white society, blacks were active agents in the making of Reconstruction whose quest for individual and community autonomy did much to establish the era's political and economic agenda. Although thwarted in their bid for land, blacks seized the opportunity created by the end of slavery to establish as much independence as possible in their working lives, consolidate their families and communities, and stake a claim to equal citizenship. Black participation in Southern public life after 1867 was the most radical development of the Reconstruction years.

The transformation of slaves into free laborers and equal citizens was the most dramatic example of the social and political changes unleashed by the Civil War and emancipation. A second purpose of this study is to trace the ways Southern society as a whole was remodeled, and to do so without neglecting the local variations in different parts of the South. By the end of Reconstruction, a new Southern class structure and several new systems of organizing labor were well on their way to being consolidated. The ongoing process of social and economic change, moreover, was intimately related to the politics of Reconstruction, for various groups of blacks and whites sought to use state and local government to promote their own interests and define their place in the region's new social order.

The evolution of racial attitudes and patterns of race relations, and the complex interconnection of race and class in the postwar South, form a third theme of this book. Racism was pervasive in mid-nineteenth-century America and at both the regional and national levels constituted a powerful barrier to change. Yet despite racism, a significant number of Southern whites were willing to link their political fortunes with those of blacks, and Northern Republicans came, for a time, to associate the fate of the former slaves with their party's raison d'être and the meaning of Union victory in the Civil War. Moreover, in the critical, interrelated issues of land and labor and the persistent conflict between planters' desire to reexert control over their labor force and blacks' quest for economic independence, race and class were inextricably linked. As a Washington newspaper noted in 1868, "It is impossible to separate the question of color from the question of labor, for the reason that the majority of the laborers . . . throughout the Southern States are colored people, and nearly all the colored people are at present laborers."

The chapters that follow also seek to place the Southern story within a national context. The book's fourth theme is the emergence during the Civil War and Reconstruction of a national state possessing vastly expanded authority and a new set of purposes, including an unprecedented commitment to the ideal of a national citizenship whose equal rights belonged to all Americans regardless of race. Originating in wartime exigencies, the activist state came to embody the reforming impulse deeply rooted in postwar politics. And Reconstruction produced enduring changes in the laws and Constitution that fundamentally altered federal–state relations and redefined the meaning of American citizenship. Yet because it threatened traditions of local autonomy, produced political corruption, and was so closely associated with the new rights of blacks, the rise of the state inspired powerful opposition, which, in turn, weakened support for Reconstruction.

Finally, this study examines how changes in the North's economy and class structure affected Reconstruction. That the Reconstruction of the North receives less attention than its Southern counterpart reflects, in part, the absence of a detailed historical literature on the region's social and political structure in these years. Nonetheless, Reconstruction cannot be fully understood without attention to its distinctively Northern and national dimensions.

This account of Reconstruction begins not in 1865, but with the Emancipation Proclamation of 1863. I do this to emphasize the Proclamation's importance in uniting two major themes of this study—grass-roots black activity and the newly empowered national state—and to indicate that Reconstruction was not only a specific time period, but also the beginning of an extended historical process: the adjustment of American society to the end of slavery. The destruction of the central institution of antebellum Southern life permanently transformed the war's character and produced far-reaching conflicts and debates over the role former slaves and their descendants would play in American life and the meaning of the freedom they had acquired. These were the questions on which Reconstruction persistently turned.

Introduction to the
2014 Anniversary Edition

Historians, by and large, tend not to be very self-reflective. Autobiography, in vogue nowadays among anthropologists and English professors, seems to have little appeal in history departments. But the reissue of *Reconstruction: America's Unfinished Revolution* to mark the 150th anniversary of the volatile era that followed the American Civil War offers the occasion for some brief reflections on how the book was originally written, how historical scholarship on Reconstruction has evolved in the last quarter century, and why an understanding of the period remains essential today.

It was the late Richard Morris, a distinguished scholar of early American history, who asked me to write the volume on Reconstruction for the New American Nation Series, for which he and Henry Steele Commager served as editors. The year was 1975 and the invitation totally unexpected. To be sure, my first book dealt with the pre–Civil War Republican party, many of whose leaders went on to play pivotal roles in Reconstruction. But when Morris's letter arrived, I was nearing completion of a book on Tom Paine and was planning to embark on a history of American radicalism. I had written nothing on Reconstruction except for an essay on Thaddeus Stevens, the leader of the era's Radical Republicans.

Years before, it is true, I had made an initial foray into Reconstruction history in my American history class at Long Beach High School, in the suburb of New York City where I grew up. Our teacher was Mrs. Bertha Berryman, affectionately known among the students as Big Bertha (after a piece of World War I artillery). Following the then-dominant view of the era, Mrs. Berryman described the Reconstruction Act of 1867, which gave the right to vote to black men in the South, as the worst law in all of American history. I raised my hand and disagreed, suggesting that "the Alien and Sedition Acts were worse." Mrs. Berryman replied, "If you don't like the way I'm teaching, why don't you come in tomorrow and give your own lesson on Reconstruction?" This I proceeded to do, admittedly with the help of my father, himself a historian. My presentation was based largely on W. E. B. Du Bois's monumental work, *Black Reconstruction in America,* which insisted that Reconstruction was a pivotal moment in the long struggle for political and economic democracy in the United States and, indeed, the entire world.[1] At the end of the class, Mrs. Berryman, herself a believer in democratic decision-making, announced: "Class, you have heard me, and you have heard Eric. Now let us vote to see who is right." I wish I could report that my presentation carried the day. In fact, only one student voted for my interpretation, my intrepid friend Neil Kleinman.

It therefore seemed almost preordained when Morris offered me the chance to get even with Mrs. Berryman. I accepted, and soon discovered that I had agreed to take on a project with a checkered past. In 1948, Howard K. Beale had signed on to do the book; he died eleven years later without having written a word. Beale was succeeded by another great scholar of nineteenth-century America, David Donald. In 1969, Donald published an article reporting on a "personal problem"— in attempting to conceptualize the book, he had reached an impasse.[2] He found it impossible, he wrote, to synthesize in a single account the political, economic, social, and intellectual developments of the Reconstruction era, and the course of national, northern, and southern events.

---

[1] W. E. B. Du Bois, *Black Reconstruction in America* (New York, 1935).

[2] David Donald, "The Grand Theme in American Historical Writing," *Journal of Historical Studies,* 2 (Autumn 1969), 186-201.

Six years later he abandoned the project entirely to devote himself to a more manageable one, a biography of the writer Thomas Wolfe.

Most books in the New American Nation Series summarize, often very ably, the current state of historical scholarship, rather than rely on new research. I assumed I could do two or three years of reading and complete the book soon afterward. In fact, it took more than ten years to research and write. The turning point in the project came in 1978, when I taught for a semester at the University of South Carolina, in Columbia. There, in the State Archives, I encountered 121 thickly packed boxes of correspondence received by the state's Reconstruction governors. The letters contained an incredibly rich record, almost entirely untapped by scholars, of the grievances and aspirations of black and white Carolinians attempting to rebuild their lives after the Civil War. I read of utopian hopes and shattered dreams, struggles for human dignity and terrorist violence, racism and black-white cooperation, and how everyday life had become politicized in ways barely hinted at in the Reconstruction literature. I realized that to tell the story of Reconstruction I could not rely on existing scholarship—even though important works on one or another aspect of the period were appearing every year while I pursued the project—but would have to delve further into archival sources to discover the rich texture of everyday life. Like Du Bois half a century earlier, I became convinced that the freedpeople were the central actors in the drama of Reconstruction. Rather than simply victims of manipulation or passive recipients of the actions of others, as they had long been portrayed, the freedpeople were agents of change, whose struggle to breathe substantive meaning into the freedom they had acquired helped to establish the agenda of Reconstruction politics and to change the definition of freedom for all Americans.

Another unexpected development affected the project's development. For the 1980–81 academic year, I was invited to teach as the Pitt Professor of American History and Institutions at Cambridge University. Prompted by some of my colleagues there, I began to read about the aftermath of emancipation in the British Empire. I soon discovered that this literature, much of it untapped by scholars of American history (in contrast to the then-flourishing comparative study of slavery), approached social conflict in the post-slavery world in rather different ways than our own historical writing. Instead of defining the problem primarily as one of race relations, the predominant view in this country, scholars in Britain, Africa, and the Caribbean focused attention on the interrelated questions of access to land and control of labor. Former slaves everywhere struggled to secure economic autonomy while former planters, often aided by the British government, sought to encourage them to return to work on the plantations and, when unsuccessful, imported indentured laborers from China and India to take their place. The same issues of land and labor, I became convinced, were central to the aftermath of slavery in the Reconstruction South. In 1982, while working on this book, I published a brief volume, *Nothing But Freedom*, which focused on the labor question after the Civil War, and whose first chapter examined the transition from slavery to freedom outside the United States.[3]

My reading also underscored the uniqueness of Reconstruction, for unlike in most countries that abolished slavery, former slaves in the United States enjoyed a significant body of white allies, who brought into being the experiment of Radical Reconstruction. This enabled the freedpeople, within a few years of emancipation, to exercise a significant degree of local political power. Historians at that time were prone to describe Reconstruction as essentially conservative, since it adhered to constitutional forms and failed to distribute land to the former slaves. I became convinced that enfranchising the freedmen constituted, both in a comparative perspective and in the context of the racism of antebellum America, a radical experiment in interracial democracy.

Soon afterward, I returned to Columbia University, where I had received my doctorate, to teach, and there over the next few years the book was written. Anyone familiar with the historiography of Reconstruction will appreciate the irony in the fact that my research expenses were partly covered by the Department of History's Dunning Fund and that much of my reading took place in Burgess Library. For it was at Columbia at the turn of the century that William A. Dunning and John W. Burgess established the traditional school of Reconstruction scholarship. Dunning, Burgess, and their students were among the first generation of university-trained historians in the United States, and they developed insights still valuable to current historians—for example, that slavery was the fundamental cause of the Civil War, and that regional and class differences within white society helped to shape Reconstruction politics. Anticipating recent scholarship, Dun-

---

[3] Eric Foner, *Nothing But Freedom: Emancipation and Its Legacy* (Baton Rouge, 1983).

ning and Burgess insisted that Reconstruction must be understood in a national context, as part of the nineteenth century's nation-building process. The Dunning scholars also pioneered in the use of primary sources (at least those emanating from white Southerners) to tell the story of Reconstruction. Nonetheless, ingrained racism undermined the value of their works. Most of these scholars taught that blacks were "children" incapable of appreciating the freedom that had been thrust upon them, and that the North did a "monstrous thing" in granting them the right to vote.[4] The views of the Dunning School helped to freeze the white South for generations in unalterable opposition to any change in race relations, and justified decades of Northern indifference to Southern nullification of the Fourteenth and Fifteenth Amendments. By the time my book appeared, numerous scholars had exposed one or another weakness of the Dunning interpretation. *Reconstruction* was to drive the final nail into the coffin of the Dunning School and to offer an alternative account of the era.

With the publication of *Reconstruction*, I assumed I would turn my scholarly attention to other areas. But things did not turn out that way. In the course of my research, I had gathered an immense body of biographical information about black political leaders in the postwar South—justices of the peace, school board officials, sheriffs, and state legislators, as well as members of Congress—most of them unknown even to scholars. In 1993, I brought this information together in *Freedom's Lawmakers,* a directory containing capsule biographies of some 1,500 individuals. Generations of historians had ignored or denigrated these black officeholders, citing their alleged incompetence to justify the violent overthrow of Reconstruction and the South's long history of disenfranchising black voters. Claude Bowers' sensationalist bestseller of the 1920s, *The Tragic Era*, described Louisiana's Reconstruction legislature as a "zoo"; E. Merton Coulter wrote in 1947 that black officeholding was "the most exotic development in government in the history of white civilization . . . [and the] longest to be remembered, shuddered at, and execrated." My hope was to put these men, as it were, on the map of history, to make available the basic data concern-

---

[4] William A. Dunning, *Essays on the Civil War and Reconstruction* (New York, 1904), 384–85; John W. Burgess, *Reconstruction and the Constitution 1866–1876* (New York, 1902), 133. For a recent reassessment of the Dunning School, see John David Smith and J. Vincent Lowery, ed., *The Dunning School: Historians, Race, and the Meaning of Reconstruction* (Lexington, 2013).

ing their lives, and to bury such misconceptions as that Reconstruction's leaders were illiterate, propertyless, and incompetent.[5]

In addition, with Olivia Mahoney of the Chicago History Museum, I served as cocurator of an exhibition, "America's Reconstruction"—the first ever to be devoted exclusively to the period—that opened in 1995 at the Virginia Historical Society in Richmond and subsequently traveled to venues in New York City, Columbia, Raleigh, Tallahassee, and Chicago. It has recently been digitalized and can be viewed on the Internet.[6] In 2004, I served as an adviser for the first PBS television series on Reconstruction. The following year I published a history of emancipation and Reconstruction aimed at an audience outside the academic world, meant to accompany a film project on the era (which, unfortunately never came to fruition). And in *The Story of American Freedom*, I attempted to trace the contested meanings of freedom, a key theme of *Reconstruction*, over the entire course of American history from the Revolution to the close of the twentieth century.[7]

Reconstruction: America's Unfinished Revolution seeks to weave into a coherent narrative the political struggle over Reconstruction, the transition from slave to free labor in the South, the evolution of a new system of race relations, and the rise of a newly empowered national state, and to delineate how these processes interacted with one another. It deals with Reconstruction at all levels of society, from debates in Congress to struggles on individual plantations. And while the focus of Reconstruction lay in the South, it also addresses the dramatic changes that took place in the North and West in these years. It places the former slaves at the center of the story, but deals as well with numerous classes of white Americans—politicians, industrialists, laborers, and small farmers, among others.

In the quarter century since the book was published, new writing has continued to appear on virtually every aspect of the Reconstruction

---

[5] Eric Foner, *Freedom's Lawmakers: A Directory of Black Officeholders during Reconstruction* (rev. ed.: Baton Rouge, 1996); Claude G. Bowers, *The Tragic Era* (Cambridge, 1929), 364; E Merton Coulter, *The South During Reconstruction 1865–1877* (Baton Rouge, 1947), 141–44.

[6] The online version of the exhibit can be found at http://www.digitalhistory.uh.edu/exhibits/reconstruction/index.html. Eric Foner and Olivia Mahoney, *America's Reconstruction: People and Politics After the Civil War* (Baton Rouge, 1997) is a catalog of the exhibition.

[7] Eric Foner, *Forever Free: The Story of Emancipation and Reconstruction* (New York, 2005). (This volume contains inserts assembled by Joshua Brown examining the era's visual iconography.) Eric Foner, *The Story of American Freedom* (New York, 1998).

era. What impresses me about recent scholarship is how it reflects a series of expansions of historians' approaches that continue to improve our understanding of emancipation, Reconstruction, and the problem of freedom.[8]

One can begin with the expansion of the source base available to scholars brought about by the digital revolution. When I began work on Reconstruction, the World Wide Web did not exist (nor did email, so that scholars wasted a lot less of their time than nowadays). High tech meant consulting documents on microfilm or microfiche. When I wrote *Freedom's Lawmakers* in the early 1990s, I searched the manuscript census for weeks for black officials. Today, that research could be done at home on a computer in a few days. Numerous other sources for the Reconstruction era are also now available and searchable online, including congressional debates and documents (among them the indispensable Ku Klux Klan hearings), plantation records, and nineteenth-century pamphlets and newspapers.

Of course, historical sources are only as useful as the questions historians ask of them. And like our source base, historians' approaches have expanded significantly in recent years. First, there is the expansion of Reconstruction's cast of characters itself. Some of the best recent work has examined changes in gender roles and gender relations resulting from the Civil War and emancipation among both white and black families. These works see the family and kinship ties as central to the early emergence and long persistence of black political activism. They also emphasize that a gendered division of social space was widely assumed to be part of the legacy of emancipation. My book touched on gender issues, discussing, for example, how women were affected by changes in family structure that came with the end of slavery, and bringing the movement for women's rights into the Reconstruction story (it may be the only history of the era in which Victoria Woodhull makes an appearance). But when I wrote, the study of how women were affected by the transition from slavery to freedom was still in its infancy. Since then numerous books have appeared that place far more emphasis on

---

[8] The notes that follow mention only a small part of the voluminous recent literature on Reconstruction. For a comprehensive bibliography through the year 2000, see David A. Lincove, *Reconstruction in the United States: An Annotated Bibliography* (Westport, 2000). Thomas J. Brown, ed., *Reconstructions: New Perspectives on the Postbellum United States* (New York, 2008) contains historiographial essays tracing the evolution of Reconstruction scholarship.

the intersections of gender, race, labor, and politics, and make it clear that in significant ways women experienced emancipation differently from men.[9]

One of the most interesting such books is Thavolia Glymph's *Out of the House of Bondage,* which examines the difficult, sometimes violent transformation in relations between black and white women, how freedwomen struggled to create new gender roles while many white women strove to re-create antebellum lives of privilege in very difficult circumstances. Another important work is Martha Jones's *All Bound Up Together,* which examines the debate within black organizations over the role and rights of women. Jones demonstrates how the abolitionist discourse of equal rights, written into the laws and Constitution during Reconstruction, affected discussions of the "woman question" in black churches and societies.[10] This scholarship asks us to expand our definition of politics beyond the electoral arena—a male preserve—to the many locations where struggles for power occur, thus opening the door to the inclusion of women in Reconstruction's political history.

My book defines Reconstruction as both a specific time period (1863–1877) and a historical process—the nation's adjustment to the destruction of slavery and the preservation of national unity, the twin results of the Civil War. Recent work reflects an expansion of the geography of emancipation. A number of important books have explored the aftermath of slavery elsewhere in the western hemisphere, sometimes offering explicit comparisons with American Reconstruction.[11] Studies

---

[9] Laura F. Edwards, *Gendered Strife and Confusion: The Political Culture of Reconstruction* (Urbana, 1997); LeeAnn Whites, *The Civil War as a Crisis in Gender: Augusta, Georgia, 1860–1890* (Athens, 1995); Nancy Bercaw, *Gendered Freedoms: Race, Rights, and the Politics of the Household in the Delta, 1861–1875* (Gaineswille, 2003); Elizabeth Regosin, *Freedom's Promise: Ex-Slave Families and Citizenship in the Age of Emancipation* (Charlottesville, 2002); Tera Hunter, *To 'Joy My Freedom: Southern Black Women's Lives and Laborers After the Civil War* (Cambridge, 1997); Susan E. O'Donovan, *Becoming Free in the Cotton South* (Cambridge, 2007); Jane T. Censer, *The Reconstruction of White Southern Womanhood, 1865–1895* (Baton Rouge, 2003).

[10] Thavolia Glymph, *Out of the House of Bondage: The Transformation of the Plantation Household* (New York, 2008); Martha S. Jones, *All Bound Up Together: The Woman Question in African American Public Culture, 1830–1900* (Chapel Hill, 2007).

[11] Rebecca J. Scott, *Degrees of Freedom: Louisiana and Cuba After Slavery* (Cambridge, 2005); Demetrius L. Eudell, *Political Languages of Emancipation in the British Caribbean and the U.S. South* (Chapel Hill, 2002); Frederick Cooper, Thomas C. Holt, and Rebecca J. Scott, *Beyond Slavery: Explorations of Race, Labor, and Citizenship in Postemancipation Societies* (Chapel Hill, 2000).

of the development of new labor systems in the tobacco and sugar districts of the South has complemented previous studies of the rise of sharecropping in the cotton belt.[12]

The chronological boundaries of Reconstruction have also expanded. Steven Hahn's *A Nation Under Our Feet,* probably the most influential volume on nineteenth-century black politics to appear in the last quarter century, begins with black political ideas under slavery as the seedbed of Reconstruction politics, and takes the story of black political organization down to the twentieth century.[13] The implications of this chronological redefinition are significant. Studies that center on Reconstruction now continue into the 1880s and 1890s to encompass Readjusters, the Knights of Labor, Populists, and struggles over the imposition of the Jim Crow system.[14] More attention, too, has been paid to the contested twentieth-century "memory" of Reconstruction, a subject recently examined by Bruce Baker in *What Reconstruction Meant,* which shows how in South Carolina politicians used a particular understanding of Reconstruction as a weapon in the construction of the Jim Crow South. In this white supremacist narrative, the Redeemers and Red Shirts took on heroic status. However, Baker shows, a counter narrative survived in black communities, to be rediscovered in the 1930s by Southern radicals who found in Reconstruction a model for the interracial cooperation they hoped to bring to the twentieth-century South.[15] Overall, we now have what might be called a

---

[12] Lynda J. Morgan, *Emancipation in Virginia's Tobacco Belt, 1850–1870* (Athens, 1992); Jeffrey Kerr-Ritchie, *Freedpeople in the Tobacco South, Virginia, 1860–1890* (Chapel Hill, 1999); John Rodrigue, *Reconstruction in the Cane Fields: From Slavery to Free Labor in Louisiana's Sugar Parishes, 1862–1880* (Baton Rouge, 2001); Moon-Ho Jung, *Coolies and Cane: Race, Labor, and Sugar in the Age of Emancipation* (Baltimore, 2006). For the transition in one part of the cotton South see Julie Saville, *The Work of Reconstruction: From Slave to Wage Laborer in South Carolina, 1860–1870* (New York, 1994).

[13] Steven Hahn, *A Nation Under Our Feet: Black Political Struggles in the Rural South, From Slavery to the Great Migration* (Cambridge, 2003).

[14] Jane Dailey, *Before Jim Crow: The Politics of Race in Postemancipation Virginia* (Chapel Hill, 2000); Gregory P. Downs, *Declarations of Dependence: The Long Reconstruction of Popular Politics in the South, 1861–1908* (Chapel Hill, 2011); Michael W. Fitzgerald, *Urban Emancipation: Popular Politics in Reconstruction Mobile, 1860–1890* (Baton Rouge, 2002); Wang Xi, *The Trial of Democracy: Black Suffrage and Northern Republicans, 1860–1910* (Athens, 1997).

[15] Bruce E. Baker, *What Reconstruction Meant: Historical Memory in the American South* (Charlottesville, 2007), W. Fitzhugh Brundage, *The Southern Past: A Clash of Race and Memory* (Cambridge, 2005). David Blight, *Race and Reunion: The Civil War in American Memory* (Cambridge, 2001), the most influential recent book on historical memory, begins with a discussion of Reconstruction.

Long Reconstruction, like historians' long civil rights movement (which begins in the 1930s or 1940s) or their long nineteenth century (dated from 1789 to 1914).

Expanding the chronological definition of Reconstruction allows for a fuller comparison of Southern events with developments in other parts of the country. Economic transformation was not confined to the South in these years, and historians have looked to changes in Northern society and politics—especially the acceleration of industrial capitalism and accompanying labor conflict, to understand the Northern retreat from Reconstruction. The right to vote, moreover, was a point of contention throughout the country, not only in the South. The persistence of racialized labor systems—peonage among Hispanics in the Southwest, long-term indentures of Chinese immigrants on the West Coast—as well as the dispossession of the lands of Native Americans raise important questions about the limits to the triumph of free labor during the Civil War. These subjects were touched on in *Reconstruction* but they have received more detailed treatment since.[16]

Like any work of history, *Reconstruction* is a product of the moment in which it was written. My book appeared at the end of an incredibly creative thirty-year period of scholarship on emancipation and Reconstruction. By the time it was published, the foundations had been laid in dozens of monographs for a new overall account of the era. As I was researching and writing, the Freedmen and Southern Society project was uncovering thousands of remarkable primary sources in National Archives on the transition from slavery to freedom.[17] Debates flourished on the rise of sharecropping, the nature of black political leadership, the American state itself. More than most works of history, my book rests on the shoulders of others.

Whether scholars emphasized the accomplishments or limits of Re-

---

[16] Heather C. Richardson, *The Death of Reconstruction: Race, Labor, and Politics in the Post–Civil War North, 1865–1901* (Cambridge, 2001); Sven Beckert, *The Monied Metropolis: New York City and the Consolidation of the American Bourgeoisie, 1850–1896* (New York, 2001); Andrew L. Slap, *The Doom of Reconstruction: The Liberal Republicans in the Civil War Era* (New York, 2006); Mitchell Snay, *Fenians, Freedmen, and Southern Whites: Race and Nationality in the Era of Reconstruction* (Baton Rouge, 2007); Amy D. Stanley, *From Bondage to Contract: Wage Labor, Marriage, and the Market in the Age of Slave Emancipation* (New York, 1998); Gunther Peck, *Reinventing Free Labor: Padrone and Immigrant Workers in the North American West, 1880–1930* (New York, 2000).

[17] Many of these documents have been published in the Freedom Series, a work still in progress: Ira Berlin, *et al.*, ed, *Freedom: A Documentary History of Emancipation, 1861–1867* (New York and Chapel Hill, 1982–).

construction, the scholarship of the 1970s and 1980s was written in the afterglow of the modern civil rights revolution. Inevitably, the preoccupations of recent scholars have reflected our own tumultuous times. In the aftermath of the terrorist attacks of September 11, 2001, it is perhaps not surprising that historians turned renewed attention to home-grown American terrorism. Recent books on Reconstruction, including a number aimed at an audience outside the academy, have infused their subjects with drama by focusing on violent confrontations (rather than, for example, the operations and accomplishments of biracial governments). One thinks of works like Nicholas Lemann's *Redemption* on the violent overthrow of Reconstruction in Mississippi, Stephen Budiansky's *Bloody Shirt*, a survey of violence during the entire period, and two recent works on the Colfax Massacre, the single bloodiest incident in an era steeped in terrorism by the Klan and kindred white supremacist groups.[18]

In addition, as the language of "empire" reentered American political discourse with the wars in Afghanistan and Iraq, scholars looked to the enhancement of the power of the national state in Reconstruction and the "moral capital," to borrow a phrase from my colleague Christopher Brown, accumulated via the end of slavery, to locate ideological origins of America's imperial expansion in the 1890s. My book devoted little attention to foreign policy, but it did point out that during Reconstruction the reborn Union began to project its power abroad. Even as the struggle between President Andrew Johnson and Congress reached its climax, the United States acquired Alaska, one part of an imperial agenda long advocated by Secretary of State William H. Seward. Under President Grant, the government attempted to annex the Dominican Republic.

The emancipation of the slaves greatly strengthened the idea of an expansionist America as an "empire of liberty" (as Jefferson had put it). At the same time, scholars showed, the alleged failure of Reconstruction became part of the ideology of the white man's burden, cited

---

[18] Nicholas Lemann, *Redemption: The Last Battle of the Civil War* (New York, 2006); Stephen Budiansky, *Bloody Shirt: Terror After Appomattox* (New York, 2008); LeeAnna Keith, *Colfax Massacre: The Untold Story of Black Power, White Terror, and the Death of Reconstruction* (New York, 2008); Charles Lane, *The Day Freedom Died: The Colfax Massacre, the Supreme Court, and the Betrayal of Reconstruction* (New York, 2008); James K. Hogue, *Uncivil War: Five New Orleans Street Battles and the Rise and Fall of Radical Reconstruction* (Baton Rouge, 2006); Lou F. Williams, *The Great South Carolina Ku Klux Klan Trials, 1871–1872* (Athens, 2004).

all over the world to demonstrate the incapacity of nonwhite peoples for self-government. *Drawing the Global Color Line*, an important recent book by two Australian scholars, points out that the late nineteenth and early twentieth centuries were a time of a global sense of fraternity among "Anglo-Saxon" nations, including Australia, New Zealand, Canada, the United States, and South Africa. Political leaders in these countries studied and copied each others' racial policies. Their "bible," Marilyn Lake and Henry Reynolds write, was James Bryce's *American Commonwealth,* published in 1888, and especially his account of Reconstruction as a time of corruption and misgovernment caused by the enfranchisement of the former slaves. Bryce's book "proved" that blacks, coolies, aborigines, etc., were unfit to be citizens. It was frequently invoked by the founders of Australia's federal nation in support of their vision of a White Australia, and by white South Africans. Around the world, the "key history lesson" (as Lake and Reynolds put it) of Reconstruction was taken to be the impossibility of multiracial democracy. Thus, as Du Bois pointed out long ago, consequences of the overthrow of Reconstruction in the United States reverberated across the globe.[19]

Despite the undeniable setbacks that followed, my book sees the destruction of slavery as a transcendent accomplishment and debates over the definition of freedom as a central feature of Reconstruction. Many works since 1988 have built upon this theme, seeking to parse out the meanings of freedom in education, labor, religious life, politics, and the family.[20] But today's historians of Reconstruction tend to give as much emphasis to the disappointments of freedom as the accomplishment of emancipation. Or, they emphasis goals other than freedom—equality, justice, fraternity—and emphasize how far Reconstruction remained from accomplishing them. Where once the abolition of slavery was seen

---

[19] Christopher L. Brown, *Moral Capital: Foundations of British Abolitionism* (Williamsburg, 2006); Moon-Ho Jung, "Reckoning with Empire: Race, Freedom, and State Power Across the Pacific," paper delivered at Wiles Symposium, Queen's University, Belfast, 2008; Marilyn Lake and Henry Reynolds, *Drawing the Global Colour Line: White Men's Countries and the International Challenge of Racial Equality* (New York, 2008).

[20] Many of the works cited above pursue this theme. See also Heather A. Williams, *Self-Taught: African-American Education in Slavery and Freedom* (Chapel Hill, 2005); William E. Montgomery, *Under Their Own Vine and Fig Tree: The African-American Church in the South, 1865–1900* (Baton Rouge, 1993); Reginald F. Hildebrand, *The Times Were Strange and Stirring: Methodist Preachers and the Crisis of Emancipation* (Durham, 1995); Dylan C. Penningroth, *The Claims of Kinfolk: African American Property and Community in the Nineteenth-Century South* (Chapel Hill, 2003).

as the great watershed of African-American life—a point of view epitomized in the title of John Hope Franklin's highly influential black history textbook, *From Slavery to Freedom*—historians of late have taken to emphasizing the inadequacy, of the freedom brought about by the Civil War. Racism and black subordination persisted despite emancipation. Steven Kantrowitz entitles his recent study of Boston's nineteenth-century black activists *More than Freedom* and the section on the post–Civil War years "The Disappointments of Citizenship."[21]

Important work exploring Reconstruction politics in various Southern states has continued to appear since 1988, most of it generally sympathetic to the era's Republican governments.[22] But, perhaps reflecting an understandable cynicism about today's political world, what the historian Michael Fitzgerald calls an "ethical recalibration" of Reconstruction studies has begun to take place, one that downplays the era's idealism and emphasizes how corruption and factionalism undermined the effectiveness of the Reconstruction governments.[23] These themes sit uneasily with the continued emphasis on the creativity and persistence of black political organization and community-building after the Civil War. Thus, many recent works add important new dimensions to the Reconstruction story. Some offer criticisms and corrections to my own book. But I think it is fair to say that no one has yet produced a comprehensive account of Reconstruction that brings new perspectives together in a coherent narrative synthesis.[24] For a history of the era, readers must still turn to *Reconstruction: America's Unfinished Revolution*.

Reconstruction historiography has always spoken directly to current concerns—another way of saying that the era remains remarkably

---

[21] Steven Kantrowitz, *More than Freedom: Fighting for Black Citizenship in a White Republic, 1829–1889* (New York, 2012). Other examples of this perspective include Jim Downs, *Sick from Freedom: African-American Illness and Suffering during the Civil War and Reconstruction* (New York, 2012) and Matthew J. Mancini, *One Dies, Get Another: Convict Leasing in the American South, 1866–1928* (Columbia, 1996).

[22] Richard Zuczek, *State of Rebellion: Reconstruction in South Carolina* (Columbia, 2009); Richard Lowe, *Republicans and Reconstruction in Virginia, 1856–1870* (Charlottesville, 1991); Richard Abbott, *For Free Press and Equal Rights: Republican Newspapers in the Reconstruction South* (Athens, 2004); and James A. Baggett, *The Scalawags: Southern Dissenters in the Civil War and Reconstruction* (Baton Rouge, 2004).

[23] Michael W. Fitzgerald, "Reconstruction Politics and the Politics of Reconstruction," in Brown, ed., *Reconstructions*, 91–116. On corruption, see Mark W. Summers, *The Era of Good Stealings* (New York, 1993).

[24] A recent brief survey of the era is Michael W. Fitzgerald, *Splendid Failure: Postwar Reconstruction in the American South* (Chicago, 2007).

relevant. Even if we remain unaware of it, Reconstruction is part of our lives even today. Issues that agitate American politics—who is an American citizen and what rights come along with citizenship, the relative powers of the national government and the states, affirmative action, the relationship between political and economic democracy, the proper response to terrorism—are Reconstruction questions. Reconstruction is embedded in our judicial processes. Every session of the Supreme Court adjudicates issues arising from the Fourteenth Amendment and the civil rights legislation of Reconstruction. Assumptions about Reconstruction dating back to the Dunning School long influenced the Court's understanding of the Fourteenth Amendment with regard to race, and even today remain embedded in established jurisprudence, leading to a cramped understanding of this key constitutional provisions when it comes to governmental efforts to promote racial justice.[25] At the same time, the definition of the "liberty" guaranteed to all American citizens in the Amendment has continued to expand. In the past decade the Fourteenth Amendment has provided the basis for the Court to overturn state and local laws making illegal homosexual acts between consenting adults, and barring the possession of handguns.

Citizenship, rights, freedom, democracy—as long as these questions remain central to our society, so too will the necessity of an accurate understanding of Reconstruction. These are not only historical and political questions, but moral ones. Reconstruction history has always been morally inflected, because writing about the period forces the historian to think about where he or she stands in relation to key problems of our own time. The Dunning School, with its emphasis on the alleged horrors of Republican Reconstruction, provided scholarly legitimation for Jim Crow, black disenfranchisement, and the now long-departed solid Democratic South. Reconstruction revisionism arose in tandem with and provided a usable past for the civil rights movement. More than most historical subjects, Reconstruction history matters. Whatever the ebb and flow of historical interpretations, I hope we never lose sight of the fact that something very important for the future of our society was taking place during Reconstruction.

---

[25] See Eric Foner, "The Supreme Court and the History of Reconstruction—and Vice Versa," *Columbia Law Review,* 112 (November, 2012), 1585–1606, and Pamela Brandwein, *Reconstructing Reconstruction: The Supreme Court and the Production of Historical Truth* (Durham, 1999).

A SHORT HISTORY OF RECONSTRUCTION, 1863–1877

1

The World the War Made

The Coming of Emancipation

On January 1, 1863, after a winter storm swept up the east coast of
the United States, the sun rose in a cloudless sky over Washington,
D.C. At the White House, Abraham Lincoln spent most of the day
welcoming guests to the traditional New Year's reception. Finally,
in the late afternoon, the President retired to his office to sign the
Emancipation Proclamation. Excluded from its purview were the
450,000 slaves in the loyal border states of Delaware, Kentucky,
Maryland, and Missouri, 275,000 in Union-occupied Tennessee,
and tens of thousands more in portions of Louisiana and Virginia
under the control of federal armies. But, the Proclamation decreed,
the remainder of the nation's slave population, well over 3 million
men, women, and children, "are and henceforth shall be free."

Nearly two and a half centuries had passed since twenty black
men and women were landed in Virginia from a Dutch ship. From
this tiny seed had grown the poisoned fruit of plantation slavery,
which, in profound and contradictory ways, shaped the course of
American development. Even as slavery mocked the ideals of a
nation supposedly dedicated to liberty and equality, slave labor
played an indispensable part in its rapid growth, expanding westward with the young republic, producing the cotton that fueled the
early industrial revolution. The slavery question divided the nation's
churches, sundered political ties between the sections, and finally
shattered the bonds of the Union. On the principle of opposing the
further expansion of slavery, a new political party rose to power in

the 1850s, placing in the White House a son of the slave state Kentucky who had grown to manhood on the free Illinois prairies and believed the United States could not endure forever half slave and half free. In the crisis that followed Lincoln's election, eleven slave states seceded from the Union, precipitating in 1861 the bloodiest war the Western Hemisphere has ever seen.

The Emancipation Proclamation not only culminated decades of struggle, but evoked Christian visions of an era of unbounded progress for a nation purged at last of the sin of slavery. Even the staid editors of the *New York Times* believed it marked a watershed in American life, "an era in the history . . . of this country and the world." For emancipation meant more than the end of a labor system, more even than the uncompensated liquidation of the nation's largest concentration of private property. Begun to preserve the Union, the Civil War now portended a far-reaching transformation in Southern life and a redefinition of the place of blacks in American society and of the very meaning of freedom in the American republic.

In one sense, however, the Proclamation only confirmed what was already happening on farms and plantations throughout the South. War, it has been said, is the midwife of revolution, and well before 1863 the disintegration of slavery had begun. As the Union Army occupied territory on the periphery of the Confederacy, first in Virginia, then in Tennessee, Louisiana, and elsewhere, slaves by the thousands headed for the Union lines. Even in the heart of the Confederacy, the conflict undermined the South's "peculiar institution." The drain of white men into military service left plantations under the control of planters' wives and elderly and infirm men, whose authority slaves increasingly felt able to challenge. Reports of "demoralized" and "insubordinate" behavior multiplied throughout the South.

But generally it was the arrival of federal soldiers that spelled havoc for the slave regime, for blacks quickly grasped that the presence of occupying troops destroyed the coercive power of both the individual master and the slaveholding community. On the Magnolia plantation in Louisiana, the arrival of the Union Army in 1862 sparked a work stoppage and worse: "We have a terrible state of affairs here negroes refusing to work. . . . The negroes have erected a gallows in the quarters and give as an excuse for it that they are told they must drive their master . . . off the plantation hang their master etc. and that then they will be free." Slavery in southern Louisiana, wrote a Northern reporter in November 1862, "is forever destroyed and worthless, no matter what Mr. Lincoln or anyone else may say on the subject."

"Meanwhile," in the words of W. E. B. Du Bois, "with perplexed and laggard steps, the United States government followed in the footsteps of the black slave." The slaves' determination to seize the opportunity presented by the war initially proved an embarrassment to the Lincoln administration and a burden to the army. Lincoln fully appreciated, as he would observe in his second inaugural address, that slavery was "somehow" the cause of the war. But he also understood the vital importance of keeping the border slave states in the Union, generating support among the broadest constituency in the North, and weakening the Confederacy by holding out to irresolute Southerners the possibility that they could return to the Union with their property, including slaves, intact. In 1861, the restoration of the Union, not emancipation, was the cause that generated the widest support for the war effort.

Yet as the Confederacy set slaves to work as military laborers, and the presence of Union soldiers precipitated large-scale desertion of the plantations, the early policy quickly unraveled. Increasingly, military authorities adopted the plan, inaugurated in Virginia by Gen. Benjamin F. Butler, of designating fugitive slaves "contraband of war" who would be employed as laborers for the Union armies. Then, too, Northern abolitionists and Radical Republicans recognized that secession offered a golden opportunity to strike a fatal blow at slavery. Their agitation kept at the forefront of Northern politics the question of the struggle's ultimate purpose.

The steps by which Congress and the President moved toward abolition have often been chronicled. In March 1862, Congress enacted an article of war expressly prohibiting the army from returning fugitives to their masters. Then came abolition in the District of Columbia (with compensation for loyal owners) and the territories, followed by the Second Confiscation Act, liberating slaves who resided in Union-occupied territory or escaped to Union lines, if their masters were disloyal. Finally, in September, came the Preliminary Emancipation Proclamation, and on January 1, 1863, the final edict, a turning point in national policy as well as in the character of the war. In effect, it transformed a war of armies into a conflict of societies. In December 1861, Lincoln had admonished Congress that the Civil War must not degenerate into "a violent and remorseless revolutionary struggle." The Emancipation Proclamation announced that this was precisely what it must become.

Of the Proclamation's provisions, few were more essential to breathing life into the promise of emancipation than the massive enrollment of blacks into military service. By the war's end, some 180,000 blacks had served in the Union Army. The highest percentage originated in the border states, where enlistment was, for most of the war, the only route to freedom.

Although obliged to serve in segregated units under white officers and initially paid less than white troops, black soldiers played a crucial role not only in winning the Civil War, but also in defining the war's consequences. The "logical result" of their military service, one Senator observed in 1864, was that "the black man is henceforth to assume a new *status* among us." For the first time in American history, large numbers of blacks were treated as equals before the law—if only military law. It was in the army that numerous former slaves first learned to read and write, either from teachers employed by Northern aid societies or in classrooms and literary clubs established and funded by the soldiers themselves. For men of talent and ambition, the army flung open a door to advancement and respectability. From the army would come many of the black political leaders of Reconstruction, including at least forty-one delegates to state constitutional conventions, sixty legislators, three lieutenant governors, and four Congressmen. In time, the black contribution to the Union war effort would fade from the nation's collective memory, but it remained a vital part of the black community's sense of its own history. "They say," an Alabama planter reported in 1867, "the Yankees never could have whipped the South without the aid of the negroes." Here was a crucial justification for blacks' self-confident claim to equal citizenship during Reconstruction.

For upholders of the South's "peculiar institution," the Civil War was a terrible moment of truth. The most perceptive among them realized they had never really known their slaves. "I believed that these people were content, happy, and attached to their masters," South Carolina rice planter A. L. Taveau confessed two months after the war's close. But if this were the case, why did the slaves desert their masters "in [their] moment of need and flock to an enemy, whom they did not know?" Blacks, Taveau now understood, had, for generations, been "looking for the Man of Universal Freedom."

The Inner Civil War

Like a massive earthquake, the Civil War and the destruction of slavery permanently altered the landscape of Southern life, exposing and widening fault lines that had lain barely visible just beneath the surface. White society was transformed no less fully than black, as traditional animosities grew more acute, longstanding conflicts acquired altered meanings, and new groups emerged into political consciousness.

From the earliest days of settlement, there had never been a single white South, and in the nineteenth century the region as a whole, and each state within it, was divided into areas with sharply differing political economies. The plantation belt, which encompassed the South's most fertile lands, supported a flourishing agriculture integrated into the world market for cotton, rice, sugar, and tobacco. It contained the majority of slaves, as well as the planters who dominated Southern society and politics and commanded most of the region's wealth and economic resources. A larger number of white Southerners lived in the upcountry, an area of small farmers and herdsmen who owned few or no slaves and engaged largely in mixed and subsistence agriculture. The upcountry itself encompassed the Piedmont, where slavery was a significant presence, and the mountains and hill country, where small communities of white families lived in frontier conditions, isolated from the rest of the South. Self-sufficiency remained the primary goal of upcountry farm families, a large majority of whom owned their land and worked it with their own labor, without slaves or hired hands.

Within the South, state borders did not coincide with lines of economic specialization. The Appalachian South, a vast mountain region of extraordinary beauty, stretched from western Virginia through parts of Kentucky, Tennessee, North Carolina, Georgia, and Alabama. The cotton kingdom, dominated by slave plantations, reached from the Carolinas southwest into Louisiana and eastern Texas. Tennessee had a western region with numerous cotton plantations, a middle section with prosperous medium-sized farms growing corn and livestock for the market, and a large mountainous area to the east, with small subsistence-oriented farms and few slaves.

Many small farmers (nearly half in both Mississippi and South Carolina) owned a slave or two, and even in the mountains slavery was "firmly entrenched" among a small but influential local elite: the few large-scale farmers, professional men, merchants, and small-town entrepreneurs. Outside the plantation belt, however, the majority of yeomen had little economic stake in the institution. Yet slavery affected society everywhere in the South, and even mountaineers shared many attitudes with the planters, beginning with a commitment to white supremacy. So long as slavery and planter rule did not interfere with the yeomanry's self-sufficient agriculture and local independence, the latent class conflict among whites failed to find coherent expression.

It was in the secession crisis and Civil War that large numbers of upcountry yeomen discovered themselves as a political class. The elections for delegates to secession conventions in the winter of 1860–61 produced massive repudiations of disunion in yeoman areas. Once the war had begun, most of the upcountry rallied to the Confederate cause. But from the outset, disloyalty was rife in the Southern mountains. Its western counties seceded from Virginia in 1861 and two years later reentered the Union as a separate state. From East Tennessee, long conscious of its remoteness from the rest of the state, thousands of men made their way through the mountains to enlist in the Union Army. Secret Union societies flourished in the Ozark mountains of northern Arkansas, from which 8,000 men eventually joined the federal army.

Discontent developed more slowly outside the mountains. It was not simply devotion to the Union but the impact of the war and the consequences of Confederate policies that awakened peace sentiment and social conflict. In any society, war demands sacrifice, and public support often rests on the conviction that sacrifice is equitably shared. But the Confederate government increasingly molded its policies in the interest of the planter class. Slavery's disintegration compelled the Confederate government to take steps to preserve the institution, and these policies, in turn, sundered white society.

The impression that planters were not bearing their fair share of the war's burdens spread quickly among Southern yeomen. The upcountry became convinced that it bore an unfair share of taxation;

it particularly resented the tax-in-kind and the policy of impressment that authorized military officers to appropriate farm goods to feed the army. During the war, poverty descended upon thousands of upcountry families, especially those with men in the army. Food riots broke out in Virginia and North Carolina, and in Randolph County, Alabama, crowds of women seized government stores of corn "to prevent starvation of themselves and families." But, above all, conscription convinced many yeomen that the struggle for Southern independence had become "a rich man's war and a poor man's fight." Beginning in 1862, the Confederacy enacted the first conscription laws in American history, including provisions that a draftee could avoid service by producing a substitute, and that one able-bodied white male would be exempted for every twenty slaves. This "class legislation" was deeply resented in the upcountry, for the cost of a substitute quickly rose far beyond the means of most white families, while the "twenty Negro" provision, a response to the decline of discipline on the plantations, allowed many overseers and planters' sons to escape military service.

In large areas of the Southern upcountry, initial enthusiasm for the war was succeeded by disillusionment, draft evasion, and eventually outright resistance to Confederate authority—a civil war within the Civil War. By war's end, more than 100,000 men had deserted, almost entirely, one officer observed, from among "the poorest class of non slaveholders whose labor is indispensable to the daily support of their families." In western and central North Carolina, whose white inhabitants supported the Confederacy at the outset, the Heroes of America, numbering perhaps 10,000 men, established an "underground railroad" to enable Unionists to escape to federal lines.

More than ever before, the Southern upcountry was divided against itself between 1861 and 1865. Yeomen supplied both the bulk of Confederate soldiers and the majority of deserters and draft resisters. Lying at the war's strategic crossroads, portions of upcountry Tennessee, Alabama, and Mississippi were laid waste by the march of opposing armies. In other areas, marauding bands of deserters plundered the farms and workshops of Confederate sympathizers, driving off livestock and destroying crops, while Confederate troops and vigilantes routed Union families from their homes. In this internal civil war, atrocities were committed on both sides, but since the bulk of the upcountry remained within Confederate lines for most of the war, Unionists suffered more intensely. In East Tennessee, hundreds were imprisoned by military tribunals and their property seized "to the total impoverishment of the sufferers."

Thus the war permanently redrew the economic and political map of the white South. Military devastation and the Confederacy's economic policies plunged much of the upcountry into poverty, thereby threatening the yeomanry's economic independence and opening the door to the postwar spread of cotton cultivation and tenancy. The war ended the upcountry's isolation, weakened its localism, and awakened its political self-consciousness. Out of the Union opposition would come many of the most prominent white Republican leaders of Reconstruction. The party's Southern governors would include Edmund J. Davis, who during the war raised the First Texas Cavalry for the Union army; William W. Holden, whose unsuccessful 1864 peace campaign for governor of North Carolina became the backbone of white Republicanism in the state; and William G. Brownlow, a circuit-riding Methodist preacher and Knoxville editor who gave violent speeches in the North against the Confederacy. Regions like East Tennessee and western North Carolina and individual counties in the hill country of other states would embrace the Republican party after the Civil War and remain strongholds well into the twentieth century. Their loyalty first to the Union and then to Republicanism did not, however, imply abolitionist sentiment during the war (although they were perfectly willing to see slavery sacrificed to preserve the Union) or a commitment to the rights of blacks thereafter. Upcountry Unionism, Northern reporter Sidney Andrews explained in the fall of 1865, rested above all on "hatred of those who went into the Rebellion" and of "a certain ruling class" that had brought upon the region the devastating impact of the Civil War.

The North's Transformation

For the Union too, the Civil War was a time of change. The Northern states did not experience a revolution as far-reaching as emancipation, but no aspect of life emerged untouched from the conflict. The policies of a national government whose powers were magnified each year the war continued offered unparalleled economic opportunities to some Northerners while spurring deter-

mined opposition among others. As in the South, how Northerners
reacted to the war and its consequences reflected prior divisions of
class, race, and politics, even as these were themselves reshaped by
the conflict.

If economic devastation stalked the South, for the North the Civil
War was a time of unprecedented prosperity. Railroads thrived on
carrying troops and supplies, and profited from the closing of the
Mississippi River. On a tide of demand from the army, the
meat-packing industry boomed; Chicago, the city of railroad and
slaughterhouse, experienced unprecedented growth in population,
construction, banking, and manufacturing. By 1865 it stood unchal-
lenged as the Midwest's preeminent commercial center. The woolen
mills of New England and the mid-Atlantic states worked day and
night to meet the military's demand for blankets and uniforms,
reaping enormous profits. Agriculture also flourished, for even as
farm boys by the thousands were drawn into the army, the frontier
of cultivation pushed westward, with machinery and immigration
replacing lost labor.

Deep structural changes accompanied the North's wartime boom.
Accelerating the emergence of an American industrial bourgeoisie,
the war tied the fortunes of this class to the Republican party and
the national state. More was involved than profits wrung from
government contracts, for faced with the war's unprecedented
financial demands, Congress adopted economic policies that promoted further industrial expansion and permanently altered the
conditions of capital accumulation. To mobilize the financial resources of the Union, the government created a national paper
currency, an enormous national debt, and a national banking
system. To raise funds it increased the tariff and imposed new taxes
on nearly every branch of production and consumption. To help
compensate for the drain of men into the army, a federal bureau was
established to encourage immigration under labor contracts. To
promote agricultural development, the Homestead Act offered free
land to settlers on the public domain, and the Land Grant College
Act assisted the states in establishing "agricultural and mechanical
colleges." And to further consolidate the Union, Congress lavished
grants of public land and government bonds upon internal improvements, most notably the transcontinental railroad, which, when
completed in 1869, expanded the national market, facilitated the
penetration of capital into the West, and heralded the final doom of

the Plains Indians. The policies of the Union embodied a spirit of national economic activism unprecedented in the prewar years.

In their expansion of federal power and their effort to organize a decentralized economy and fragmented polity, these measures reflected the birth of the modern American state. On the eve of the Civil War, the federal government was "in a state of impotence." Most functions of government were handled at the state and local level; one could live out one's life without ever encountering an official representative of national authority. But the exigencies of war created, as Sen. George S. Boutwell later put it, a "new government," with a greatly expanded income, bureaucracy, and set of responsibilities. A government whose regular army in 1860 numbered only 16,000 found itself mobilizing, training, equipping, and coordinating the activities of millions of men. The federal budget, amounting to $63 million in 1860, rose to well over $1 billion by 1865. At war's end the federal government, with 53,000 employees including new Custom House officials, internal revenue agents, clerks, and inspectors, was the largest employer in the nation.

Especially after the Emancipation Proclamation clothed national authority with an indisputably moral purpose, Republicans exalted the state's continuing maturation as one of the most salutary of the war's consequences. "The policy of this country," declared Sen. John Sherman, "ought to be to make everything national as far as possible; to nationalize our country so that we shall love our country." Within Congress, Sherman's broad nationalism was embraced, above all, by the Radical Republicans. For Radicals, the nation had become the "custodian of freedom," and some questioned whether the states deserved continued existence at all. The war vindicated their conviction that freedom stood in greater danger of abridgment from local than national authority. In the full flush of nationalist exuberance, a magazine founded in 1865 by antislavery crusaders, and entitled, significantly, *The Nation*, announced in its second issue:

> The issue of the war marks an epoch by the consolidation of nationality under democratic forms. . . . This territorial, political, and historical oneness of the nation is now ratified by the blood of thousands of her sons. . . . The prime issue of the war was between nationality one and indivisible, and the loose and changeable federation of independent States.

As never before, the war mobilized the energies of Northern reformers. Especially among women, it inspired an outpouring of voluntary undertakings. Much of their activity centered on the United States Sanitary Commission, which organized medical relief and other services for soldiers, and the freedmen's aid movement, an attempt to help the government cope with the daunting problem of the destitute blacks liberated from slavery. Although men controlled these organizations at the highest levels, the war years inculcated among these women a heightened interest in public events and a sense of independence and accomplishment, while also offering training in organization. Even though the prewar agitation for the suffrage came to a virtual standstill, the war enlarged the ranks of women who resented their legal and political subordination to men and believed themselves entitled to the vote in recognition of their contribution to Union victory and the destruction of slavery.

If the war opened doors of opportunity for women, it held out hope for an even more radical transformation in the condition of the tiny, despised black population of the free states. Numbering fewer than a quarter million in 1860, blacks comprised less than two percent of the North's population, yet they found themselves subjected to pervasive discrimination. Barred in most states from the suffrage, schools, and public accommodations, confined to menial occupations, living in the poorest, unhealthiest quarters of cities like New York, Philadelphia, and Cincinnati, many Northern blacks had by the 1850s all but despaired of ever finding a secure and equal place within American life.

The Civil War produced an abrupt shift from the pessimism of the 1850s to a renewed spirit of patriotism and a restored faith in the larger society. Even before the Emancipation Proclamation, a black Californian foresaw the dawning of a new day for his people:

> Everything among us indicates a change in our condition, and [we must] prepare to act in a different sphere from that in which we have heretofore acted. . . . Our relation to this government is changing daily. . . . Old things are passing away, and eventually old prejudices must follow. The revolution has begun, and time alone must decide where it is to end.

Emancipation further transformed the black response to American nationality. Throughout his life, Frederick Douglass had been the

most insistent advocate of what one historian calls the Great
Tradition of black protest—the idea that blacks formed an integral
part of the nation and were entitled to the same rights and
opportunities white citizens enjoyed. Now Douglass emerged as
black America's premier spokesman, welcomed at the White House,
his speeches widely reprinted in the Northern press. Throughout
the war Douglass insisted that from emancipation should flow the
end of all color discrimination, the establishment of equality before
the law, and the enfranchisement of the black population—the "full
and complete adoption" of blacks "into the great national family of
America."

The war galvanized a black assault upon the Northern color line
which, in the conflict's final months, won some modest but impressive victories. In February 1865, John S. Rock of Boston became the
first black lawyer admitted to the bar of the Supreme Court. Slowly,
the North's racial barriers began to fall. In 1863, California for the first
time permitted blacks to testify in criminal cases; early in 1865 Illinois
repealed its laws barring blacks from entering the state, serving on
juries, or testifying in court, while Ohio eliminated the last of its
discriminatory "black laws." In May 1865, Massachusetts passed the
first comprehensive public accommodations law in American history.
New York City, San Francisco, Cincinnati, and Cleveland all deseg-
regated their streetcars during the war. For reformers, this initial
progress was an augury of the reborn republic they believed was
emerging from the war. Essential to this transformation would be
some as yet undefined measure of equality before the law for blacks,
and the "regeneration" of the South, transplanting there, as Douglass
put it, "the higher civilization of the North."

Republicans had brought into the war an ideology grounded in a
conviction of the superiority of free to slave labor, which saw the
distinctive quality of Northern society as the opportunity it offered
the wage laborer to rise to the status of independent farmer or
craftsman. In 1861, Lincoln placed the struggle firmly within the
familiar context of the free labor ideology. Slavery, he insisted,
embodied the idea that the condition of the worker should remain
forever the same; in the North, by contrast, there was "no such . . .
thing as a free man being fixed for life in the condition of a hired
laborer. . . . Men, with their families . . . work for themselves on
their farms, in their houses, and in their shops, taking the whole
product to themselves, and asking no favors of capital on the one

hand nor of hired laborers or slaves on the other." Here was a social vision already being rendered obsolete by the industrial revolution and the appearance of a class of permanent wage laborers. Indeed, even as the war vindicated the free labor ideology, it strengthened tendencies that inexorably transformed the society of small producers from which that ideology had sprung. "The youngest of us," abolitionist Wendell Phillips wrote in 1864, "are never again to see the republic in which we were born."

Yet the world that spawned the free labor ideology remained close enough in time, and its assumptions authentic enough in the experience of men like Lincoln and the millions of small-town and rural men and women who still made up the majority of the North's population, for the ideology to retain a broad plausibility. Sanctified by the North's triumph, it would emerge from the war further strengthened as an underpinning of Republican party policy and as a starting point for discussions of the postwar South. Now the prospect opened of an affluent, democratic, free labor South, with small farms replacing the great plantations and Northern capital and migrants energizing the society. And presiding over the transformation would stand a benevolent and powerful national state. With "the whole continent opened to free labor and Northern enterprise," an abolitionist journal exulted just two days after the Emancipation Proclamation, "the imagination can hardly exaggerate the glory and power of the American republic. Its greatness will overshadow the world."

Thus the Civil War consolidated the national state while identifying that state, via emancipation, with the interests of all humanity and, more prosaically, with a coalition of diverse groups and classes. An emerging industrial bourgeoisie, adherents of the Republican party, men and women of the reform milieu, a Northern black community demanding a new status in American life—all these embraced the changes brought on by the war. But these developments also galvanized bitter wartime opposition. The enrichment of industrialists and bondholders appeared unfair to workers devastated by a regressive tax system and inflation. The process of national state formation clashed with cherished traditions of local autonomy and cultural diversity. And even small improvements in the status of Northern blacks, not to mention the vast changes implied by emancipation, stirred ugly counterattacks from advocates of white supremacy.

The Democratic party, the preeminent conservative institution of the era, reaped the political harvest of opposition to the changes wrought by the war. Tainted with disloyalty in Republican eyes, unable to develop a coherent alternative to the policies of the Lincoln administration, the Democracy's survival testified to the resilience of the deeply rooted traditions the war threatened to undermine. Its greatest strength lay in areas like the "butternut" farming regions of the Ohio Valley, closely tied to the South and bypassed by wartime economic expansion, and among urban Catholic immigrants and other voters hostile to the perfectionist reform tradition, with its impulse toward cultural homogeneity.

To unite these groups, the Democracy built upon an ideological appeal developed in the 1850s, which identified the Republican party as an agent of economic privilege and political centralization, and a threat to individual liberty and the tradition of limited government. During the war, Democrats perfected economic appeals based on the inequity of protective tariffs, high railroad freight rates, and state and federal aid to private corporations that would provide the staples of agrarian protest in years to come. White supremacy provided the final ideological glue in the Democratic coalition. "Slavery is dead," the Cincinnati *Enquirer* announced at war's end, "the negro is not, there is the misfortune."

All the elements of opposition to the war and its consequences came together for a few terrifying days in July 1863. The New York City draft riot, the largest civil insurrection in American history apart from the South's rebellion itself, originated in opposition to conscription. But it reflected as well resentment of the emerging industrial bourgeoisie and the Republican party that appeared as its handmaiden, and violent hostility to emancipation, abolitionists, and blacks.

Beginning with an attack on a conscription office, the riot quickly developed into a wholesale assault on all the symbols of the new order being created by the Republican party and the Civil War. Its targets included government officials, factories and docks (some the scene of recent strikes), the opulent homes of the city's Republican elite, and such symbols of the reform spirit as the Colored Orphan Asylum, which was burned to the ground. Above all, the riot degenerated into a virtual racial pogrom, with uncounted numbers of blacks murdered on the streets or driven to take refuge in Central Park or across the river in New Jersey. Only the arrival of troops fresh from the Union victory at Gettysburg restored order to the city.

Like the inner civil war within the Confederacy, the draft riot underscored the fact that for North and South alike, the war's legacy was fraught with ambiguity. Could a society in which racial hatred ran so deep secure justice for the emancipated slaves? What would it mean to remake Southern society in the Northern image when the North was itself so bitterly divided by the changes brought on by the Civil War? The war's most conspicuous legacies—the preservation of the Union and the abolition of slavery—posed a host of unanswered questions. And their wartime corollaries—a more powerful national state and a growing sense among Republicans that blacks were entitled to some measure of civil equality—produced countervailing tendencies, as localism, laissez-faire, and racism, persistent forces in nineteenth-century American life, reasserted themselves.

Thus, two societies, each divided internally, entered the Reconstruction years to confront the myriad consequences of the Civil War. As Sidney Breese, an Illinois jurist and politician, observed, all Americans "must live in the world the War made."

Rehearsals for Reconstruction

Dilemmas of Wartime Reconstruction

Of the Civil War's many legacies, none proved so divisive as the series of questions that came to form the essence of Reconstruction. On what terms should the defeated Confederacy be reunited with the Union? Should Congress or the President establish these terms? What system of labor should replace plantation slavery? What should be the place of blacks in the political and social life of the South and of the nation? One definitive conclusion emerged from the war: The reconstructed South would be a society without slavery. But even this raised as many questions as it answered.

The Emancipation Proclamation permanently transformed not only the character of the Civil War, but the problem of Reconstruction. For it suggested that the rebelling Southern states could not resume their erstwhile position without far-reaching changes in their society and politics. But nearly a year elapsed between emancipation and Lincoln's first announcement of a comprehensive program for Reconstruction. Issued on December 8, 1863, his Proclamation of Amnesty and Reconstruction offered full pardon and the restoration of all rights "except as to slaves" to persons who took an oath of future loyalty and pledged to accept the abolition of slavery. A few groups, including high-ranking civil and military officers of the Confederacy, were excluded. When in any state the number of loyal Southerners amounted to ten percent of the votes cast in 1860, this minority could establish a new state government. Its constitution must abolish slavery, but it could adopt temporary measures regarding blacks "consistent . . . with their present condition as a laboring, landless, and homeless class."

A few abolitionists criticized this Ten Percent Plan for failing to implement black suffrage and equality before the law. Lincoln seems to have assumed that the South's former Whigs, many of whom, although large slaveholders, had been reluctant secessionists, would accept his lenient terms. Black suffrage would alienate such men, while the implied invitation to return to the Union to oversee and regulate the transition from slave to free labor might well attract them. In actual operation, the plan quickly stirred Radical Republican opposition, but at its announcement, few demurred. For on the crucial question of 1863—emancipation—Lincoln and the Radicals now agreed.

It would be a mistake to see the Ten Percent Plan as a hard-and-fast policy from which Lincoln was determined never to deviate. Rather than as a design for a reconstructed South, it might better be viewed as a device to shorten the war and solidify white support for emancipation. As functioning governments, those established under the terms of Lincoln's proclamation approached the absurd. Inverted pyramids, the New York *World* called them, for a few thousand voters would control the destiny of entire states. But in strictly military terms, for ten percent of the voters of 1860 to renounce their loyalty to the Confederacy would indeed augment the Union war effort and undermine the Confederacy's will to fight. No one, least of all Lincoln, believed that the 1863 proclamation laid out a comprehensive blueprint for the postwar South. But the process of establishing loyal governments had unanticipated consequences, producing serious divisions among Southern Unionists, creating political forums in which long-excluded groups laid claim to a share of political power, and inspiring blacks and their Radical allies to demand sweeping changes in Southern life.

The four slave states and part of a fifth (West Virginia) that had remained within the Union and were unaffected by the Emancipation Proclamation and the Ten Percent Plan were the first to reveal the revolutionary implications of tying Reconstruction to abolition, as well as the bitter strength of resistance to change. The black border population was far smaller than in the Deep South, and slavery less central to the economy. All the border states contained large and rapidly growing regions organized on a free-labor basis and susceptible to antislavery politics. Nonetheless, in all the loyal slave states, slaveholders had dominated antebellum politics. Throughout the war, Delaware and Kentucky clung to the decaying body of slavery. West Virginia, Maryland, and Missouri, by contrast, underwent internal reconstructions that brought to power new classes anxious to overturn slavery and revolutionize state politics. The experience of the border states provided graphic insights into the potential and limitations of a Reconstruction that excluded the participation of both Confederates and blacks.

An amalgam of hostility to the antebellum regime, commitment to democratic change for Unionist whites, reluctance to push beyond emancipation for blacks, and wholesale proscription of former Confederates characterized wartime Unionism throughout the border region. Nowhere was this more evident than in Maryland, a state as divided internally as any in the South. Its 87,000 slaves were concentrated in the counties of southern Maryland, whose large tobacco plantations recalled the social order of the Deep South. The area was economically stagnant, but its political leaders dominated the state, thanks to an archaic system of legislative apportionment that reduced the influence of Baltimore and the rapidly growing white farming counties to its north and west.

Occupied by federal troops when the war began, Maryland soon experienced the disintegration of slavery from within and the mobilization of free blacks against the institution. It also witnessed the rapid growth of emancipationist sentiment among the white population. The "great army in blue," remarked antislavery leader Hugh Lennox Bond, brought in its wake "a great army of ideas." These found a receptive audience among small farmers and the manufacturers and white laborers of Baltimore. "It seems to give great satisfaction to the laboring whites," one slaveholder noted, "that the non laboring slave owners are losing their slaves, and they too will be reduced to the necessity of going into the fields."

Bolstered by loyalty oaths administered to voters by army provost marshals, Unionists committed to immediate and uncompensated emancipation swept the Maryland elections of 1863 and called a constitutional convention to reconstruct the state. Abolition headed the agenda, but the convention also voiced longstanding sectional and class grievances. It established a free, tax-supported public school system, exempted property worth up to $500 from seizure for debt, and, by basing legislative representation on the white population alone, drastically reduced the power of the plantation counties. Voting was confined to those who took a strict loyalty oath, which included an avowal that one had never expressed a "desire" for Confederate victory.

Except for a few emancipationists, however, little concern was evinced for the fate of the former slaves. Many delegates denied that support for abolition implied "any sympathy with *negro equality.*" The school system excluded blacks, and the legislature did nothing to alter a prewar statute that authorized local courts to apprentice free black children, even over the objections of their parents. Within a month of November 1, 1864, the date of emancipation, thousands of former slaves had been bound to white masters, an injustice that galvanized blacks to protest and bedeviled relations between Maryland and federal authorities. All in all, as one Maryland Unionist remarked after the constitution won narrow approval in September 1864:

> [It] must be a source of mortification that emancipation has . . . not been from high principle, . . . but party spirit, vengeful feeling against disloyal slaveholders, and regard for material interest. There has been no expression, at least in this community, of regard for the negro—for human rights, but . . . many expressive of the great prosperity to result to the state by a change of the system of labor.

Early in 1865, the antislavery party moved to solidify its position by disenfranchising all who had served in the Southern armies or given even verbal support to the Confederacy. No thought was given to expanding the Unionist base by allowing the black fifth of Maryland's population to vote.

Unlike the border states, the Confederate Upper South, especially Tennessee, experienced wartime Reconstruction under direct military rule. But in many ways, events followed a similar course. By an accident of war, Tennessee's Reconstruction began not in the staunchly Unionist eastern mountains, but in the slaveholding middle and western parts of the state, where Confederate sentiment prevailed. After the Union capture of Nashville early in February 1862, Lincoln appointed Andrew Johnson military governor. Johnson's decision to remain in the Senate after Tennessee seceded had made him a national symbol of what both he and the Republican North supposed to be a legion of courageous Southern Unionists. He soon took to using the phrase that won him a national reputation for Radicalism: "Treason must be made odious and traitors punished."

Time would reveal that Johnson's Radicalism was cut from a different cloth from that of Northerners who wore the same label, but this was not completely evident during the Civil War. Although Tennessee was exempted from the Emancipation Proclamation, by the end of 1863 Johnson had declared for abolition in the state. His conversion, however, was based less on concern for the slave than on hatred of the Confederacy and of the slaveholders he believed had dragged poor whites unwillingly into rebellion. As he remarked to Gen. John M. Palmer: "Damn the Negroes, I am fighting those traitorous aristocrats, their masters." Yet, as middle Tennessee whites remained resolutely pro-Confederate, while Nashville's free black community mobilized to support his administration and put an end to slavery, Johnson's prejudices softened. By 1864 he was speaking of elevating Tennesseans of both races. Addressing a black gathering in October, Johnson unilaterally decreed the end of slavery in Tennessee. "I will indeed be your Moses," he went on, "and lead you through the Red Sea of war and bondage to a fairer future of liberty and peace."

In November 1864 Johnson was elected Vice President by the Republicans. His presence on the ticket symbolized the party's determination to reward Southern Unionists and extend its organization into the South. The following March, Johnson assumed the Vice Presidency and William G. Brownlow was elected the first governor of a free Tennessee. With its support confined to the eastern part of the state, the Brownlow regime moved swiftly to consolidate its power by securing the ballot box, in the governor's words, against "the approach of treason." A franchise law limited the right to vote to white males "publicly known to have entertained unconditional Union sentiments" throughout the war. As for blacks, Brownlow urged Congress to set aside a territory for their settlement as a "nation of freedmen."

Of all the states where wartime Reconstruction was attempted, only Louisiana lay in the Deep South. Here Lincoln invested the greatest hopes, and here he suffered the greatest disappointments. In a way, it was a cruel trick of fate that decreed that the Reconstruction of the Confederate heartland should be attempted in a state "long divided along economic, cultural and racial lines . . . its politics . . . faction-ridden, corrupt, and occasionally violent." In contrast to Tennessee, however, the initial federal occupation of Louisiana at least took place in a Unionist stronghold. When the forces of Gen. Benjamin F. Butler seized New Orleans in April 1862, the Union took possession of the South's largest city. Its predominantly white population of 144,000 included a large number of the foreign-born, as well as a sizable contingent of Northerners prominent in banking, mercantile activities, and the professions. The Union Army also occupied the sugar parishes of southeastern Louisiana, whose planters, unlike the cotton aristocrats, depended on national tariff protection and tended to be pro-Union Whigs.

As in other states, however, Louisiana's Unionists were divided. Conservatives, notably sugar planters and wealthy merchants, hoped at first to preserve slavery and then insisted that planters should receive compensation for their slaves and retain their traditional political power. The Free State Association embodied the more radical view that a free Louisiana should be more than simply the old order without slavery. Its diverse membership included immigrants, artisans, small merchants, reform-oriented professionals and intellectuals, Northerners (or men educated in the free states and married to Northern women), and federal officeholders. Such men accepted the free labor ideology and saw emancipation as the key to remolding the backward South in the image of the progressive North. For them, the Civil War offered the opportunity to overthrow a reactionary and aristocratic ruling class.

In August 1863 Lincoln endorsed the program of the Free State Association, urging Gen. Nathaniel P. Banks to organize a constitutional convention to abolish slavery in Louisiana. The lenient Ten Percent Plan of December was motivated, in part, by Lincoln's desire to speed up Reconstruction in Louisiana. But the plan exacerbated an emerging split between Radicals and moderates in the Free State movement over what rights, if any, blacks would enjoy in the new Louisiana.

In New Orleans lived the largest free black community of the Deep South. Its wealth, social standing, education, and unique history set it apart not only from the slaves but from free persons of color elsewhere. Most were the descendants of unions between French settlers and black women or of wealthy mulatto emigrants from Haiti. Although denied suffrage, they enjoyed far more rights than free blacks in other states, including the ability to travel freely and testify in court against whites. On the eve of the Civil War, they owned some $2 million worth of property and dominated skilled crafts like bricklaying, cigarmaking, carpentry, and shoemaking.

This community, with a strong sense of its collective history and a network of privately supported schools, orphanages, and benevolent societies, was well positioned to advance its interests under Union rule. Late in 1863 a mass meeting of free blacks heard speakers, including P. B. S. Pinchback, a future lieutenant governor of the state, call for political rights for the free community. At this point, the free blacks were speaking only for themselves, for, as one who knew them well later recounted:

> They tended to separate their struggle from that of the Negroes; some believed that they would achieve their cause more quickly if they abandoned the black to his fate. In their eyes, they were nearer to the white man; they were more advanced than the slave in all respects. . . . A strange error in a society in which prejudice weighed equally against all those who had African blood in their veins, no matter how small the amount.

By January 1864 Lincoln appears to have privately endorsed the enrollment of freeborn blacks as voters in Louisiana. But to Gen. Banks, even limited black suffrage was both personally distasteful and a threat to his efforts to win white support for reconstructing Louisiana under the Ten Percent Plan. Meanwhile, two representatives of the free black community, Arnold Bertonneau, a wealthy wine dealer, and Jean-Baptiste Roudanez, a plantation engineer, arrived in Washington to present a petition for the suffrage. On March 13, 1864, the day after they met with Lincoln, the President wrote Louisiana Gov. Michael Hahn concerning the coming constitutional convention: "I barely suggest for your private consideration, whether some of the colored people not be let in—as for instance, the very intelligent, and especially those who have fought gallantly in our ranks. . . . But this is only a suggestion, not to the public, but to you alone." Hardly a ringing endorsement of black suffrage, Lincoln's letter nonetheless illustrated the capacity for both growth and compromise that was the hallmark of his political leadership. This quality, unfortunately, was in short supply in Louisiana.

The constitutional convention ratified the overthrow of Louisiana's old order. The delegates included reform-minded professionals, small businessmen, artisans, civil servants, and a sprinkling of farmers and laborers, but hardly any planters. Reflecting the urban orientation of the Unionist coalition, the constitution made New Orleans the state capital and sharply increased the city's power in the legislature at the expense of the plantation parishes by basing representation upon voting population rather than total number of inhabitants. In addition, the new constitution established a minimum wage and nine-hour day on public works and adopted a progressive income tax and a system of free public education. And, of course, slavery was abolished. The convention's president spoke of abolition as "the commencement of a new era in civilization . . . [a] dividing line between the old and worn out past and the new and glorious future."

When it came to the role of blacks in free Louisiana, however, the ideas of the "old and worn out past" displayed remarkable resiliency. "Prejudice against the colored people is exhibited continually," reported a correspondent of Secretary of the Treasury Salmon P. Chase, "prejudice bitter and vulgar." Radicals were shocked when men who favored abolition demanded the expulsion of all blacks from the state, even though black troops were at that very moment guarding the convention hall. The delegates ignored Lincoln's "suggestion" concerning limited black suffrage. The result widened the breach in Unionist ranks, turned the Radicals more sharply against the Banks government, and propelled them, within a few months, down the road to universal manhood suffrage.

Land and Labor During the Civil War

Of the many questions raised by emancipation, none was more crucial for the future of both blacks and whites in Southern society than the organization of the region's economy. Slavery had been first and foremost a system of labor. And while all Republicans agreed that "free labor" must replace slavery, few were certain how the transition should be accomplished. "If the [Emancipation] Proclamation makes the slaves actually free," declared the *New York Times* in January 1863, "there will come the further duty of making them work. . . . All this opens a vast and most difficult subject."

As the war progressed, the Union Army extended its control from coastal Virginia and South Carolina to the plantation belt along the Mississippi River. Theoretically, the Second Confiscation Act of

1862 threatened the wholesale forfeiture of property owned by Confederates. Lincoln, however, fearful that large-scale confiscation would antagonize loyal planters and other Southern whites, did not vigorously enforce the act. Far more land came into federal hands from seizures for nonpayment of taxes (in which case it could be sold at auction) or as abandoned property (which the Treasury Department would then administer). How to dispose of this land and organize its black labor became points of conflict as former slaves, former slaveholders, military commanders, and Northern entrepreneurs and reformers competed to influence the wartime transition to free labor.

By 1865, hundreds of thousands of slaves scattered throughout the South had become, under federal auspices, free workers. The most famous of these "rehearsals for Reconstruction" occurred on the South Carolina Sea Islands. When the U.S. Navy occupied Port Royal in November 1861, virtually all the white inhabitants fled to the mainland, leaving behind some 10,000 slaves long accustomed to organizing their own labor. The system of labor employed on mainland rice and Sea Island cotton plantations, in which slaves were assigned daily tasks rather than working in closely supervised gangs, gave these blacks a unique control over the pace and length of the workday.

Sea Island blacks, it quickly became clear, possessed their own definition of the meaning of freedom. When the planters fled, the slaves sacked the big houses and destroyed cotton gins; they then commenced planting corn and potatoes for their own subsistence, but evinced considerable resistance to growing the "slave crop," cotton. But blacks were not to chart their own path to free labor, for in the navy's wake came Northern military officers, Treasury agents, investors, and a squad of young teachers and missionaries known collectively as Gideon's Band, the men fresh from Harvard, Yale, or divinity school, the women from careers as teachers and work in the abolitionist movement. Each group had its own ideas about how the transition to freedom should take place.

The most highly publicized Northerners on the islands, the Gideonites were also the least powerful. More influential were Treasury officials, army officers, and those, lured by the fabulously high price of cotton, who proposed to employ the ex-slaves as paid plantation laborers. In 1863 and 1864, Treasury agents auctioned Sea Island land seized for nonpayment of taxes. Despite efforts by the Gideonites to secure preferential treatment for blacks, only a small portion of the land went to groups of freedmen. Many plantations ended up in the hands of army officers, government officials, and Northern speculators and cotton companies. Eleven were purchased by a consortium of Boston investors that included Edward Atkinson, agent for six Massachusetts textile firms, and Edward S. Philbrick, assistant superintendent of the Boston & Worcester Railroad.

Motivating Atkinson and Philbrick was a typically American combination of reform spirit and desire for profit. In the eyes of these antislavery entrepreneurs, Port Royal offered the perfect opportunity to demonstrate that "the abandonment of slavery did not imply the abandonment of cotton" and that blacks would work more efficiently and profitably as free laborers than as slaves. Sent to the Sea Islands to oversee the experiment, Philbrick sought to create a model free labor environment, with blacks neither exploited by their employers nor lapsing into dependency upon the government. He opposed efforts to allow blacks access to land at below the market price, insisting, "no man . . . appreciates property who does not work for it." He failed to consider the possibility that the former slaves had worked for the land during their 250 years of bondage.

Was the free labor experiment a success? One Gideonite, William C. Gannett, believed so, pointing to an improvement in black living conditions—wooden chimneys replaced by brick, better clothing, a more varied diet. Philbrick himself remained uncertain. Personally, it was lucrative enough, earning him $20,000 in 1863 alone. But the freedmen continued to prefer growing provision crops to cotton. By 1865, concluding that blacks "will not produce as much cotton in this generation as they did five years ago," he divided his plantations into small parcels, sold them to the laborers, and returned to Massachusetts. In the end, the experiment underscored both the ambiguities within the concept of free labor itself and the conflicting interests lurking beneath the effort to reconstruct Southern society. Northern investors understood free labor to mean working for wages on plantations; to blacks it meant farming their own land and living largely independent of the marketplace.

Despite the attention lavished upon it by both contemporaries and historians, the Sea Island experience was anything but typical. It involved relatively few freedmen and remained insulated from both the presence of the former slaveholders and, until late in the war, the disruptive impact of the massive flight of slaves to Union lines. Far more indicative of the future course of Southern labor relations was the system that evolved in southern Louisiana. Here, as in the Sea Islands, blacks aspired to own the land. But occupied Louisiana also contained a large group of Unionist planters, who expected the army to enforce plantation discipline. The federal military commander, Gen. Banks, was convinced that maintaining the plantation system would relieve the army of the burden of caring for black refugees, restore the vitality of the state's economy, and assist in creating a Free State movement with broad support among the white population. When Banks issued labor regulations for 1863, many critics charged that they bore a marked resemblance to slavery. The former slaves, he announced, must avoid vagrancy and idleness and enter into yearly contracts with loyal planters, for either five percent of the proceeds of the year's crop or a wage of $3.00 per month, plus food, shelter, and medical care. Once hired, the blacks were forbidden to leave the plantations without permission of their employers.

Depending on one's point of view, Banks's system was either "the first step in the transition from slave to free labor" or a cynical device to win planters' support for Reconstruction by using the army to restore plantation discipline. The zeal of provost marshals in rounding up "vagrant" blacks produced complaints that the army was acting more like a slave patrol than an agent of emancipation. Yet Banks later claimed to have sent a group of free blacks into the plantation belt "to ascertain what the negroes wanted." His emissaries discovered the former slaves wanted the sanctity of their families respected, education for their children, the end of corporal punishment, and payment of reasonable wages. All these, the general insisted, were provided for by his policy.

A compulsory system of free labor was an anomaly born of the exigencies of war, ideology, and politics. Blacks, who resented having yearly contracts forced upon them and found the wages inadequate, labored irregularly, devoting much of their time to their garden plots and often refusing to obey their employers. Planters, for their part, believed the ban on corporal punishment rendered the entire system useless since blacks would never labor efficiently without it. Banks's system, moreover, was always subordinate to military needs, for, when required, the army impressed black laborers into its ranks directly from the plantations. For all these reasons, the army never succeeded in reviving the state's agriculture. The rich sugar parishes, wrote one planter, were enveloped in "darkness and gloom . . . plantations abandoned, fences and buildings destroyed, . . . the negroes conscripted into the army or wandering about. . . . Such is war, civil war." Yet after the fall of Vicksburg in July 1863, the army extended the Banks labor system to the entire Mississippi Valley.

Despite local variations in policy, most army officials assumed that the emancipated slaves should remain as plantation laborers. Only occasionally did glimmerings of an alternative point of view appear. The largest laboratory of black economic independence was Davis Bend, Mississippi, which contained the huge plantations of Confederate President Jefferson Davis and his brother Joseph. Before the war, the Davis brothers had attempted to establish a model slave community, with blacks far better fed and housed than elsewhere in the state and permitted an extraordinary degree of self-government, including a slave jury system that enforced plantation discipline. Other planters mocked "Joe Davis's free negroes," but the system enhanced the family's reputation among blacks. After the war, one group of freedmen pressed for Jefferson Davis's release from prison because "altho he tried hard to keep us all slaves . . . some of us well know of many kindness he shown his slaves on his plantation."

The Civil War destroyed the "model" slave system at Davis Bend. By the time Union troops arrived, Joseph Davis had fled and the blacks were running the plantation. In 1863, General Grant decided that Davis Bend should become a "negro paradise," and the following year the entire area was set aside for the exclusive settlement of freedmen. By 1865, Davis Bend had become a remarkable example of self-reliance, whose laborers raised nearly 2,000 bales of cotton and earned a profit of $160,000. The community had its own system of government, complete with elected judges and sheriffs.

Davis Bend demonstrated that not all blacks, if given the choice, would eschew the marketplace and cotton. But it was not Davis Bend, any more than the South Carolina Sea Islands, that proved to be the true rehearsal for Reconstruction so far as labor relations were concerned. Despite their apparent failure, the Louisiana and Mississippi Valley experiments in free labor not only involved far larger numbers of blacks, but established a system of plantation agriculture based on yearly labor contracts, which would carry over into the postwar policies of the army and the Freedmen's Bureau. Almost by default, military men had made crucial policy decisions that began to resolve one of the most complex problems to arise from the Civil War. And their labor policies exacerbated a developing split within the Republican party over the course of wartime Reconstruction and the implications of emancipation.

The Politics of Emancipation and the End of the War

By mid-1864, a white resident of Chattanooga noted, life in the Union-occupied South was "so different from what it used to be." Yankee teachers directed schools for blacks, and hundreds of thousands of former slaves were working for wages. Nonetheless, the course of events in the South threatened to divide Northern Republicans. With emancipation now an article of party faith, political debate increasingly centered on the freedmen's postwar status. Many Republicans were particularly troubled by developments in Louisiana.

In 1864, the major concern even of Radical Republicans was equality before the law, not black suffrage, and the control of new Southern governments by genuine Unionists. On both counts, the new government of Louisiana appeared wanting. Banks's labor system and the overtly antiblack views of his supporters convinced many Republicans that the freedmen could not receive equitable treatment from governments organized under Lincoln's Ten Percent Plan.

Dissatisfaction with events in Louisiana and concern for the fate of the freedmen came together in July 1864 to produce the Wade-Davis Bill. This proposed to delay the start of Reconstruction until a majority of a state's white males had pledged to support the federal Constitution. Then, elections would be held for a constitutional convention, with suffrage restricted to those who swore under the Ironclad Oath that they had never aided the Confederacy. The bill also guaranteed blacks equality before the law, although not the suffrage. Fearing the measure would force him to repudiate the Louisiana regime, Lincoln pocket-vetoed it, whereupon its Radical authors, Ohio Sen. Benjamin F. Wade and Maryland Congressman Henry Winter Davis, issued an intemperate "manifesto" accusing the President of exercising "dictatorial usurpation."

Despite the harsh language of the Wade-Davis Manifesto, these events did not sever relations between Lincoln and the Radical Republicans. The points of unity among Republicans, especially their commitment to winning the war and securing emancipation, were far greater than their differences. Nonetheless, the controversy underscored the party's divisions concerning Reconstruction. Lincoln viewed Reconstruction as part of the effort to win the war and secure emancipation. His aim was to weaken the Confederacy by establishing state governments that attracted broad Southern support. To the Radicals, Reconstruction implied a far-reaching transformation in Southern society; as a result, they wished to delay the process until after the war and to limit participation to a smaller number of "iron-clad loyalists." Wade-Davis limited suffrage to loyal whites. Many Radicals, however, were already convinced that black suffrage must come. In many states, George S. Boutwell insisted, the freedmen "are almost the only people who are trustworthy supporters of the Union." But it was not the Radicals who forced black suffrage onto the center stage of politics. That was accomplished by the political mobilization of New Orleans's free blacks.

Soon after Louisiana's 1864 constitutional convention, the New Orleans *Tribune* was created as a rallying point for Radicalism. Its founder was Louis C. Roudanez, the wealthy son of a French merchant and a free woman of color, who had earned medical degrees at both the University of Paris and Dartmouth. In November 1864, Jean-Charles Houzeau, one of the most remarkable men to take part in the saga of Reconstruction, became the editor. Born to an aristocratic Belgian family, this journalist and astronomer had emigrated to Texas in 1858, opposed secession, and in 1864 arrived in Louisiana. In Dr. Roudanez and the others associated with the newspaper, Houzeau recognized "the vanguard of the African population of the United States."

Even before Houzeau's arrival, the *Tribune* had determined to demand suffrage for the former slaves, the free blacks' "*dormant* partners." But it was Houzeau who transformed the *Tribune* into a journal widely respected in Northern Republican circles and who broadened its message to encompass a coherent radical program embracing black suffrage, equality before the law, desegregation of Louisiana's schools and New Orleans's streetcars, and division of the plantations among the freedmen. And it was he who made the alliance between free blacks and the freedmen the cornerstone of *Tribune* politics, as the only means of preventing the revolution unleashed by the Civil War from succumbing to reaction. Once the paper made its commitment to suffrage for the freedmen, it did not turn back, and it brought in tow the Radical party of Louisiana. In December 1864, mass meetings in New Orleans heard white Radical Thomas J. Durant and free blacks Oscar J. Dunn and James H. Ingraham demand black suffrage. "We regard all black and colored men," Dunn declared, "as fellow sufferers."

Thus, as the Civil War drew to a close, the nation's most articulate and politicized black community was thoroughly estranged from the military and civil authorities of free Louisiana. In Washington, their complaints found a sympathetic audience. Contact with this cultured, economically successful group challenged the racist assumptions widespread even in Republican circles and doubtless influenced Lincoln's evolution toward a more egalitarian approach to Reconstruction. Because of Louisiana, the issue of Reconstruction remained unresolved, and when Congress adjourned in March 1865, the Radicals prepared themselves for a massive effort to persuade the North of the necessity of black suffrage.

Despite the Louisiana impasse, the second session of the Thirty-Eighth Congress was indeed a historic occasion. In 1864 the Senate had approved the Thirteenth Amendment, abolishing slavery throughout the Union. On January 31, 1865, by a margin of 119 to 56, the Amendment won House approval and was forwarded to the states for ratification. "The one question of the age is *settled*," declared antislavery Congressman Cornelius Cole. But like so many other achievements of the Civil War, the Amendment closed one issue only to open a host of others. "What is freedom?" James A. Garfield later asked. "Is it the bare privilege of not being chained? . . . If this is all, then freedom is a bitter mockery, a cruel delusion." Many Republicans believed the Thirteenth Amendment made blacks part of a national citizenship whose fundamental rights were protected by a beneficent federal government.

Even the abolitionist movement could not decide whether the Amendment was an end or a beginning. "My vocation, as an Abolitionist, thank God, is ended," declared William Lloyd Garrison, urging the American Anti-Slavery Society at its May 1865 annual meeting to dissolve in triumph. To which Frederick Douglass replied, "Slavery is not abolished until the black man has the ballot." Garrison's proposal was defeated, Wendell Phillips replaced him as the society's president, and the *National Anti-Slavery Standard* appeared with a new motto on its masthead: "No Reconstruction Without Negro Suffrage."

Lurking behind these debates was a broader question suggested by the end of slavery: Should the freedmen be viewed as ready to take their place as citizens and participants in the competitive marketplace, or did their unique historical experience oblige the federal government to take special action on their behalf? Although they had generally accepted the expansion of national authority during the war, many reformers still espoused laissez-faire ideas. Assistance begets dependence, insisted Sea Island teacher William C. Gannett; the sooner blacks were "thrown upon themselves, the speedier will be their salvation."

At the other end of this ideological spectrum stood Radicals advocating an act of federal intervention comparable in scope to emancipation—the division of planter lands among the freedmen. The most persistent Congressional supporter of such a measure was George W. Julian, chairman of the House Committee on Public Lands, who insisted that without land reform, the freedmen would find themselves reduced to "a system of wages slavery . . . more galling than slavery itself." The creation of the Freedmen's Bureau in March 1865 symbolized the widespread belief among Republicans that the federal government must shoulder broad responsibility for the emancipated slaves, including offering them some kind of access to land.

The Bureau was empowered to distribute clothing, food, and fuel to destitute freedmen and oversee "all subjects" relating to their condition in the South. Despite its unprecedented responsibilities, it was clearly seen as a temporary expedient, for its life-span was initially limited to one year. Massachusetts Sen. Charles Sumner had proposed establishing the Bureau as a permanent agency with a secretary of Cabinet rank, but such an idea ran counter to strong inhibitions against long-term guardianship. In one respect, however, the Freedmen's Bureau appeared to promise a permanent transformation of the condition of the emancipated slaves. For Congress authorized it to divide abandoned and confiscated land into forty-acre plots for rental to freedmen and loyal refugees and eventual sale. While hardly a definitive commitment to land distribution, the law establishing the Bureau clearly anticipated that the government would aid some blacks to become independent farmers in a "free labor" South.

While Congress deliberated, a victorious Gen. William T. Sherman added a new dimension to the already perplexing land question. On January 12, 1865, at the urging of Secretary of War Edwin M. Stanton, who had joined him in Savannah, Sherman gathered twenty leaders of the city's black community, mostly Baptist and Methodist ministers. The conversation revealed that these black leaders possessed a clear conception of the meaning of freedom. Garrison Frazier, a Baptist minister who had known bondage for sixty years before purchasing his liberty in 1857, defined freedom as "placing us where we could reap the fruit of our own labor." The best way to accomplish this, he added, was "to have land, and . . . till it by our own labor." Four days later, Sherman issued Special Field Order No. 15, setting aside the Sea Islands and a portion of the lowcountry rice coast south of Charleston, extending thirty miles inland, for the exclusive settlement of blacks. Each family would receive forty acres of land, and Sherman later authorized the army to loan them mules. (Here, perhaps, lies the origin of the phrase "forty acres and a mule" that would soon echo throughout the South.) By June, some 40,000 freedmen had been settled on 400,000 acres of "Sherman land." Here in coastal South Carolina and Georgia, the prospect beckoned of a transformation of Southern society more radical even than the end of slavery.

And now the war hastened inexorably to its close. Sherman's army moved into South Carolina, bringing in its wake, as one rice planter recorded in his journal, the "breath of Emancipation." Planters' homes, smokehouses, and storerooms were plundered; an overseer was murdered; on one plantation blacks refused to listen any longer to the local white minister, but "would shout and sing after their own fashion." What one planter called "the general wreck of our property" dealt the lowcountry rice aristocracy a blow from which it never recovered.

On February 18, 1865, Union forces entered Charleston, among them the black Fifty-Fourth Massachusetts Infantry singing "John Brown's Body." Five weeks later the city witnessed a "grand jubilee" of freedom, a vast outpouring of the city's black community. Four thousand blacks took part in a massive parade—soldiers, fire companies, members of the various trades with their respective tools, schoolchildren carrying a banner with the inscription "We

Know No Master But Ourselves." Farther north, similar scenes of jubilation occurred as Grant's army, on April 3, occupied Richmond. Blacks thronged the streets, dancing, praying, singing "Slavery chain done broke at last." The next day, Lincoln, heedless of his own safety, walked the streets of Richmond accompanied only by a dozen sailors. At every step he was besieged by former slaves who hailed him as a "Messiah" and fell on their knees before the embarrassed President, who asked them to remain standing. A Richmond black told his former owner, "all was equal. . . . All the land belongs to the Yankees now and they gwine divide it out among de coloured people." On April 9, Grant accepted Lee's surrender at Appomattox.

Amid this cavalcade of historic events, Reconstruction emerged as the central problem confronting the nation. But, as James G. Blaine later remarked, Lincoln did not turn to peacetime with a "fixed plan" of Reconstruction. The President had approved the lenient policies of General Banks in Louisiana and the far more proscriptive acts of Andrew Johnson in Tennessee, all in an attempt to quicken Union victory and secure the abolition of slavery, rather than to fashion a blueprint for the postwar South. Nor had wartime Reconstruction been particularly successful. Union governments had been created within the Confederacy in Virginia, Tennessee, Arkansas, and Louisiana, but none had attracted truly broad support and none had been recognized by Congress.

On April 11, Lincoln delivered at the White House what came to be known as his "last speech," the first occasion on which he (or any American President) publicly endorsed black suffrage, albeit in cautious and limited language: "I would myself prefer that [the vote] were now conferred on the very intelligent, and on those who serve our cause as soldiers." The speech was typical of Lincoln—an attempt to maintain public support and party unity by moving partway toward the Radical position on black suffrage, without promising to impose his "preference" on the defeated South. The *New York Times* concluded that Lincoln had judged the time not yet ripe for "the statement of a settled reconstruction policy." Four days later, the President was assassinated by the actor John Wilkes Booth.

Years before the end of slavery, black abolitionist Charles L. Reason had predicted that emancipation would impose "severe trials" on the freedmen: "The prejudice now felt against them for bearing on their persons the brand of slaves, cannot die out immediately." Yet in a society resting on ideals of individual autonomy and competitive equality, could there be a permanent resting place between slavery and citizenship? The elusive concept of "freedom" differed substantially in the United States from societies accustomed to fixed social classes and historically defined gradations of civil and political rights. Here, emancipation led inexorably to demands for civil equality and the vote. And, on a more pragmatic level, without black suffrage could the old ruling class of the South be prevented from reestablishing its political hegemony? These questions had been repeatedly raised as the war neared its close, but the war did not provide an answer.

It was becoming apparent, moreover, that whites would not debate these questions alone. In 1864 Isaac Brinckerhoff, a Northern Baptist missionary in Union-occupied Florida, delivered a series of lectures on the United States Constitution and the principles of republican government. The blacks, he recorded, "were deeply interested. Old Meredith, my colored servant, when asked how he was enjoying the lectures, spread both his hands and said, 'I grow bigger and bigger every time.' " Here was a people just emerging onto the stage of politics, and they, too, would have a say in defining the meaning of freedom.

As postwar Reconstruction commenced, Sidney George Fisher, a conservative Philadelphia lawyer, observed that the war had left fundamental issues unresolved:

> It seems our fate never to get rid of the Negro question. No sooner have we abolished slavery than a party, which seems [to] be growing in power, proposes Negro suffrage, so that the problem—What shall we do with the Negro?—seems as far from being settled as ever. In fact it is *incapable* of any solution that will satisfy both North and South.

Fisher understood the inevitability of continuing conflict over the legacy of emancipation. "Verily," as Frederick Douglass put it, "the work does not end with the abolition of slavery, but only begins."

The Meaning of Freedom

Freedom came in different ways to different parts of the South. In large areas, slavery had disintegrated long before Lee's surrender, but elsewhere, far from the presence of federal troops, blacks did not learn of its irrevocable end until the spring of 1865. Despite the many disappointments that followed, this generation of blacks would always regard the moment when "de freedom sun shine out" as the great watershed of their lives. Houston H. Holloway, who had been sold three times before he reached the age of twenty in 1865, later recalled with vivid clarity the day emancipation came to his section of Georgia: "I felt like a bird out of a cage. Amen. Amen. Amen. I could hardly ask to feel any better than I did that day. . . . The week passed off in a blaze of glory."

"Freedom," said a black minister, "burned in the black heart long before freedom was born." But what did "freedom" mean? "It is necessary to define that word," Freedmen's Bureau Commissioner O. O. Howard told a black audience in 1865, "for it is most apt to be misunderstood." Howard assumed a straightforward definition existed. But "freedom" itself became a terrain of conflict, its substance open to different and sometimes contradictory interpretations, its content changing for whites as well as blacks in the aftermath of the Civil War.

Blacks carried out of bondage an understanding of their new condition shaped both by their experience as slaves and by observation of the free society around them. What one planter called their "wild notions of rights and freedom" encompassed, first of all, an end to the myriad injustices associated with slavery. Some, like black minister Henry M. Turner, stressed that freedom meant the enjoyment of "our rights in common with other men." "If I cannot do like a white man I am not free," Henry Adams told his former master in 1865. "I see how the poor white people do. I ought to do so too, or else I am a slave."

But underpinning the specific aspirations lay a broader theme: a desire for independence from white control, for autonomy both as individuals and as members of a community being transformed by emancipation. Before the war, free blacks had created churches, schools, and mutual benefit societies, while slaves had forged a culture centered on the family and church. With freedom, these institutions were consolidated, expanded, and liberated from white supervision, and new ones—particularly political organizations—joined them as focal points of black life. In stabilizing their families, seizing control of their churches, greatly expanding their schools and benevolent societies, staking a claim to economic independence, and forging a political culture, blacks during Reconstruction laid the foundation for the modern black community, whose roots lay deep in slavery but whose structure and values reflected the consequences of emancipation.

From Slavery to Freedom

Long after the end of the Civil War, the experience of bondage remained deeply etched in blacks' collective memory. The freedmen resented not only the brutal incidents of slavery but the fact of having been held as slaves at all. During a visit to Richmond, Scottish minister David Macrae was surprised to hear a former slave complain of past mistreatment, while acknowledging he had never been whipped. "How were you cruelly treated then?" asked Macrae. "I was cruelly treated," answered the freedman, "because I was kept in slavery."

In countless ways, the newly freed slaves sought to overturn the real and symbolic authority whites had exercised over every aspect of their lives. Blacks relished opportunities to flaunt their liberation from the innumerable regulations, significant and trivial, associated with slavery. Freedmen held mass meetings and religious services unrestrained by white surveillance, acquired previously forbidden dogs, guns, and liquor, and refused to yield the sidewalks to whites.

They dressed as they pleased, black women sometimes wearing gaudy finery, carrying parasols, and replacing the slave kerchief with colorful hats and veils. Whites complained of "insolence" and "insubordination" among the freedmen, by which they meant any departure from the deference and obedience expected under slavery. On the Bradford plantation in Florida, one untoward incident followed another. First, the family cook told Mrs. Bradford "if she want any dinner she kin cook it herself." Then the former slaves went off to a meeting with Northern soldiers to discuss "our freedom." Told that she and her daughter could not attend, one woman replied "they were now free and if she saw fit to take her daughter into that crowd it was nobody's business." "Never before had I a word of impudence from any of our black folk," recorded nineteen-year-old Susan Bradford, "but they are not ours any longer."

Among the most resented of slavery's restrictions was the rule, enforced by patrols, than no black could travel without a pass. With emancipation, it seemed that half the South's black population took to the roads. Southern towns and cities experienced an especially large influx of freedmen during and immediately after the Civil War. In the cities, many blacks believed, "freedom was free-er." Here were schools, churches, and fraternal societies, as well as the army (including, in 1865, black soldiers) and the Freedmen's Bureau, offering protection from the violence so pervasive in much of the rural South. Between 1865 and 1870, the black population of the South's ten largest cities doubled, while the number of white residents rose by only ten percent. Smaller towns, from which blacks had often been excluded as slaves, experienced even more dramatic increases.

Black migrants who hoped to find urban employment often encountered severe disappointment. The influx from the country-side flooded the labor market, consigning most urban blacks to low-wage, menial employment. Unable to obtain decent housing, black migrants lived in squalid shantytowns on the outskirts of Southern cities, where the incidence of disease and death far exceeded that among white city dwellers. The result was a striking change in Southern urban living patterns. Before the war, blacks and whites had lived scattered throughout Southern cities. Reconstruction witnessed the rise of a new, segregated, urban geography.

No aspect of black mobility was more poignant than the effort to reunite families separated during slavery. "In their eyes," wrote a Freedmen's Bureau agent, "the work of emancipation was incomplete until the families which had been dispersed by slavery were reunited." One freedman, writing from Texas, asked the Bureau's aid in locating "my own dearest relatives," providing a long list of sisters, nieces, nephews, uncles, and in-laws, none of whom he had seen since his sale in Virginia twenty-four years before. A typical plea for help appeared in the Nashville *Colored Tennessean*:

> During the year 1849, Thomas Sample carried away from this city, as his slaves, our daughter, Polly, and son. . . . We will give $100 each for them to any person who will assist them . . . to get to Nashville, or get word to us of their whereabouts.

Although vulnerable to disruption, strong family ties had existed under slavery. Emancipation allowed blacks to solidify their family connections, and most freedmen seized the opportunity. Many families, in addition, adopted the children of deceased relatives and friends rather than see them apprenticed to white masters or placed in Freedmen's Bureau orphanages. By 1870, a large majority of blacks lived in two-parent households.

But while emancipation strengthened the preexisting black family, it also transformed the roles of its members and relations among them. One common, significant change was that slave families, separated because their members belonged to different owners, could now live together. More widely noticed by white observers in early Reconstruction was the withdrawal of black women from field labor.

Beginning in 1865, and for years thereafter, Southern whites throughout the South complained of the difficulty of obtaining female field laborers. Planters, Freedmen's Bureau officials, and Northern visitors all ridiculed the black "female aristocracy" for "acting the *lady*" or mimicking the family patterns of middle-class whites. White employers also resented their inability to force black children to labor in the fields, especially after the spread of schools in rural areas. Contemporaries appeared uncertain whether black women, black men, or both were responsible for the withdrawal of females from agricultural labor. There is no question that many black men considered it manly to have their wives work at home and believed that, as head of the family, the male should decide how its labor was organized. But many black women desired to devote more time than under slavery to caring for their children and to domestic responsibilities like cooking, sewing, and laundering.

The shift of black female labor from the fields to the home proved a temporary phenomenon. The rise of renting and sharecropping, which made each family responsible for its own plot of land, placed a premium on the labor of all family members. The dire poverty of many black families, deepened by the depression of the 1870s, made it essential for both women and men to contribute to the family's income. Throughout this period, a far higher percentage of black than white women and children worked for wages outside their homes. Where women continued to concentrate on domestic tasks, and children attended school, they frequently engaged in seasonal field labor. Thus, emancipation did not eliminate labor outside the home by black women and children, but it fundamentally altered control over their labor. Now blacks themselves, rather than a white owner or overseer, decided where and when black women and children worked.

For blacks, liberating their families from the authority of whites was an indispensable element of freedom. But the family itself was in some ways transformed by emancipation. Although historians no longer view the slave family as matriarchal, it is true that slave men did not function as economic breadwinners and that their masters wielded authority within the household. In a sense, slavery had imposed on black men and women the rough "equality" of powerlessness. With freedom came developments that strengthened patriarchy within the black family and consigned men and women to separate spheres.

Outside events strongly influenced this development. Service in the Union Army enabled black men to participate more directly than women in the struggle for freedom. The Freedmen's Bureau designated the husband as head of the black household, insisting that men sign contracts for the labor of their entire families and establishing lower wage scales for women. After 1867 black men could serve on juries, vote, hold office, and rise to leadership in the Republican party, while black women, like their white counterparts, could not. And black preachers, editors, and politicians emphasized women's responsibility for making the home "a place of peace and comfort" for men and urged them to submit to their husbands' authority.

Not all black women placidly accepted the increasingly patriarchal quality of black family life. Indeed, many proved more than willing to bring family disputes before public authorities. The records of the Freedmen's Bureau contain hundreds of complaints by black women of beatings, infidelity, and lack of child support. Some black women objected to their husbands' signing labor contracts for them, demanded separate payment of their wages, and refused to be liable for their husbands' debts at country stores. Yet if emancipation not only institutionalized the black family but also spawned tensions within it, black men and women shared a passionate commitment to the stability of family life as the solid foundation upon which a new black community could flourish.

Building the Black Community

Second only to the family as a focal point of black life stood the church. And, as in the case of the family, Reconstruction was a time of consolidation and transformation for black religion. With the death of slavery, urban blacks seized control of their own churches, while the "invisible institution" of the rural slave church emerged into the light of day. The creation of an independent black religious life proved to be a momentous and irreversible consequence of emancipation.

In antebellum Southern Protestant congregations, slaves and free blacks had enjoyed a kind of associate membership. Subject to the same rules and discipline as whites, they were required to sit in the back of the church or in the gallery during services and were excluded from Sabbath schools and a role in church governance. In the larger cities, the number of black members often justified the organization of wholly black congregations and the construction of separate churches, although these were legally required to have white pastors. In the aftermath of emancipation, the wholesale withdrawal of blacks from biracial congregations redrew the religious map of the South. Two causes combined to produce the independent black church: the refusal of whites to offer blacks an equal place within their congregations and the black quest for self-determination.

Throughout the South, blacks emerging from slavery pooled their resources to purchase land and erect their own churches. Before the buildings were completed, they held services in structures as diverse as a railroad boxcar, where Atlanta's First Baptist Church gathered, or an outdoor "bush arbor," where the First Baptist Church of Memphis congregated in 1865. The first new building to rise amid Charleston's ruins was a black church on Calhoun Street; by 1866 ten more had been constructed. In the countryside, a community would often build a single church, used in rotation by the various black denominations. By the end of Reconstruction in 1877, the vast majority of Southern blacks had withdrawn from churches dominated by whites. On the eve of the war, 42,000 black Methodists worshipped in biracial South Carolina churches; by the 1870s, only 600 remained.

The church was "the first social institution fully controlled by black men in America," and its multiple functions testified to its centrality in the black community. Churches housed schools, social events, and political gatherings. In rural areas, church picnics, festivals, and excursions often provided the only opportunity for fellowship and recreation. The church served as an "Ecclesiastical Court House," promoting moral values, adjudicating family disputes, and disciplining individuals for adultery and other illicit behavior. In every black community, ministers were among the most respected individuals, esteemed for their speaking ability, organizational talents, and good judgment on matters both public and private.

Inevitably, too, preachers played a central role in Reconstruction black politics. Many agreed with Rev. Charles H. Pearce, who held several Reconstruction offices in Florida, that it was "impossible" to separate religion and politics: "A man in this State cannot do his whole duty as a minister except he looks out for the political interests of his people." Even those preachers who lacked ambition for political position sometimes found it thrust upon them. Often among the few literate blacks in a community, they were called on to serve as election registrars and candidates for office. Over 100 black ministers, hailing from North and South, from free and slave backgrounds, and from every black denomination from African Methodist Episcopal to Primitive Baptist, would be elected to legislative seats during Reconstruction.

Throughout Reconstruction, religious convictions shaped blacks' understanding of the momentous events around them, the language in which they voiced aspirations for justice and autonomy. Blacks inherited from slavery a distinctive version of Christian faith, in which Jesus appeared as a personal redeemer offering solace in the face of misfortune, while the Old Testament suggested that they were a chosen people, analogous to the Jews in Egypt, whom God, in the fullness of time, would deliver from bondage. "There is no part of the Bible with which they are so familiar as the story of the deliverance of the Children of Israel," a white army chaplain reported in 1866.

Emancipation and the defeat of the Confederacy strongly reinforced this messianic vision of history. Even nonclerics used secular and religious vocabulary interchangeably, as in one 1867 speech recorded by a North Carolina justice of the peace:

> He said it was not now like it used to be, that . . . the negro was about to get his equal rights. . . . That the negroes owed their freedom to the courage of the negro soldiers and to God. . . . He made frequent references to the II and IV chapters of Joshua for a full accomplishment of the principles and destiny of the race. It was concluded that the race have a destiny in view similar to the Children of Israel.

The rise of the independent black church was accompanied by the creation of a host of fraternal, benevolent, and mutual aid societies. In early Reconstruction, blacks created literally thousands of such organizations; a partial list includes burial societies, debating clubs, Masonic lodges, fire companies, drama societies, trade associations, temperance clubs, and equal rights leagues. Offering social fellowship, sickness and funeral benefits, and, most of all, a chance to manage their own affairs, these voluntary associations embodied a spirit of collective self-improvement. Robert G. Fitzgerald, who had been born free in Delaware, served in both the U.S. Army and Navy, and came to Virginia to teach in 1866, was delighted to see rural blacks establishing churches, lyceums, and schools. "They tell me," he recorded in his diary, "before Mr. Lincoln made them free they had nothing to work for, to look up to, now they have everything, and will, by God's help, make the best of it." Moreover, the spirit of mutual self-help extended outward from the societies to embrace destitute nonmembers. In 1865 and 1866, blacks in Nashville, Jackson, New Orleans, and Atlanta, as well as in many rural areas, raised money to establish orphanages, soup kitchens, employment agencies, and poor relief funds.

Perhaps the most striking illustration of the freedmen's quest for self-improvement was their seemingly unquenchable thirst for education. Before the war, every Southern state except Tennessee had prohibited the instruction of slaves, and although many free blacks had attended school and a number of slaves became literate through their own efforts or the aid of sympathetic masters, over ninety percent of the South's adult black population was illiterate in 1860. Access to education for themselves and their children was, for blacks, central to the meaning of freedom, and white contemporaries were astonished by their "avidity for learning." Adults as well as children thronged the schools. A Northern teacher in Florida reported how one sixty-year-old woman, "just beginning to spell, seems as if she could not think of any thing but her book, says she spells her lesson all the evening, then she dreams about it, and wakes up thinking about it."

Northern benevolent societies, the Freedmen's Bureau, and, after 1868, state governments provided most of the funding for black education during Reconstruction. But the initiative often lay with blacks themselves. Urban blacks took immediate steps to set up schools, sometimes holding classes temporarily in abandoned warehouses, billiards rooms, or, in New Orleans and Savannah, former slave markets. In rural areas, Freedmen's Bureau officials repeatedly expressed surprise at discovering classes organized by blacks already meeting in churches, basements, or private homes. And everywhere there were children teaching their parents the alphabet at home, laborers on lunch breaks "poring over the elementary pages," and the "wayside schools" described by a Bureau officer:

A negro riding on a loaded wagon, or sitting on a hack waiting for a train, or by the cabin door, is often seen, book in hand delving after the rudiments of knowledge. A group on the platform of a depot, after carefully conning an old spelling book, resolves itself into a class.

Throughout the South, blacks in 1865 and 1866 raised money to purchase land, build schoolhouses, and pay teachers' salaries. Some communities voluntarily taxed themselves; in others black schools charged tuition, while allowing a number of the poorest families to enroll their children free of charge. Black artisans donated their labor to construct schoolhouses, and black families offered room and board to teachers to supplement their salaries. By 1870, blacks had expended over $1 million on education, a fact that long remained a point of collective pride. "Whoever may hereafter lay claim to the honor of 'establishing' . . . schools," wrote a black resident of Selma in 1867, "I trust the fact will never be ignored that Miss Lucy Lee, one of the emancipated, was the pioneer teacher of the colored children, . . . without the aid of Northern societies."

Inevitably, the first black teachers appeared incompetent in Northern eyes, for a smattering of education might place an individual in front of a class. One poignantly explained, "I never had the chance of goen to school for I was a slave until freedom. . . . I am the only teacher because we can not doe better now." Yet even an imperfect literacy, coupled with the courage often required to establish a rural school in the fact of local white opposition, marked these teachers as community leaders. Black teachers played numerous roles apart from education, assisting freedmen in contract disputes, engaging in church work, and drafting petitions to the Freedmen's Bureau, state officials, and Congress. Like the ministry, teaching frequently became a springboard to political office. At least seventy black teachers served in state legislatures during Reconstruction. And many black politicians were linked in other ways to the quest for learning, like Alabama Congressman Benjamin S. Turner, an ex-slave "destitute of education," who financed a Selma school.

Not surprisingly, the majority of black teachers who held political office during Reconstruction had been free before the Civil War. Indeed the schools, like the entire institutional structure established by blacks during Reconstruction, symbolized the emergence of a community that united the free and the freed, and Northern and Southern blacks. The process occurred most smoothly in the Upper South, where the cultural and economic gap between free blacks and slaves had always been less pronounced than in the urban Deep South. While generally lighter in color than slaves, most Upper South free blacks were poor urban workers or farm laborers, often tied to the slave community through marriage and church membership. In cities like New Orleans, Mobile, Savannah, and Charleston, however, affluent mulatto elites responded with deep ambivalence to the new situation created by emancipation. Even in New Orleans, where politically conscious free blacks had already moved to make common cause with the freedmen, a sense of exclusivity survived the end of slavery. The Freedmen's Bureau found many free blacks reluctant to send their children to school with former slaves.

After New Orleans, the South's largest and wealthiest community of free blacks resided in Charleston, although the free elite there was neither as rich nor as culturally distinct as its Louisiana counterpart. Arriving in Charleston in November 1865, Northern journalist John R. Dennett found some members of the free elite cultivating their old exclusiveness. Others, however, took the lead in organizing assistance for destitute freedmen and in teaching the former slaves. Sons and daughters of prominent free families, mostly young people in their twenties, fanned out into the South Carolina countryside as teachers and missionaries. Several thereby acquired positions of local political leadership and later returned to Charleston as constitutional convention delegates and legislators. Thus the children of the Charleston elite cast their lot with the freedmen, bringing, as they saw it, modern culture to the former slaves. This encounter was not without its tensions. But in the long run it hastened the emergence of a black community stratified by class rather than color, in which the former free elite took its place as one element of a new black bourgeoisie, instead of existing as a separate caste as in the antebellum port cities.

In the severing of ties that had bound black and white families and churches to one another under slavery, the coming together of blacks in an explosion of institution building, and the political and cultural fusion of former free blacks and former slaves, Reconstruction witnessed the birth of the modern black community. All in all, the months following the end of the Civil War were a period of remarkable accomplishment for Southern blacks. Looking back in January 1866, the Philadelphia-born black missionary Jonathan C. Gibbs could only exclaim: "we have progressed a century in a year."

The Economics of Freedom

Nowhere were blacks' efforts to define their freedom more explosive for the entire society than in the economy. Freedmen brought out of slavery a conception of themselves as a "Working Class of People" who had been unjustly deprived of the fruits of their labor. To white predictions that they would not work, blacks responded that if any class could be characterized as lazy, it was the planters, who had "lived in idleness all their lives on stolen labor." It is certainly true that many blacks expected to labor less as free men and women than they had as slaves, an understandable aim considering the conditions they had previously known. "Whence comes the assertion that the 'nigger won't work'?" asked an Alabama freedman. "It comes from this fact: . . . the freedman refuses to be driven out into the field two hours before day, and work until 9 or 10 o'clock in the night, as was the case in the days of slavery."

Yet freedom meant more than shorter hours and payment of wages. Freedmen sought to control the conditions under which they labored, end their subordination to white authority, and carve out the greatest measure of economic autonomy. These aims led them to prefer tenancy to wage labor, and leasing land for a fixed rent to sharecropping. Above all, they inspired the quest for land. Owning land, the freedmen believed, would "complete their independence."

To those familiar with the experience of other postemancipation societies, blacks' "mania for owning a small piece of land" did not appear surprising. Freedmen in Haiti, the British and Spanish Caribbean, and Brazil all saw ownership of land as crucial to economic independence, and everywhere former slaves sought to avoid returning to plantation labor. Unlike freedmen in other countries, however, American blacks emerged from slavery convinced that the federal government had committed itself to land distribution. Belief in an imminent division of land was most pervasive in the South Carolina and Georgia lowcountry, but the idea was shared in other parts of the South as well, including counties that had never been occupied by federal troops. Blacks insisted that their past labor entitled them to at least a portion of their owners' estates. As an Alabama black convention put it: "The property which they hold was nearly all earned by the sweat of *our* brows."

In some parts of the South, blacks in 1865 did more than argue the merits of their case. Hundreds of freedmen refused either to sign labor contracts or to leave the plantations, insisting that the land belonged to them. On the property of a Tennessee planter, former slaves not only claimed to be "joint heirs" to the estate but, the owner complained, abandoned the slave quarters and took up residence "in the rooms of my house." Few freedmen were able to maintain control of land seized in this manner. A small number did, however, obtain property through other means, squatting on unoccupied land in sparsely populated states like Florida and Texas, buying tiny city plots, or cooperatively purchasing farms and plantations. Most blacks, however, emerged from slavery unable to purchase land even at the depressed prices of early Reconstruction and confronted by a white community unwilling to advance credit or sell them property. Thus, they entered the world of free labor as wage or share workers on land owned by whites. The adjustment to a new social order in which their persons were removed from the market but their labor was bought and sold like any other commodity proved in many respects difficult. For it required them to adapt to the logic of the economic market, where the impersonal laws of supply and demand and the balance of power between employer and employee determine a laborer's material circumstances.

Most freedmen welcomed the demise of the paternalism and mutual obligations of slavery and embraced many aspects of the free market. They patronized the stores that sprang up throughout the rural South, purchasing "luxuries" ranging from sardines, cheese, and sugar to new clothing. They saved money to build and support churches and educate their children. And they quickly learned to use and influence the market for their own ends. The early years of Reconstruction witnessed strikes or petitions for higher wages by black urban laborers including Richmond factory workers, Jackson washerwomen, New Orleans and Savannah stevedores, and mechanics in Columbus, Georgia. In rural areas, too, plantation freedmen sometimes bargained collectively over contract terms, organized strikes, and occasionally even attempted to establish wage schedules for an entire area. Blacks exploited competition between planters and nonagricultural employers, seeking work on railroad construction crews and at turpentine mills and other enterprises offering pay far higher than on the plantations.

Slavery, however, did not produce workers fully socialized to the virtues of economic accumulation. Despite the profits possible in early postwar cotton farming, many freedmen strongly resisted growing the "slave crop." "If ole massa want to grow cotton," said one Georgia freedman, "let him plant it himself." Many freedmen preferred to concentrate on food crops and only secondarily on cotton or other staples to obtain ready cash. Rather than choose irrevocably between self-sufficiency and market farming, they hoped to avoid a complete dependence on either while taking advantage of the opportunities each could offer. As A. Warren Kelsey, a representative of Northern cotton manufacturers, shrewdly observed:

> The sole ambition of the freedman at the present time appears to be to become the owner of a little piece of land, there to erect a humble home, and to dwell in peace and security at his own free will and pleasure. If he wishes, to cultivate the ground in cotton on his own account, to be able to do so without anyone to dictate to him hours or system of labor, if he wishes instead to plant corn or sweet potatoes—to be able to do *that* free from any outside control. . . . That is their idea, their desire and their hope.

Historical experience and modern scholarship suggest that acquiring small plots of land would hardly, by itself, have solved the economic plight of black families. Without control of credit and access to markets, land reform can often be a hollow victory. And where political power rests in hostile hands, small landowners often find themselves subjected to oppressive taxation and other state policies that severely limit their economic prospects. In such circumstances, the autonomy offered by land ownership tends to be defensive, rather than the springboard for sustained economic advancement. Yet while hardly an economic panacea, land redistribution would have had profound consequences for Southern society, weakening the land-based economic and political power of the old ruling class, offering blacks a measure of choice as to whether, when, and under what circumstances to enter the labor market, and affecting the former slaves' conception of themselves.

Blacks' quest for economic independence not only threatened the foundations of the Southern political economy, it put the freedmen at odds with both former owners seeking to restore plantation labor discipline and Northerners committed to reinvigorating staple crop production. But as part of the broad quest for individual and collective autonomy, it remained central to the black community's effort to define the meaning of freedom. Indeed, the fulfillment of other aspirations, from family autonomy to the creation of schools and churches, all greatly depended on success in winning control of their working lives and gaining access to the economic resources of the South.

"Emancipated Negroes Celebrating the Emancipation Proclamation of President Lincoln": a scene in northern Virginia near Winchester. (*Le Monde Illustré*, March 21, 1863)

Unidentified Civil War Sergeant (Chicago Historical Society)

Robert G. Fitzgerald in His Navy Uniform, 1863. After serving in both the Union Army and Navy, Fitzgerald became a schoolteacher in Virginia and North Carolina. (Estate of Pauli Murray)

Black Refugees Crossing the Rappahannock River, Virginia, 1862. (Library of Congress

"Secret Meeting of Southern Unionists." (*Harper's Weekly*, August 4, 1866)

"The Riots in New York: The Mob Lynching a Negro in Clarkson Street."
(*Illustrated London News*, August 8, 1863)

Richmond Ruins, 1865. (Library of Congress)

PILLARS OF THE BLACK COMMUNITY: SCHOOL, CHURCH, AND FAMILY

Laura M. Towne and Pupils, 1866. One of the original "Gideonites," Towne taught on the South Carolina Sea Islands until her death in 1901. (New York Public Library, Schomburg Center for Research in Black Culture)

"Prayer Meeting." (*Harper's Weekly*, February 2, 1867)

Unidentified Black Family. (New-York Historical Society)

"The Freedmen's Bureau": the Bureau as promoter of racial peace in the postwar South. (*Harper's Weekly*, July 25, 1868)

Democratic Broadside, from Pennsylvania's Congressional and gubernatorial campaign of 1866. (Library of Congress)

"Rice Culture on the Ogeechee, near Savannah, Georgia." (*Harper's Weekly*, January 5, 1867)

"The Sugar Harvest in Louisiana." (*Harper's Weekly*, October 30, 1875)

Cotton Pickers. (New-York Historical Society)

An Upcountry Family, Dressed in Homespun, Cedar Mountain, Virginia.
(Library of Congress)

PROTAGONISTS OF THE RECONSTRUCTION DEBATE

Andrew Johnson, Seventeenth President of the United States. (Library of Congress)

Thaddeus Stevens, Congressman from Pennsylvania, floor leader of House Republicans, and outspoken Radical. (Library of Congress)

Lyman Trumbull, Senator from Illinois, Chairman of the Judiciary Committee, and author of the Civil Rights and Freedmen's Bureau Bills of 1866. (Library of Congress)

Charles Sumner, Senator from Massachusetts and eloquent proponent of equality before the law. (Library of Congress)

Origins of Black Politics

If the goal of autonomy inspired blacks to withdraw from religious and social institutions controlled by whites and to attempt to work out their economic destinies for themselves, in the polity, "freedom" meant inclusion rather than separation. Recognition of their equal rights as citizens quickly emerged as the animating impulse of Reconstruction black politics. In the spring and summer of 1865, blacks organized a seemingly unending series of mass meetings, parades, and petitions demanding civil equality and suffrage as indispensable corollaries of emancipation. By midsummer, "secret political Radical Associations" had been formed in Virginia's major cities. Richmond blacks first organized politically to protest the army's rounding up of "vagrants" for plantation labor, but soon expanded their demands to include the right to vote and the removal of the "Rebel-controlled" local government.

Statewide conventions held throughout the South in 1865 and early 1866 offered the most visible evidence of black political organization. Several hundred delegates attended these gatherings, some selected by local meetings, others by churches, fraternal societies, Union Leagues, and black army units, still others simply appointed by themselves. The delegates "ranged all colors and apparently all conditions," but urban free mulattoes took the most prominent roles, and former slaves were almost entirely absent from leadership positions. But other groups also came to the fore in 1865. In Mississippi, a state with few free blacks before the war, ex-slave army veterans and their relatives comprised the majority of the delegates. Alabama and Georgia had a heavy representation of black ministers, and all the conventions included numerous skilled artisans.

The prominence of free blacks, ministers, artisans, and former soldiers in these early conventions foreshadowed black politics for much of Reconstruction. From among these delegates emerged such prominent officeholders as Alabama Congressman James T. Rapier and Mississippi Secretary of State James D. Lynch. In general, however, what is striking is how few of these early leaders went on to positions of prominence. In most states, political mobilization had advanced far more rapidly in cities and in rural areas occupied by federal troops during the war than in the bulk of the plantation counties, where the majority of the former slaves lived. The free blacks of Louisiana and South Carolina who stepped to the fore in 1865 remained at the helm of black politics throughout Reconstruction; elsewhere, however, a new group of leaders, many of them freedmen from the black belt, soon superseded those who took the lead in 1865.

The debates at these conventions illuminated conflicting currents of black public life in the immediate aftermath of emancipation. Tensions within the black community occasionally rose to the surface. One delegate voiced resentment that a Northern black had been chosen president of North Carolina's convention. By and large, however, the proceedings proved harmonious, the delegates devoting most of their time to issues that united blacks rather than divided them. South Carolina's convention demanded access to all the opportunities and privileges enjoyed by whites, from education to the right to bear arms, serve on juries, establish newspapers, assemble peacefully, and "enter upon all the avenues of agriculture, commerce, [and] trade."

The delegates' central preoccupation, however, was equality before the law and the suffrage. In justifying their demand for the vote, the delegates invoked America's republican traditions, especially the Declaration of Independence—"the broadest, the deepest, the most comprehensive and truthful definition of human freedom that was ever given to the world." The North Carolina freedmen's convention portrayed the Civil War and emancipation as chapters in the onward march of "progressive civilization," embodiments of "the fundamental truths laid down in the great charter of Republican liberty, the Declaration of Independence." Such language was not confined to the convention delegates. Eleven Alabama blacks, who complained of contract frauds, injustice before the courts, and other abuses, concluded their petition with a revealing masterpiece of understatement: "This is not the persuit of happiness."

Like their Northern counterparts during the Civil War, Southern blacks proclaimed their identification with the nation's history, destiny, and political system. The abundance of letters and petitions addressed by black gatherings and ordinary freedmen to military officials, the Freedmen's Bureau, and state and federal authorities, as well as the decision of a number of conventions to send representatives to Washington to lobby for black rights, revealed a belief that the political order was at least partially open to their influence. "We are Americans," declared a meeting of Norfolk blacks, "we know no other country, we love the land of our birth." Their address reminded white Virginians that in 1619, "our fathers as well as yours were toiling in the plantations on James River" and that a black man, Crispus Attucks, had shed "the first blood" in the American Revolution. And, of course, blacks had fought and died to save the Union. America, resolved one meeting, was "now *our* country—made emphatically so by the blood of our brethren."

Despite the insistence on equal rights, the convention resolutions and public addresses generally adopted a moderate tone, offering "the right hand of fellowship" to Southern whites. Even the South Carolina convention, forthright in claiming civil and political equality and in identifying its demand with "the cause of millions of oppressed men" throughout the world, took pains to assure the state's white minority of blacks' "spirit of meekness," their consciousness of "your wealth and greatness, and our poverty and weakness."

To some extent, this cautious tone reflected a realistic assessment of the political situation at a time when Southern whites had been restored to local power by President Johnson and Congress had not yet launched its own Reconstruction policy. But the blend of radicalism and conciliation also mirrored the indecision of an emerging black political leadership still finding its own voice in 1865 and 1866 and dominated by urban free blacks, ministers, and others who had in the past enjoyed harmonious relations with at least some local whites and did not always feel the bitter resentments of rural freedmen.

Nor did a coherent economic program emerge from these assemblies. Demands for land did surface at local meetings that chose convention delegates. Yet such views were rarely expressed among the conventions' leadership. By and large, economic concerns figured only marginally in the proceedings, and the addresses and resolutions offered no economic program apart from stressing the "mutual interest" of capital and labor and urging self-improvement as the route to personal advancement. The ferment rippling through the Southern countryside found little echo at the state conventions of 1865, reflecting the paucity of representation from plantation counties and the prominence of political leaders more attuned to political equality and self-help formulas than to rural freedmen's thirst for land.

Nonetheless, these early black conventions both reflected and advanced the process of political mobilization. Some Tennessee delegates, for example, took to heart their convention's instruction to "look after the welfare" of their constituents. After returning home, they actively promoted black education, protested to civil authorities and the Freedmen's Bureau about violence and contract frauds, and struggled against unequal odds to secure blacks a modicum of justice in local courts. Chapters of the Georgia Equal Rights and Educational Association, established at the state's January 1866 convention, became "schools in which the colored citizens learn their rights." Spreading into fifty counties by the end of the year, the Association's local meetings attracted as many as 2,000 freedmen, who listened to speeches on issues of the day and readings from Republican newspapers.

All in all, the most striking characteristic of this initial phase of black political mobilization was unevenness. In some states, organization proceeded steadily in 1865 and 1866; in others, such as Mississippi, little activity occurred between an initial flurry in the summer of 1865 and the advent of black suffrage two years later. Large parts of the black belt remained untouched by organized politics, but many blacks were aware of Congressional debates on Reconstruction policy and quickly employed on their own behalf the Civil Rights Act of 1866. "The negro of today," remarked a correspondent of the New Orleans *Tribune* in September 1866, "is not the same as he was six years ago. . . . He has been told of his rights, which have long been robbed." Only in 1867 would blacks enter the "political nation," but in organization, leadership, and an ideology that drew on America's republican heritage to demand an equal place as citizens, the seeds that flowered then were planted in the first years of freedom.

Violence and Everyday Life

The black community's religious, social, and political mobilization was all the more remarkable for occurring in the face of a wave of violence that raged almost unchecked in large parts of the postwar South. In the vast majority of cases freedmen were the victims and whites the aggressors.

In some areas, violence against blacks reached staggering proportions in the immediate aftermath of the war. "I saw white men whipping colored men just the same as they did before the war," testified ex-slave Henry Adams, who claimed that "over two thousand colored people" were murdered in 1865 in the area around Shreveport, Louisiana. In some cases, whites wreaked horrible vengeance for offenses real or imagined. In 1866, after "some kind of dispute with some freedmen," a group near Pine Bluff, Arkansas, set fire to a black settlement and rounded up the inhabitants. A man who visited the scene the following morning found "a sight that apald me 24 Negro men woman and children were hanging to trees all round the Cabbins."

The pervasiveness of violence reflected whites' determination to define in their own way the meaning of freedom and to resist black efforts to establish their autonomy, whether in matters of family, church, labor, or personal demeanor. Georgia freedman James Jeter was beaten "for claiming the right of whipping his own child instead of allowing his employer and former master to do so." Black schools, churches, and political meetings also became targets. Conduct deemed manly or dignified on the part of whites became examples of "insolence" and "insubordination" in the case of blacks. One North Carolina planter complained bitterly to a Union officer that a black soldier had "bowed to me and said good morning," insisting blacks must never address whites unless spoken to first. In Texas, Bureau records listed the "reasons" for some of the 1,000 murders of blacks by whites between 1865 and 1868: One victim "did not remove his hat"; another "wouldn't give up his whiskey flask"; a white man "wanted to thin out the niggers a little"; another wanted "to see a d—d nigger kick." Gender offered no protection—one black woman was beaten by her employer for "using insolent language," another for refusing to "call him master," a third "for crying because he whipped my mother." Probably the largest number of violent acts stemmed from disputes arising from blacks' efforts to assert their freedom from control by their former masters. Freedmen were assaulted and murdered for attempting to leave plantations, disputing contract settlements, not laboring in the manner desired by their employers, attempting to buy or rent land, and resisting whippings.

The pervasive violence underscored what might be called the politicization of everyday life that followed the demise of slavery. A seemingly insignificant incident reported to the state's governor in 1869 by black North Carolinian A. D. Lewis graphically illustrates this development:

Please allow me to call your kine attention to a transaction which occured to day between me and Dr. A. H. Jones. . . . I was in my field at my own work and this Jones came by me and drove up to a man's gate that live close by . . . and ordered my child to come there and open that gate for him . . . while there was children in the yard at the same time not more than twenty yards from him and jest because they were white and mine black he wood not call them to open the gate. . . . I spoke gently to him that [the white children] would open the gate. . . . He got out of his buggy . . . and walked nearly hundred yards rite into my field where I was at my own work and double his fist and strick me in the face three times . . . cursed me [as] a dum old Ratical. . . . Now governor I wants you to please rite to me how to bring this man to jestus.

No record exists of the disposition of this complaint, but Lewis's letter conveys worlds of meaning about Reconstruction: his powerful sense of place, his quiet dignity in the face of assault, his refusal to allow his son to be treated differently from white children or to let a stranger's authority be imposed on his family, the way an everyday encounter rapidly descended into violence and acquired political meaning, and Lewis's assumption (reflecting the situation after 1867) that blacks could expect justice from the government under which they lived. Most of all, it illustrates how day-to-day encounters between the races became infused with the tension inevitable when a social order, with its established power relations and commonly understood rules of conduct, has been swept away and a new one has not yet come into being. As David L. Swain, former governor of North Carolina, remarked in 1865, "With reference to emancipation, we are at the beginning of the war."

Ambiguities of Free Labor

Northern journalists who hurried south at the end of the Civil War telegraphed back reports of a devastated society. Where the great armies had fought and marched, vast scenes of desolation greeted the observer. The Shenandoah Valley, Virginia's antebellum bread-basket, appeared "almost a desert," its barns and dwellings burned, bridges demolished, fences, tools, and livestock destroyed. North-ern Alabama, having endured three years of fighting, and the state's central counties, which felt the wrath of the Union cavalry early in 1865, offered vistas of "absolute destitution." Along Sherman's track in Georgia and South Carolina, the scars of battle were everywhere. A white Georgian in August described in his diary a railroad journey through "a desolated land. Every village and station we stopped at presented an array of ruined walls and chimneys standing useless and solitary . . . thanks to that destroying vandal."

Even apart from physical devastation, the widespread destruction of work animals, farm buildings, and machinery, and the deterio-ration of levees and canals, ensured that the revival of agriculture would be slow and painful. So too did the appalling loss of life, a disaster without parallel in the American experience. Thirty-seven thousand blacks, the great majority from the South, perished in the Union Army, as did tens of thousands more in contraband camps, on Confederate Army labor gangs, and in disease-ridden urban shanty-towns. Nearly 260,000 men died for the Confederacy—over one-fifth of the South's adult white male population. The region, moreover, was all but bankrupt, for the collapse of Confederate bonds and currency wiped out the savings of countless individuals and the resources and endowments of colleges, churches, and other institutions.

Agricultural statistics reveal the full extent of the economic disaster the South had suffered. Between 1860 and 1870, while farm output expanded in the rest of the nation, the South experienced precipitous declines in the value of farm land and the amount of acreage under cultivation. The number of horses fell by twenty-nine percent, swine by thirty-five percent, and farm values by half. The real value of all property, even discounting that represented by slaves, stood thirty percent lower in 1870 than its prewar figure, and the output of the staple crops cotton, rice, sugar, and tobacco, and food crops like corn and potatoes, remained far below their ante-bellum levels. Confederate Gen. Braxton Bragg returned from the war to his "once prosperous" Alabama home to find "*all, all* was lost, except my debts."

Despite the grim reality of desolation and poverty, the South's economic recovery involved more than rebuilding shattered farms and repairing broken bridges. An entire social order had been swept away, and on its ruins a new one had to be constructed. The process by which a new social and economic order replaced the old followed different paths in different parts of the South. But for black and white alike, the war's end ushered in what South Carolina planter William H. Trescot called "the perpetual trouble that belongs to a time of social change."

Masters Without Slaves

Plantation slavery never dominated the entire South as it did, for example, most islands of the West Indies. But the plantation belt, containing the region's most productive land, the bulk of its economic wealth, and the majority of its slave population, gave rise to a ruling class that had shaped regional institutions, from the school and church to the state, in its own interests. A large landed estate specializing in the production of a staple crop for the world market, the plantation has historically required a disciplined, dependent labor force, since planters have found it nearly impossible to attract free laborers, especially where either land or alternative employment opportunities are available. Like their counterparts in other societies, American planters believed that the South's

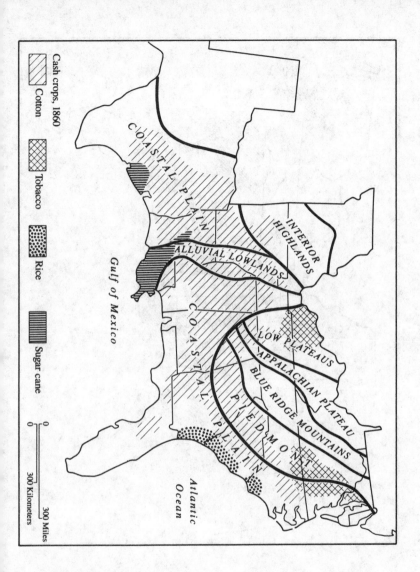

Major Physical
and Cash Crop
Regions of the
South, 1860

Cash crops, 1860

Cotton

Tobacco

Rice

Sugar cane

Gulf of Mexico

Atlantic Ocean

COASTAL PLAIN

INTERIOR HIGHLANDS

ALLUVIAL LOWLANDS

COASTAL PLAIN

LOW PLATEAUS

APPALACHIAN PLATEAU

BLUE RIDGE MOUNTAINS

PIEDMONT

0   300 Miles

0   300 Kilometers

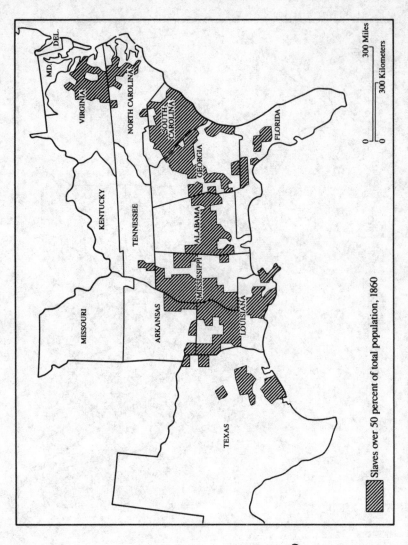

Slave Population, 1860

Slaves over 50 percent of total population, 1860

300 Miles

300 Kilometers

prosperity and their own survival as a class depended, as a Georgia newspaper put it, on "one single condition—*the ability of the planter to command labor*." And the conflict between former masters attempting to re-create a disciplined labor force and blacks seeking to infuse meaning into their freedom by carving out autonomy in every aspect of their lives profoundly affected the course of Reconstruction.

Southern planters emerged from the Civil War a devastated class—physically, economically, and psychologically. Thousands of wealthy young men had perished in battle. The loss of planters' slaves and life savings (to the extent that they had invested in Confederate bonds) wiped out the inheritance of generations. William Gilmore Simms, the South Carolina poet and novelist who had married a planter's daughter, lost "slaves, stock, furniture, books, pictures, horses . . . a property which was worth $150,000 in gold."

For the majority of planters, as for their former slaves, the Confederacy's defeat and the end of slavery ushered in a difficult adjustment to new race and class relations and new ways of organizing labor. The first casualty of this transformation was the paternalist ethos of prewar planters. A sense of obligation based on mastership over an inferior, paternalism had no place in a social order in which labor relations were mediated by the impersonal market and blacks aggressively pressed claims to autonomy and equality. "The Law which freed the negro," a Southern editor wrote in 1865, "at the same time freed the master, all obligations springing out of the relations of master and slave, except those of kindness, cease mutually to exist." And kindness proved all too rare in the aftermath of war and emancipation. Numerous planters evicted from their plantations those blacks too old or infirm to labor, and transformed "rights" enjoyed by slaves—clothing, housing, access to garden plots—into commodities for which payment was due.

"The former relation has to be unlearnt by both parties," wrote one planter, but except for the obligations of paternalism, ideas inherited from slavery displayed remarkable resiliency. For those accustomed to the power of command, the normal give-and-take of employer and employee was difficult to accept. The employer, many planters believed, should be the sole judge of the value of his laborers' services. One white North Carolinian hired a freedman in the spring of 1865, promising to give him "whatever was right" after the crop had been gathered. Behavior entirely normal in the North, such as a freedman leaving the employ of a Georgia farmer because "he thought he could do better," provoked cries of outrage and charges of ingratitude.

Carl Schurz and other Northerners who toured the South in 1865 concluded that white Southerners "do not know what free labor is." To which many planters replied that Northerners "do not understand the character of the negro." Free labor assumptions—economic rationality, internal self-discipline, responsiveness to the incentives of the market—could never, planters insisted, be applied to blacks. "They are improvident and reckless of the future," complained a Georgia newspaper. Nor was another free labor axiom, opportunity for social mobility, applicable in the South. A Natchez newspaper informed its readers: "The true station of the negro is that of a servant. The wants and state of our country demand that he should remain a servant."

The conviction that preindustrial lower classes share an aversion to regular, disciplined toil had a long history in both Europe and America. In the Reconstruction South, this ideology took a racial form, and although racism was endemic throughout nineteenth-century America, the requirements of the plantation economy shaped its specific content in the aftermath of emancipation. Charges of "indolence" were often directed not against blacks unwilling to work, but at those who preferred to labor for themselves. "Want of ambition will be the devil of the race, I think," wrote Kemp P. Battle, a North Carolina planter and political leader, in 1866. "Some of my most sensible men say they have no other desire than to cultivate their own land in grain and raise bacon." On the face of it, such an aspiration appears ambitious enough, and hardly unusual in the nineteenth-century South. But in a plantation society, a black man seeking to work his way up the agricultural ladder to the status of self-sufficient farmer seemed not an admirable example of industriousness, but a demoralized freedman unwilling to work—work, that is, under white supervision on a plantation.

The questions of land and labor were intimately related. Planters quickly concluded that their control of black labor rested upon maintaining their own privileged access to the productive land of the plantation belt. Even if relatively few freedmen established themselves as independent farmers, plantation discipline would dissolve since, as William H. Trescot explained, "it will be utterly impossible for the owner to find laborers that will work contentedly for wages alongside of these free colonies." At public meetings in 1865, and in their private correspondence, planters resolved never to rent or sell land to freedmen. In effect, they sought to impose upon blacks their own definition of freedom, one that repudiated the former slaves' equation of liberty and autonomy. "They have an idea that a hireling is not a freedman," Mississippi planter Samuel Agnew noted in his diary. He went on to observe:

> Our negroes have a fall, a tall fall ahead of them, in my humble opinion. They will learn that freedom and independence are different things. A man may be free and yet not independent.

Between the planters' need for a disciplined labor force and the freedmen's quest for autonomy, conflict was inevitable. Planters attempted through written contracts to reestablish their authority over every aspect of their laborers' lives. "Let everything proceed as formerly," one advised, "the contractual relation being substituted for that of master and slave." These early contracts prescribed not only labor in gangs from sunup to sundown as in antebellum days, but complete subservience to the planter's will. One South Carolina planter required freedmen to obey the employer "and go by his direction the same as in slavery time." Many contracts not only specified modes of work and payment, but prohibited blacks from leaving plantations, entertaining visitors, or holding meetings without permission of the employer.

Such provisions proved easier to compose than to enforce. Planters quickly learned that labor contracts could not by themselves create a submissive labor force. On the aptly named Vexation plantation in Texas, blacks in September 1865 were said to be "insolent and refusing to work." The employees of Louisiana's former Confederate governor, Thomas O. Moore, set their own pace of work, refused to plow when the ground was hard, and answered his complaints in a "disrespectful and annoying" manner. Conflict was endemic on plantations throughout the South. Some blacks refused to weed cotton fields in the rain. Others would not perform the essential but hated "mud work" of a rice plantation— dredging canals and repairing dikes—forcing some rice planters "to hire Irishmen to do the ditching." House servants, too, had their own ideas of where their obligations began and ended. Butlers refused to cook or polish brass, domestics would not black the boots of plantation guests, chambermaids declared that it was not their duty to answer the front door, serving girls insisted on the right to entertain male visitors in their rooms.

Southern whites were not the only ones to encounter difficulty disciplining the former slaves. During and immediately after the war, a new element joined the South's planter class: Northerners who purchased land, leased plantations, or formed partnerships with Southern planters. These newcomers were a varied, ambitious group, mostly former soldiers anxious to invest their savings in this promising new frontier and civilians lured South by press reports of "the fabulous sums of money to be made in the South in raising cotton." Joined with the quest for profit, however, was a reforming spirit, a vision of themselves as agents of sectional reconciliation and the South's "economic regeneration." As an Illinois man farming in Texas wrote: "I am going to introduce new ideas here in the farming line and show the beauties of free over slave labor."

Southern planters predicted that the newcomers would soon complain about the character of black labor, and they were not far wrong. The very "scientific" methods Northerners hoped to intro-duce, involving closely supervised work and changes in customary plantation routines, challenged the more irregular pace of work preferred by blacks and their desire to direct their own labor. As time passed, the Northern planters sounded and acted more and more like Southern. Some sought to restore corporal punishment, only to find that the freedmen would not stand for it. Perhaps the problem arose from the fact that, like Southern whites, most of the newcomers did not believe recently emancipated blacks capable of "self-directed labor." If the freedmen were to become productive free laborers, said the *New York Times* with unintended irony, "it must be done by giving them new masters." Blacks, however, wanted to be their own masters. And, against employers both Southern and Northern, they used whatever weapons they could find in the chaotic economic conditions of the postwar South to influence the conditions of their labor.

Blacks did, indeed, enjoy considerable bargaining power because of the "labor shortage" that followed the end of slavery. Particularly acute in sparsely populated Florida and the expanding cotton empire of the Southwest, competition for labor affected planters throughout the South. "The struggle seems to be who will get the negro at any price," lamented Texas planter Frank B. Conner. Planters, he concluded, must band together to "establish some maximum figure," stop "enticing" one another's workers, and agree that anyone "breaking the established custom should be driven from the community."

The scarcity of labor was no mirage. Measured in hours worked per capita, the supply of black labor dropped by about one-third after the Civil War, largely because all former slaves were determined to work fewer hours than under slavery, and many women and children withdrew altogether from the fields. But the "labor shortage" was a question not only of numbers, but of power. It arose from black families' determination to use the rights resulting from emancipation to establish the conditions, rhythms, and compensation of their work.

If the shortage of labor enhanced blacks' bargaining power, successive postwar crop failures seriously undermined it. Spurred by the high cotton prices of 1865, Southern planters and Northern newcomers plunged into cotton production, only to find that wartime destruction of tools and animals, the use of old seed that failed to produce vigorous crops, and persistent conflicts over labor discipline combined to produce a disappointing harvest. In 1866 nature compounded the problems of Southern farmers. The weather alternated between periods of drought and heavy rain, stunting the crops. Battered by the war, levees on the Mississippi, Red, and Arkansas Rivers gave way, flooding prime cotton lands and drowning cattle and mules. Finally, the dreaded army worm attacked what cotton had survived.

Many planters suffered devastating losses in these years. In black belt Alabama, Henry Watson, Jr., surveyed the condition of his neighbors at the beginning of 1867. Of fourteen plantations, only one had turned a profit. Large numbers of Northern planters and investors suffered the same fate. Whitelaw Reid lost $20,000, mostly borrowed from a Washington bank, and decided to return north to make his living as a journalist. As the poorest part of the region's population, blacks suffered the most. On the South Carolina Sea Islands, where the corn and cotton crops had failed, "the negroes soon were almost starving," and in the state as a whole, the Freedmen's Bureau estimated, not one freedman in ten who had labored on the plantations in 1866 "realized enough to support their families."

"If Providence had smiled on this region in 1866, by giving it a reasonable crop . . . ," Northern planter George Benham later remarked, "injustice to the negro and the new-comer, bitterness of heart and hatred of the government would all have disappeared. In the absence of a good crop . . . all these were intensified." Benham may have been overly sanguine about the prospects for social harmony in the postwar South, but there is no doubt that crop failures further embittered relations between planters and their black employees. Those working for a share of the crop discovered that poor harvests reduced their income virtually to nothing; others, laboring for wages, found planters, themselves impoverished, unable to meet their obligations. Thousands of blacks were evicted from the plantations without pay as soon as crops had been harvested. Decades later, freedwoman Ella Wilson would recall how her employer drove her family from a Louisiana plantation: "We didn't get no half. We didn't git nothin'. . . . We hadn't done nothin' to him. He just wanted all the crop for hisself and he run us off. That's all."

The "Misrepresented Bureau"

Despite the intensity of their conflict, neither former master nor former slave possessed the power to define the South's new system of labor. A third protagonist, the victorious North, also attempted to shape the transition from slavery to freedom. To the Freedmen's Bureau, more than any other institution, fell the task of assisting at the birth of a free labor society. The Bureau's commissioner was Gen. Oliver Otis Howard, whose close ties to the freedmen's aid societies had earned him the sobriquet "Christian General." Although temporary, Howard's agency was an experiment in social policy that, a modern scholar writes, "did not belong to the America of its day." Its responsibilities can only be described as daunting; they included introducing a workable system of free labor in the South, establishing schools for freedmen, providing aid to the destitute, aged, ill, and insane, adjudicating disputes among blacks and between the races, and attempting to secure for blacks and white Unionists equal justice from the state and local governments established during Presidential Reconstruction. The local Bureau agent was expected to win the confidence of blacks and whites alike in a situation where race and labor relations had been poisoned by mutual distrust and conflicting interests. Moreover, the Bureau employed, at its peak, no more than 900 agents in the entire South. Only a dozen served in Mississippi in 1866, and the largest contingent in Alabama at any time comprised twenty. "It is not . . . in your power to fulfill one tenth of the expectations of those who framed the Bureau," Gen. William T. Sherman advised Howard. "I fear you have Hercules' task."

At first glance, the Bureau's activities appear as a welter of contradictions, reflecting differences among individual agents in interpreting general policies laid down in Washington. But unifying the Bureau's activities was the endeavor to lay the foundation for a free labor society. To the extent that this meant putting freedmen back to work on plantations, the Bureau's policies coincided with the interests of the planters. To the extent that it prohibited coercive labor discipline, took up the burden of black education, sought to protect blacks against violence, and promoted the removal of legal barriers to blacks' advancement, the Bureau reinforced the freedmen's aspirations. In the end, the Bureau's career exposed the ambiguities and inadequacies of the free labor ideology itself. But simultaneously, the former slaves seized the opportunity offered by the Bureau's imperfect efforts on their behalf to bolster their own quest for self-improvement and autonomy.

Education, for Gen. Howard, was essential to the advancement of the freedmen, and the oversight of schools for blacks occupied a significant portion of local agents' time. Limited resources precluded the Bureau from establishing schools, but it did coordinate the activities of Northern societies committed to black education. By 1869 nearly 3,000 schools, serving over 150,000 pupils, reported to the Bureau, and these figures did not include many evening and private schools operated by the missionary societies and by blacks themselves. Plagued by financial difficulties and inadequate facilities, and more successful in reaching black youngsters in towns and cities than in rural areas, Bureau schools nonetheless helped lay the foundation for Southern public education. Education probably represented the agency's greatest success in the postwar South.

In a number of states local whites, some with blatantly racist attitudes, staffed the freedmen's schools, but most of the teachers were middle-class white women, the majority from New England, sent south by the Northern aid societies. Most had received some higher education, either in normal schools or in the few colleges, like Oberlin, that admitted women, and nearly all carried with them a commitment to uplifting the freedmen. "I feel that it is a precious privilege," one wrote, "to be allowed to do something for these poor people." With assistance from the Freedmen's Bureau, moreover, the societies founded and staffed the first black colleges in the South, including Fisk, Hampton, and Tougaloo, all initially designed to train black teachers. By 1869, among the approximately 3,000 freedmen's teachers in the South, blacks for the first time outnumbered whites.

A typical nineteenth-century amalgam of benevolent uplift and social control, freedmen's education aimed simultaneously to equip the freedmen to take full advantage of citizenship and to remake the culture blacks had inherited from slavery by inculcating qualities of self-reliance and self-discipline. Few Northerners involved in black education could rise above the conviction that slavery had produced a "degraded" people in dire need of instruction in frugality, temperance, honesty, and the dignity of labor. In classrooms, alphabet drills and multiplication tables alternated with exhortations to piety, cleanliness, and punctuality. Social control, however, did not exhaust the purposes of freedmen's education. The effort to acculturate former slaves to the workings of the market carried with it a complex and sometimes contradictory set of implications. Bureau educators viewed schooling as a solvent of class lines that equipped individuals to advance economically while enabling the society at large to avoid class conflict.

In the broadest sense, the schools established by the Freedmen's Bureau and Northern aid societies, to quote the American Freedmen's Union Commission, aimed "to plant a genuine republicanism in the Southern States." The divorce of schooling from ideals of equal citizenship would come only after Reconstruction when, under the auspices of Booker T. Washington and the South's white "Redeemers," the philosophy of industrial education gained ascendancy in Southern black schooling. Before then, most teachers favored equality before the law and black suffrage, and many promoted black political organization.

The Bureau activity most celebrated in the North, education was also the only one intended to leave permanent institutions in the South. Even as his agency created an extensive network of courts, hospitals, charitable institutions, and labor regulations, Howard sought to limit their life-span, convinced that blacks would benefit more by recognition as equal citizens than from being treated as a special class permanently dependent on federal assistance and protection. Yet the assumption of its own impermanence severely limited the scope and effectiveness of Bureau policies. Nowhere was this more evident than in the beleaguered Bureau agents' efforts to prevent the freedmen from being "treated with greater inhumanity and brutality than when in bondage" and to assure them the protection of the law.

Many agents found suppressing violence a difficult and frustrating task. Gen. E. O. C. Ord, the military commander in Arkansas and Mississippi, believed that without troops agents of the Bureau were "worse than useless," but very few had military force at their disposal. Despite Southern complaints of bayonet rule, the Union Army rapidly demobilized after the war, plummeting from 1 million on May 1, 1865, to 38,000, many of them stationed on the Indian frontier, by the fall of 1866. In most cases, therefore, Bureau agents had to rely on their own powers of persuasion and the cooperation of local officials in attempting to protect the freedmen.

From Howard himself to the local agents, most Bureau officials remained deeply committed to the idea of equality before the law. But instead of strengthening its own court system, the Bureau labored to persuade the Southern states to recognize racial equality in their own judicial proceedings. After initial hesitation, especially on the matter of allowing blacks to testify against whites, one state after another revised its judicial proceedings in accordance with Bureau guidelines, precisely to rid themselves of Bureau courts. By the end of 1866, local courts had regained jurisdiction over cases involving freedmen. Bureau agents now monitored state and local judicial proceedings on behalf of blacks, defending freedmen, prosecuting whites, and retaining the authority to overturn discriminatory decisions. But it quickly became clear that the formal trappings of equality could not guarantee blacks substantive justice. The basic problem, concluded Col. Samuel Thomas, who directed the Bureau in Mississippi in 1865, was that white public opinion could not "conceive of the negro having any rights at all."

Blacks recognized in the agents and their courts their best hope for impartial justice in the postwar South. They brought to the Bureau problems trivial and substantial, including many involving family and personal disputes among themselves. Most cases, however, arose from black complaints against whites, especially violence, nonpayment of wages, and unfair division of crops. Freedmen appreciated that whatever the outcome of individual cases, the very existence of these tribunals represented a challenge both to notions of local autonomy and to inherited ideas of racial domination. For their part, Southern whites perceived the necessity of answering charges brought by former slaves as an indignity. "He listened to the slightest complaint of the negroes, and dragged prominent white citizens before his court upon the mere accusation of a dissatisfied negro," whites complained about one Mississippi agent.

A similar combination of limited resources, free labor precepts, a commitment to assisting the freedmen, and the conviction that civil authorities must assume responsibility for the equitable treatment of blacks shaped the Bureau's efforts to alleviate destitution among the black population. "A man who can work has no right to support by government. No really respectable person wishes to be supported by others." This injunction, issued in 1865 by a Mississippi Bureau agent, epitomized the contemporary Northern view that poor relief undermined manly independence.

Howard himself considered public assistance to the poor "abnormal to our system of government." The Bureau's "war on dependency" led it to close with unseemly haste camps for fugitive and homeless blacks that had been established during the war and to restrict direct assistance to children, the aged, and those unable to work. Economic realities, however, undermined its premature efforts to eliminate relief altogether. In the first fifteen months following the war, the Bureau issued over thirteen million rations (corn meal, flour, and sugar sufficient to feed a person for one week), two-thirds to blacks. Then, in the fall of 1866, Howard ordered such relief discontinued, except for hospital patients and inmates of orphan asylums—a draconian measure impossible to implement in the wake of the 1866 crop failure and ensuing destitution.

Throughout its existence, the Bureau regarded poor relief as a temptation to idleness. Blacks, declared Virginia Bureau head Orlando Brown, must "feel the spur of necessity, if it be needed to make them self-reliant, industrious and provident." Clearly, this position reflected not only attitudes toward blacks, but also a more general Northern belief in the dangers of encouraging dependency among the lower classes. Yet the Bureau's assumption that blacks *wished* to be dependent on the government persisted in the face of evidence that the black community itself, wherever possible, shouldered the task of caring for orphans, the aged, and the destitute and the fact that in many localities more whites than blacks received Bureau aid. In Mobile, Whitelaw Reid observed, "a stranger might have concluded that it was the white race that was going to prove unable to take care of itself, instead of the emancipated slaves."

Yet its relief policy was only one part of a larger contradiction in the Bureau's purposes. The aim of revitalizing the South's production of agricultural staples in many ways undercut that of guaranteeing the freedmen's rights. Nowhere was this ambiguity more evident than in the Bureau's efforts to supervise the transition from slave to free labor.

The Freedmen's Bureau, Land, and Labor

In the war's immediate aftermath, federal policy regarding black labor was established by the army. And the army seemed to many freedmen to have only one object in view—to compel them to return to work on the plantations. In the spring and early summer of 1865, military commanders issued stringent orders to stem the influx of freedmen into Southern cities. Military regulations forbade blacks to travel without passes from their employers or be on the streets at night and prohibited "insubordination" on their part. In several cities, postwar black political organization began with protests against army policies. A group of Memphis free blacks condemned the rounding up of "vagrants" for plantation labor: "It seems the great slave trade is revived again in our city." In July, Secretary of War Stanton instructed Southern commanders to discontinue pass requirements and cease interfering with blacks' freedom of movement. But the assumption underpinning military policy, that the interests of all Americans would be best served by blacks' return to plantation labor, remained intact as the Freedmen's Bureau assumed command of the transition to free labor.

The idea of free labor, wrote a Tennessee agent, was "the noblest principle on earth." Like Northern Republicans generally, Bureau officers held what in retrospect appear as amazingly utopian assumptions about the ease with which Southern labor relations could be recast in the free labor mold. Blacks and whites merely had to abandon attitudes toward labor, and toward each other, inherited from slavery, and the market would do the rest. "Let it be understood that a fair day's wages will be paid for a fair day's work," Gen. Robert K. Scott, the Bureau's chief officer in South Carolina, announced, "and the planter will not want for reliable and faithful laborers." With the Bureau acting as midwife at its birth, the free market would quickly assume its role as arbiter of the South's economic destinies, honing those qualities that distinguished free labor from slave—efficiency, productivity, and economic rationality—and ensuring equitable wages and working conditions.

In fact, this social vision was to a large extent irrelevant to the social realities the Bureau confronted. The free labor ideology rested on a theory of universal economic rationality and the conviction that all classes in a free labor society shared the same interests. In reality, former masters and former slaves inherited from slavery work habits and attitudes at odds with free labor assumptions, and both recognized, more clearly than the Bureau, the irreconcilability of their respective interests and aspirations. The free labor social order, moreover, ostensibly guaranteed the ambitious worker the opportunity for economic mobility, the ability to move from wage labor to independence through the acquisition of productive property. Yet what became of this axiom in an impoverished society where even the highest agricultural wages remained pitiably low, and whose white population was determined to employ every means at its disposal to prevent blacks from acquiring land or any other means of economic independence?

Establishing themselves in the South in the summer and fall of 1865, Bureau agents hoped to induce Southerners to "give the system a fair and honest trial." To planters' desire for a disciplined labor force governed by the lash, agents responded that "*bodily coercion* fell as an incident of slavery." To the contention that blacks would never work voluntarily or respond to market incentives, they replied that the problem of economic readjustment should be viewed through the prism of labor, rather than race. As agent John E. Bryant explained:

> *No* man loves work naturally. Interest or necessity induces him to labor. . . . Why does the *white man* labor? That he may acquire property and the means of purchasing the comforts and luxuries of life. The *colored man* will labor for the same reason.

The "two evils" against which the Bureau had to contend, an army officer observed in July 1865, were "cruelty on the part of the employer and shirking on the part of the negroes." Yet the Bureau, like the army, seemed to consider black reluctance to labor the greater threat to its economic mission. In some areas agents continued the military's urban pass systems and vagrancy patrols, as well as the practice of rounding up unemployed laborers for shipment to plantations. Bureau courts in Memphis dispatched impoverished blacks convicted of crimes to labor for whites who would pay their fines. "What a mockery to call those 'Freedmen' who are still subjected to such things," commented a local minister.

United as to the glories of free labor, Bureau officials, like Northerners generally, differed among themselves about the ultimate social implications of the free labor ideology. Some believed the freedmen would remain a permanent plantation labor force; others insisted they should enjoy the same opportunity to make their way up the social ladder to independent proprietorship as Northern workers; still others hoped the federal government would assist at least some blacks in acquiring their own farms. Howard believed most freedmen must return to plantation labor, but under conditions that allowed them the opportunity to work their way out of the wage-earning class. At the same time, he took seriously the provision in the act establishing his agency that authorized it to settle freedmen on confiscated and abandoned lands. In 1865, Howard and a group of sympathetic Bureau officials attempted to breathe life into this alternative vision of a free-labor South.

Even though the Lincoln administration had left the 1862 Confiscation Act virtually unenforced, the Bureau controlled over 850,000 acres of abandoned land in 1865, hardly enough to accommodate all the former slaves but sufficient to make a start toward creating a black yeomanry. Howard's subordinates included men sincerely committed to settling freedmen on farms of their own and protecting the rights of those who already occupied land. In Louisiana, Thomas Conway, the Bureau's assistant commissioner, leased over 60,000 acres to blacks (including a plantation owned by the son of former President Zachary Taylor). Most dedicated of all to the idea of black landownership was Gen. Rufus Saxton, a prewar abolitionist who directed the Bureau in South Carolina, Georgia, and Florida during the summer of 1865. Saxton had already overseen the settlement of thousands of blacks on lands reserved for them under Gen. Sherman's Field Order 15. In June 1865 he announced his intention to use the property under Bureau control to provide freedmen with forty-acre homesteads "where by faithful industry they can readily achieve an independence."

Initially, Howard himself shared the radical aims of Conway and Saxton. At the end of July 1865 he issued Circular 13, which instructed Bureau agents to "set aside" forty-acre tracts for the freedmen as rapidly as possible. But Andrew Johnson, who had been pardoning former Confederates, soon directed Howard to rescind his order. A new policy, drafted in the White House and issued in September as Howard's Circular 15, ordered the restoration to pardoned owners of all land except the small amount that had already been sold under a court decree. Once growing crops had been harvested, virtually all the land in Bureau hands would revert to its former owners.

Most of the land occupied by blacks in the summer and fall of 1865 lay within the "Sherman reservation." To Howard fell the melancholy task of informing the freedmen that the land would be restored to their former owners and that they must either agree to work for the planters or be evicted. In October he traveled to lowcountry South Carolina, hoping to "ease the shock as much as possible, of depriving the freedmen of the ownership of the lands." On Edisto Island occurred one of the most poignant confrontations of the era. The freedmen fully anticipated Howard's message, and when he rose to speak to more than 2,000 blacks gathered at a local church, "dissatisfaction and sorrow were manifested from every part of the assembly." Finally, a "sweet-voiced negro woman" quieted the crowd by leading it in singing the spirituals "Nobody Knows the Trouble I Seen" and "Wandering in the Wilderness of Sorrow and Gloom." When the freedmen fell silent, Howard begged them to "lay aside their bitter feelings, and to become reconciled to their old masters." He was continually interrupted by members of the audience: "No, never," "Can't do it," "Why, General Howard, do you take away our lands?"

Howard requested the assembled freedmen to appoint a three-man committee to consider the fairest way of restoring the planters to ownership. The committee's eloquent response did not augur well for a tranquil settlement:

General, we want Homesteads, we were promised Homesteads by the government. If it does not carry out the promises its agents made to us, if the government haveing concluded to befriend its late enemies and to neglect to observe the principles of common faith between its self and us its allies in the war you said was over, now takes away from them all right to the soil they stand upon save such as they can get by again working for *your* late and their *all time* enemies . . . we are left in a more unpleasant condition than our former. . . . You will see this is not the condition of really freemen.

You ask us to forgive the land owners of our island. . . . The man who tied me to a tree and gave me 39 lashes and who stripped and flogged my mother and my sister and who will not let me stay in his empty hut except I will do his planting and be satisfied with his price and who combines with others to keep away land from me well knowing I would not have anything to do with him if I had land of my own—that man, I cannot well forgive. Does it look as if he has forgiven me, seeing how he tries to keep me in a condition of helplessness?

In these words, the committee expressed with simple dignity the conviction of all freedmen that land was the foundation of freedom, the evils of slavery could not be quickly forgotten, and the interests of former master and former slave were fundamentally irreconcilable. The freedmen pleaded with Howard for the right to rent or purchase land, and displayed "the greatest aversion" to signing labor contracts with the landowners, equating such agreements with "a practical return to slavery."

Genuinely moved by this experience, Howard pledged to renew the fight for land when Congress reconvened in December. Meanwhile, planters complained of the hostile attitude of General Saxton. So long as Saxton headed the Bureau in South Carolina, William H. Trescot informed the President, the land would never be restored. Early in 1866, Johnson ordered Saxton removed. On his departure, thousands of South Carolina freedmen contributed "pennies and five cent pieces" to present "two or three handsome pieces of silver" to their staunchest friend in the Freedmen's Bureau. The idea of a Bureau actively promoting black landownership had come to an abrupt end.

The restoration of land required the displacement of tens of thousands of freedmen throughout the South. The army evicted most of the 20,000 blacks settled on confiscated and abandoned property in southeastern Virginia. The 62,000 acres farmed by Louisiana blacks were restored to their former owners; as the wife of a New Orleans editor observed, Gen. Joseph S. Fullerton, who succeeded Conway, "can't seem to hustle out fast enough the occupants of confiscated property." Even Davis Bend, Mississippi, where black farmers cultivated 10,000 acres in 1865, reverted to Joseph Davis. Unlike most planters, however, Davis thereupon sold the land on long-term credit to Benjamin Montgomery, the most prominent leader of the Bend's black community. Davis died in 1870, leaving a will instructing his heirs to "extend a liberal indulgence" with respect to Montgomery's payments. But in 1878, after the $300,000 purchase price had fallen due, a Mississippi court ordered the land restored to the Davis family—a melancholy end to the dream of establishing a "Negro paradise" at Davis Bend.

Nowhere, however, was the restoration process so disruptive as in the Georgia and South Carolina lowcountry. On more than one occasion freedmen armed themselves, barricaded plantations, and drove off owners attempting to dispossess them. Black squatters told one party of Edisto Island landlords in February 1866, "you have better go back to Charleston, and go to work there, and if you can do nothing else, you can pick oysters and earn your living as the loyal people have done—by the sweat of their brows." Bureau agents, black and white, made every effort to induce lowcountry freedmen to sign contracts with their former owners, while federal troops forcibly evicted those who refused. In the end, only about 2,000 South Carolina and Georgia freedmen actually received the land they had been promised in 1865.

The events of 1865 and 1866 kindled a deep sense of betrayal among freedmen throughout the South. Land enough existed, wrote former Mississippi slave Merrimon Howard, for every "man and woman to have as much as they could work." Yet blacks had been left with

> no *land*, no *house*, not so much as place to lay our head. . . .
> Despised by the world, hated by the country that gives us birth,
> denied of all our writs as a people, we were friends on the march, . . .
> brothers on the battlefield, but in the peaceful pursuits of life it
> seems that we are strangers.

Thus, by 1866 the Bureau found itself with no alternative but to encourage virtually all freedmen to sign annual contracts to work on the plantations. Its hopes for long-term black advancement and Southern economic prosperity now came to focus exclusively on the labor contract itself. By voluntarily signing and adhering to contracts, both planters and freedmen would develop the habits of a free labor economy and come to understand their fundamental harmony of interests. Agents found themselves required to perform a nearly impossible balancing act. Disabusing blacks of the idea that they would soon obtain land from the government, and threatening to arrest those who refused to sign a contract or leave the plantations, agents simultaneously insisted on blacks' right to bargain freely for employment and attempted to secure more advantageous contracts than had prevailed in 1865. Some Bureau officers approved agreements in which the laborer would receive nothing at all if the crop failed and could incur fines for such vaguely defined offenses as failure to do satisfactory work or "impudent, profane or indecent language." More conscientious agents revoked contract provisions regulating blacks' day-to-day lives and insisted that laborers who left plantations before the harvest must be paid for their work up to the date of departure. And virtually all agents insisted that planters acknowledge that their power to employ physical coercion had come to an end.

The Bureau's role in supervising labor relations reached its peak in 1866 and 1867; thereafter, federal authorities intervened less and less frequently to oversee contracts or settle plantation disputes. To the extent that the contract system had been intended to promote stability in labor relations in the chaotic aftermath of war and allow commercial agriculture to resume, it could be deemed a success. But in other ways, the system failed. For the entire contract system in some ways violated the principles of free labor. Agreements, Howard announced soon after assuming office, "should be free, *bona fide* acts." Yet how voluntary were labor contracts signed by blacks when they were denied access to land, coerced by troops and Bureau agents if they refused to sign, and fined or imprisoned if they struck for higher wages? Propertyless individuals in the North, to be sure, were compelled to labor for wages, but the compulsion was supplied by necessity, not by public officials, and contracts did not prevent them from leaving work whenever they chose. Why, asked the New Orleans *Tribune* again and again, did the Bureau require blacks to sign year-long labor contracts when "laborers throughout the civilized world"—including agricultural laborers in the North—could leave their employment at any time? To which one may add that even the most sympathetic Bureau officials assumed that blacks would constitute the rural labor force, at least until the natural working of the market divided the great plantations into small farms. "Idle white men" were never required to sign labor contracts or ordered to leave Southern cities for the country-side, a fact that made a mockery of the Bureau's professed goal of equal treatment for the freedmen.

Howard always believed that the Bureau's policies, viewed as a whole, benefited the freedmen more than their employers, espe-cially since civil authorities offered blacks no protection against violence or fraud and the courts provided no justice to those seeking legal redress. He viewed the system of annual labor contracts as a temporary expedient, which would disappear once free labor ob-tained a "permanent foothold" in the South "under its necessary protection of equal and just laws properly executed." Eventually, as in the North, the market would regulate employment. Yet in the early years of Reconstruction, operating within the constraints of the free labor ideology, adverse crop and market conditions, the desire to restore production of the South's staple crops, and presidential policy, Bureau decisions conceived as temporary ex-erted a powerful influence on the emergence of new economic and social relations, closing off some options for blacks, shifting the balance of power in favor of employers, and helping to stabilize the beleaguered planter class.

Nonetheless, whatever the policies of individual agents, most Southern whites resented the Bureau as a symbol of Confederate defeat and a barrier to the authority reminiscent of slavery that planters hoped to impose on the freedmen. Even if, in individual cases, the Bureau's intervention enhanced the power of the em-ployer, the very act of calling on a third and ostensibly disinterested party served to undermine his standing, by making evident to the freedmen that the planter's authority was not absolute. John F. Couts, member of a prominent Middle Tennessee planter family, confirmed that for many whites the Bureau's presence was a humiliation:

The Agent of the Bureau . . . *requires* citizens (former owners) to make and enter into *written contracts* for the hire of their *own* negroes. . . . When a negro is not *properly* paid or fairly dealt with and *reports* the facts, then a squad of Negro soldiers is sent after the *offender*, who is *escorted* to town to be dealt with as per the negro testimony. In the name of God how long is such things to last?

For the same reasons that Southern whites demanded its removal, most blacks remained "doggedly loyal" to the Bureau. To the very end of Reconstruction, blacks would insist that "those who freed them shall protect that freedom." The strength of their commitment to this principle, and to the Bureau as an embodiment of the nation's responsibility, became clear in 1866 when President Johnson sent Generals James Steedman and Joseph S. Fullerton on an inspection tour of the South. Johnson hoped to elicit enough complaints to discredit the agency, but in city after city, blacks rallied to the Bureau's support. In Wilmington, North Carolina, 800 blacks crowded into the Brick Church. Gen. Steedman asked the assemblage if the army or the Freedmen's Bureau had to be withdrawn, which they would prefer to have remain in the South. From all parts of the church came the reply, "the Bureau."

Col. W. H. H. Beadle, a native of Michigan and Bureau agent at Wilmington, most likely attended the meeting at the Brick Church. Scarcely a month earlier, in testifying before the Joint Congressional Committee on Reconstruction, Beadle had lamented the fact that Southerners did not comprehend a crucial axiom of the free labor ideology—"the mutual dependence of labor and capital." Even as planters sought to limit the freedom of the former slaves in every way possible, and blacks understood that they lived "in the midst of enemies to our race," Bureau agents held fast to the conviction that "the interests of capital and labor are identical." This belief severely compromised the Bureau's understanding of the society in which it had been placed. Even those agents most sympathetic to the freedmen viewed the struggle on the plantation as an irrational legacy of slavery that would disappear as soon as both planters and freedmen absorbed free labor principles. In fact, however, the South's "labor problem" arose not from misunderstanding, but from the irreconcilable interests of former masters and former slaves as each sought to define the meaning of emancipation. Perhaps the greatest failing of the Freedmen's Bureau was that it never quite comprehended the depths of racial antagonism and class conflict in the postwar South.

Beginnings of Economic Reconstruction

So began the forging of a new class structure to replace the shattered world of slavery. It was an economic transformation that would culminate, long after the end of Reconstruction, in the consolidation of a rural proletariat composed of the descendants of former slaves and white yeomen, and of a new owning class of planters and merchants, itself subordinate to Northern financiers and industrialists. The historian, however, must avoid telescoping the actual course of events into a predetermined, linear progression. A new set of labor arrangements did not spring up overnight, and there was no preordained outcome to the workings of what one federal official described as "the new *system* of labor if system it may be called, when there is endless confusion, and absurd contradiction."

In some parts of the South, planters in the early postwar years found it almost impossible to resume production, notably in the sugar and rice kingdoms, where the estates of exceptionally wealthy aristocracies lay in ruins. The war had devastated the expensive grinding and threshing mills and the elaborate systems of dikes, irrigation canals, and levees and thoroughly disrupted the labor system. Only a handful of Louisiana's sugar plantations operated at all in 1865; the rest stood idle, overgrown with weeds, and the crop amounted to only one-tenth of that raised in 1861. In the rice region, "labor was in a disorganized and chaotic state, production had ceased, and . . . the power to compel laborers to go into the rice swamp utterly broken." Thousands of black families had been settled on abandoned rice plantations in accordance with Gen. Sherman's Field Order 15, and countless others occupied estates deserted by their owners. President Johnson's restoration of planters to control of their land failed to end the "undeclared war" between former masters and former slaves that consumed the lowcountry.

Where agricultural production did resume, a variety of arrangements often coexisted in the same area, sometimes on the same plantation. In the early years of Reconstruction, payments included cash wages, paid monthly or at year's end; a share of the crop, divided collectively among the entire labor force or among smaller groups of workers; various combinations of wage and share payments; time-sharing plans in which freedmen worked part of the week for the planter and part on their own land; wages in kind; and cash wages for specific tasks.

Beneath the welter of arrangements, however, certain broad patterns may be discerned. In 1865 and 1866, a majority of labor contracts involved agreements between planters and large groups of freedmen. Payment was generally either in "standing wages" withheld until year's end, or, more frequently, "share wages"—a share of the crop sometimes paid collectively to the workers and divided among themselves and sometimes allocated according to their working capacity. In the contracts of 1865, the shares paid to the freedmen were usually extremely low, sometimes as little as one-tenth of the crop. In effect, moreover, the postponement of payment to the end of the year represented an interest-free extension of credit from employee to employer, as well as a shifting of part of the risk of farming to the freedmen. The practice not only left share workers penniless in the event of a poor crop, but offered numerous opportunities for fraud on the part of planters, some of whom deducted excessive fines for poor work or other infractions, or presented freedmen with bills for rations that exceeded the wages due them.

In 1866 and 1867, the freedmen's demand for an improvement in their economic condition and greater independence in their working lives set in motion a train of events that fundamentally transformed the plantation labor system. Blacks' desire for greater autonomy in the day-to-day organization of work produced a trend toward the subdivision of the labor force. Gang labor for wages persisted where planters had access to outside capital and could offer high monthly wages, promptly paid. Thanks to an influx of Northern investment, this was the case on sugar plantations that managed to resume production. On many cotton plantations in 1866 and 1867, however, squads of a dozen or fewer freedmen replaced the gangs so reminiscent of slavery. Generally organized by the blacks themselves, these squads sometimes consisted entirely of members of a single family, but more often included unrelated men. By 1867 the gang system was disappearing from the cotton fields.

The final stage in the decentralization of plantation agriculture was the emergence of sharecropping. Unlike the earlier share-wage system, with which it is often confused, in sharecropping individual families (instead of large groups of freedmen) signed contracts with the landowner and became responsible for a specified piece of land (rather than working in gangs). Generally, sharecroppers retained one-third of the year's crop if the planter provided implements, fertilizer, work animals, and seed, and half if they supplied their own. The transition to sharecropping occurred at different rates on different plantations and continued well into the 1870s, but the arrangement appeared in some areas soon after the Civil War.

To blacks, sharecropping offered an escape from gang labor and day-to-day white supervision. For planters, the system provided a way to reduce the cost and difficulty of labor supervision, share risk with tenants, and circumvent the chronic shortage of cash and credit. Most important of all, it stabilized the work force, for sharecroppers utilized the labor of all members of the family and had a vested interest in remaining until the crop had been gathered. Yet whatever its economic rationale, many planters resisted share-cropping as a threat to their overall authority and inefficient besides (since they believed blacks would not work without direct white supervision). A compromise not fully satisfactory to either party, the system's precise outlines remained a point of conflict. Planters insisted sharecroppers were wage laborers who must obey the orders of their employer and who possessed no property right in the crop until they received their share at the end of the year. But sharecroppers, a planter complained in 1866, considered themselves "partners in the crop," who insisted on farming according to their own dictates and would not brook white supervision. Only a system of wages, payable at the end of the year, he concluded, would allow whites to "work them in accordance with our former management." But precisely because it seemed so far removed from "our former management," blacks came to prefer the sharecropping system.

If freedmen in the cotton fields rejected the gang labor associated with bondage, those in the rice swamps insisted on strengthening the familiar task system, the foundation of the partial autonomy they had enjoyed as slaves. "We want to work just as we have always worked," declared a group of freedmen in South Carolina's rice region, and to attract labor, rice planters found themselves obliged to let the blacks "work . . . as they choose without any overseer." Out of the wreck of the rice economy and blacks' insistence on autonomy emerged an unusual set of labor relations. Some planters simply rented their plantations to blacks for a share of the crop or divided the land among groups of freedmen to cultivate as they saw fit. Others agreed to a system of labor sharing in which freedmen worked for two days on the plantation in exchange for an allotment of land on which to grow their own crops.

Thus, the struggles of early Reconstruction planted the seeds of new labor systems in the rural South. The precise manner in which these seeds matured would be worked out not only on Southern farms and plantations, but also on the Reconstruction battlefields of local, state, and national politics.

The Failure of Presidential Reconstruction

Andrew Johnson and Reconstruction

At first glance, the man who succeeded Abraham Lincoln seemed remarkably similar to his martyred predecessor. Both knew poverty in early life, neither enjoyed much formal schooling, and in both deprivation sparked a powerful desire for fame and worldly success. During the prewar decades, both achieved material comfort, Lincoln as an Illinois corporation lawyer, Andrew Johnson rising from tailor's apprentice to become a prosperous landowner. And for both, antebellum politics became a path to power and respect.

In terms of sheer political experience, few men have seemed more qualified for the Presidency than Andrew Johnson. Beginning as a Greenville, Tennessee, alderman in 1829, he rose to the state legislature and then to Congress. He served two terms as governor, and in 1857 entered the Senate. Even more than Lincoln, Johnson gloried in the role of tribune of the common man. His speeches lauded "honest yeomen" and thundered against the "slaveocracy"— a "pampered, bloated, corrupted aristocracy." The issues most closely identified with Johnson's prewar career were tax-supported public education, a reform enacted into law during his term as governor, and homestead legislation, which he promoted tirelessly in the Senate.

Apart from the education law, however, Johnson's political career was remarkably devoid of substantive accomplishment. In part, this failure stemmed from traits that did much to destroy his Presidency. If in Lincoln poverty and the struggle for success somehow produced wit, political dexterity, and sensitivity to the views of others, Johnson's personality turned in upon itself. An accomplished public orator, privately Johnson was a self-absorbed, lonely man. No one could doubt his courage, yet early in his career other less commendable qualities had also become apparent, among them stubbornness, intolerance of differing views, and an inability to compromise. As governor, Johnson failed to work effectively with his legislature; as military governor he proved unable to elicit popular support for his administration. Hardly a political novice, he found himself, as President, thrust into a role that required tact, flexibility, and sensitivity to the nuances of public opinion—qualities Lincoln possessed in abundance, but that Johnson lacked.

When Johnson assumed office on April 15, 1865, his past career led many to expect a Reconstruction policy that envisioned far-reaching change in the defeated South. "Treason must be made odious, and traitors must be punished and impoverished," Johnson had declared in 1864; in the same year he offered himself as a "Moses" to lead blacks to a promised land of freedom. "It was supposed," John Sherman later recalled, "that President Johnson would err, if at all, in imposing too harsh terms upon these states."

In the weeks following Lincoln's assassination, leading Radicals met frequently with the new President to press the issue of black suffrage. Yet Johnson shared neither the Radicals' expansive conception of federal power nor their commitment to political equality for blacks. Despite his own vigorous exercise of authority as military governor, Johnson had always believed in limited government and a strict construction of the Constitution. In Congress, he even opposed appropriations to pave Washington's muddy streets. His fervent nationalism in no way contradicted his respect for the rights of the states. Individual "traitors" should be punished, but the states had never, legally, seceded, or surrendered their right to govern their own affairs.

Logically, as Carl Schurz later commented, Johnson had "a pretty plausible case"—secession had been illegal, the states remained intact, and Reconstruction meant enabling them to resume their full constitutional rights as quickly as possible. The situation actually confronting the nation, however, bore little resemblance to Johnson's neat syllogism. "To say because they had no right to go out therefore they could not," declared California railroad magnate Leland Stanford, "does not seem to me more reasonable than to say that because a man has no right to commit murder therefore he cannot. A man does commit murder and that is a fact which no reasoning can refute." And did not secession and war imply that the Southern states had sacrificed some of their accustomed rights? If Johnson could appoint provisional governors and lay down terms for reunion, he could also prescribe voting qualifications. In this sense, the Radicals and Johnson disagreed less on a constitutional issue than on a matter of policy: whether black suffrage should be made a requirement for the South's readmission.

Johnson never wavered from the conviction that the federal government could not impose such a policy on the states, and that the status of blacks must not obstruct the speedy completion of Reconstruction. The owner of five slaves before the war, Johnson had sincerely embraced emancipation. But in condemning slavery he dwelled almost obsessively on racial miscegenation as the institution's main evil, and he made no commitment to civil equality or a political role for the freedmen. The President's private secretary, Col. William G. Moore, later recorded that Johnson "has at times exhibited a morbid distress and feeling against the negroes." In his December 1867 annual message to Congress, Johnson insisted that blacks possessed less "capacity for government than any other race of people. . . . Wherever they have been left to their own devices they have shown a constant tendency to relapse into barbarism."

"White men alone," Johnson declared, "must manage the South." Johnson's prejudices are often ascribed to his "poor white" background and his self-defined role as spokesman for the South's yeomanry. This assessment contains considerable truth. Johnson had long believed that the planter aristocracy had dragooned a reluctant yeomanry into secession. He had once advocated separate statehood for East Tennessee, to liberate yeomen from the Slave Power's yoke. He assumed that the war had shattered the power of the slaveocracy and made possible the political ascendancy of loyal white yeomen. But the freedmen had no role in his vision of a reconstructed South. When a black delegation visited him at the White House in early 1866, Johnson proposed that their people emigrate to some other country.

Throughout his Presidency, Johnson held the view that slaves had joined with their owners to oppress nonslaveholding whites. "The colored man and his master combined kept [the poor white] in slavery," he told the black delegation, "by depriving him of a fair participation in the labor and productions of the rich land of the country." The result of black enfranchisement would therefore be an alliance of blacks and planters, restoring the Slave Power's hegemony. As Johnson put it, "the negro will vote with the late master, whom he does not hate, rather than with the non-slaveholding white, whom he does hate."

The definitive announcement of Johnson's plan of Reconstruction came in two proclamations issued on May 29, 1865. The first conferred amnesty and pardon, including restoration of all property rights except for slaves, upon former Confederates who pledged loyalty to the Union and support for emancipation. Fourteen classes of Southerners, however, most notably major Confederate officials and owners of taxable property valued at more than $20,000, were required to apply individually for Presidential pardons. Simultaneously, Johnson appointed William W. Holden provisional governor of North Carolina, instructing him to call a convention to amend the state's prewar constitution so as to create a "republican form of government." Persons who had not been pardoned under the terms of the first proclamation were excluded from voting for delegates, but otherwise, voter qualifications in effect immediately before secession (when the franchise, of course, was limited to whites) would apply. Similar proclamations for other Southern states soon followed.

The May proclamations reflected Johnson's determination to overturn the political and economic hegemony of the slaveocracy and assure the ascendancy of Unionist yeomen. Indeed, while Johnson claimed that his Reconstruction policy continued Lincoln's, in crucial respects it was very much his own. On the one hand, Lincoln, at the end of his life, favored a limited suffrage for Southern blacks; on the other, he had never suggested exemptions to Presidential amnesty as sweeping as those contained in Johnson's proclamation. The $20,000 clause, excluding the Confederacy's economic elite from a voice in Reconstruction, gave Johnson's proclamations an aura of sternness quite unlike any of Lincoln's Reconstruction statements. Many in May 1865 believed Johnson intended the clause to "keep these people out in the cold," enabling yeomen to shape Reconstruction. Others, however, believed he planned to use individual pardons to force the "aristocracy" to endorse his terms of Reconstruction. The latter course had its attractions, especially since it would contribute to Johnson's own reelection, a consideration that could not have been far from the mind of so intensely ambitious a man. Were Presidential Reconstruction successful, Johnson had it in his grasp to create an unassailable political coalition capable of determining the contours of American politics for a generation or more.

Blacks, of course, would remain outside the bounds of citizenship. A Southern Unionist pointed out the contradiction: "You say you believe in democratic government, or *consent* of loyal people. Yet you *dare not* avow with practical effect the right of the colored man to vote. Are you honest?" By the end of his life, Lincoln had moved to recognize some blacks as part of the political nation. Johnson's suggestion that individual states might take the initiative was certainly disingenuous, for not a single state, North or South, had expanded the political rights of blacks since the founding of the republic. It already seemed clear that, as one freedman recalled years afterward, "things was hurt by Mr. Lincoln gettin' kilt."

Launching the South's New Governments

Whatever their differences, Northern proposals for Reconstruction took for granted that loyal men must wield political power in the South. But what constituted loyalty? Legally, at least, the Ironclad Oath, an affirmation that an individual had never voluntarily aided the Confederacy, defined loyalty to the Union. And "unconditional" Unionists, who met this stringent requirement, assumed they would reap the political benefits of Reconstruction. Already, such men had come to power in Maryland, West Virginia, Missouri, and Johnson's own Tennessee. Yet outside mountain areas like western North Carolina and some parts of the upper Piedmont, they comprised a small faction, despised by the white majority as "Tories" and traitors. "There is almost no such thing as loyalty here, as that word is understood in the North," a Union officer reported. As Whitelaw Reid observed during a tour of the South, "it remains to be seen how long a minority, however loyal, can govern in a republican country."

An alternative definition of Unionism focused on an individual's position during the secession crisis. A large number of white Southerners had opposed disunion but "went with their states" with the coming of war. They indignantly repudiated the labels secessionist or traitor. Even Alexander H. Stephens, the South's wartime Vice President, claimed membership in Georgia's "Union element." If opposition to secession and willingness to "accept the situation" at war's end were the criteria, nearly everyone in the South appeared to qualify as loyal, for an "original secessionist" proved difficult to find in 1865.

Former Whigs comprised the majority of antisecession Southerners claiming the Unionist mantle, and they "expected to take control of affairs" at war's end. The idea of absorbing a revived Whiggery into the Republican party had influenced Lincoln's Reconstruction policies and beguiled Northern politicians well into the 1870s. But the actual extent of "persistent Whiggery" remains open to question. The slavery issue had killed Southern Whiggery, and by 1860 most of the party's leaders had joined the Democratic camp.

One thing, however, was plain: In 1865, Southern Unionism, of whatever kind, did not imply a willingness to extend civil and political equality to the freedmen. For most, Reconstruction meant the proscription of "rebels," not rights for blacks. Jealous of their local autonomy, upcountry Unionists resented the presence of black troops and Freedmen's Bureau agents. They also shared President Johnson's assumption that blacks would vote with their former owners. As for Old Line Whigs, many were confirmed elitists who had never accepted the democratizing trends of the antebellum era. Those who believed too many whites enjoyed the franchise were hardly likely to favor extending it to blacks.

For a man bent on making treason odious and displacing the South's traditional leadership, Andrew Johnson displayed remarkable forbearance in choosing provisional governors. Two appointments did appear provocative to many white Southerners: Andrew J. Hamilton of Texas, a Union Army veteran who had been appointed his state's military governor by Lincoln, and William W. Holden, outspoken champion of North Carolina's yeomanry and leader of the 1864 peace movement. Elsewhere, however, Johnson selected men acceptable to a broader segment of white public opinion. In Georgia, the President chose James Johnson, an obscure former Whig Congressman who sat out the war without taking sides. In Alabama, Johnson selected Lewis E. Parsons, a former Whig Congressman tied to the state's mercantile and railroad interests. Mississippi's new governor was William L. Sharkey, a prominent Whig planter; Florida's was William Marvin, a New York–born businessman who spent most of the war as a judge behind federal lines. The South Carolina post, of great symbolic importance in Northern eyes, went to Benjamin F. Perry. His main qualification, apart from Unionism, was that he lived in the upcountry and had long opposed planters' domination of the state's politics.

Taken together, these men were assuredly loyal, although not all could take the Ironclad Oath. All, however, faced the identical task: building political support for themselves and the President in the aftermath of Johnson's proclamation. With both black suffrage and widespread white disenfranchisement excluded, the governors had little choice but to conciliate the majority of voters who had aided the Confederacy.

In nineteenth-century America, patronage oiled the machinery of politics, and Johnson's governors possessed unprecedented patronage powers, for every state and local office stood vacant. By mid-August, Holden alone had named over 4,000 officials, ranging from mayors to judges and constables. Rather than fill these positions with unconditional Union men, the governors used patronage to attract the support of a portion of the South's antebellum and Confederate political leadership. Even Hamilton, who relied heavily on wartime Unionists, appointed prominent pro-Confederate citizens in plantation counties. And Holden used patronage primarily to reward political friends and expand his personal following. All in all, the new governors' appointment policies sounded the death knell of wartime Unionists' hopes that Reconstruction would bring to power "a new class of politicians from the *plain* people." At the same time, the new governors moved to reassure whites that emancipation did not imply any further change in the freedmen's status. Florida Governor Marvin advised blacks not to "delude themselves" into believing that abolition meant civil equality or the vote. Freedmen should return to the plantations, labor diligently, and "call your old Master—'Master.'"

To the bulk of white Southerners, these policies came as an unexpected tonic. In the immediate aftermath of defeat, many were ready to acquiesce in whatever directives emerged from Washington. Northern correspondent Whitelaw Reid probed the white South's mood in May and concluded that any conditions for reunion specified by the President, even black suffrage, would be "promptly accepted." By June, as Johnson's policy unfolded, Reid discerned a change in the Southern spirit. Relief at the mildness of Johnson's terms for reunion now mingled with defiant talk of states' rights and resistance to black suffrage. By midsummer, prominent whites realized that Johnson's Reconstruction empowered them to shape the transition from slavery to freedom and define blacks' civil status. Harvey M. Watterson, a Tennessee Unionist dispatched in June on a Southern tour by the President, found the implications of Johnson's policies well understood—the President favored "a white man's government."

Events in the summer and fall of 1865 further encouraged white Southerners to look upon the President as their ally and protector. Fearing the force would be composed of Confederate veterans who would not deal fairly with freedmen and Unionists, Maj. Gen. Henry W. Slocum prohibited the formation of a state militia in Mississippi, only to see Johnson countermand his order. In the fall, Johnson acquiesced in pleas for the removal of black troops, whose presence, "besides being a painful humiliation," was said to destroy plantation discipline. Within two years nearly all had been mustered out of the service.

Johnson's pardon policy reinforced his emerging image as the white South's champion. Despite talk of punishing traitors, the President proved amazingly lenient. No mass arrests followed the collapse of the Confederacy. Jefferson Davis spent two years in federal prison but was never put on trial; his Vice President, Alexander H. Stephens, served a brief imprisonment, returned to Congress in 1873, and ended his days as governor of Georgia. Some 15,000 Southerners, a majority barred from the general amnesty because of their wealth, filed applications for individual pardons. Soon they were being issued wholesale, sometimes hundreds in a single day. By 1866, over 7,000 had been granted.

Why the President so quickly abandoned the idea of depriving the prewar elite of its political and economic hegemony has always been something of a mystery. Most likely, Johnson came to view cooperation with the planters as indispensable to two goals—white supremacy in the South and his own reelection. Blacks' unexpected militancy in 1865 may well have hardened Johnson's prejudices and caused him to reevaluate his traditional hostility to the planter class. After conversations with Johnson and Secretary of State William H. Seward, British ambassador Sir Frederick Bruce recorded their belief that blacks needed to be kept "in order" while receiving "the care and civilizing influence of dependence on the white man."

Only planters could supervise and control the black population, but once entrusted with this responsibility, they could hardly be barred from a role in politics.

The white South's identification with Johnson as a protector against the "ultra fanatics" of the North quickly rendered serious discussion of alternatives to a "white man's government" impossible. A few prominent Southerners departed from the regional consensus to advocate some form of black suffrage based on property and educational qualifications. Imprisoned Confederate Postmaster General John H. Reagan's public letter urging limited black suffrage created a situation in which, as a former governor of the state informed him, "every man in Texas who expects to be a candidate for anything from governor to constable seems to regard it as his duty to denounce you morning, noon, and night." Had Johnson lent his support, the opinions of men like Reagan might have carried considerable weight; in the absence of presidential backing, their suggestions went unheeded.

If Presidential Reconstruction were to bring to power a new Unionist political leadership, the election of convention delegates in the summer of 1865 provided the opportunity. Few high Confederate officials or men of wealth had yet received individual pardons, and the politically discredited architects of secession did not seek election. As a result, over two-thirds of those elected had opposed secession in 1860. Most were former Whigs, many of whom had held office before the war, but the top level of the antebellum political leadership was conspicuous by its absence. If the elections repudiated the South's prewar secessionist leadership, they did not herald the coming to power of those who had actively opposed the Confederacy, or of previously subordinate social classes.

For the Unionist Whigs who dominated the conventions, Johnson's conditions for Reconstruction ought to have appeared mild indeed. Initially, delegates had only to acknowledge the abolition of slavery and repudiate secession; in October, the President also directed them to void state debts incurred in aid of the Confederacy. These measures merely confirmed Confederate defeat. Yet, although conscious that their every action received careful scrutiny in the North, the conventions became embroiled in "petty and rancorous" disputes that undermined confidence in the President's policy and cast doubt on the willingness even of self-styled Unionists to abandon prewar beliefs and prejudices.

First to assemble, in mid-August, was Mississippi's convention, composed almost entirely of former Whigs. It immediately embarked on what one delegate called "ceaseless wrangling over an immaterial issue"—the precise wording of a constitutional amendment prohibiting slavery. In the end, the convention adopted a simple acknowledgment of abolition. Most conventions adopted language declaring secession null and void, although in Mississippi "repeal" failed by only two votes. As for the repudiation of Confederate state debts, totaling some $54 million, wartime Unionists rather than the President initially raised this demand. Only when South Carolina took no action on its debt and North Carolina strongly resisted this "humiliating act" did Johnson publicly require the voiding of "every dollar."

In other ways the conventions seized the opportunities for change created by the Confederacy's defeat. Upcountry delegates pressed for long-desired changes in the region's political structure. They were most successful in South Carolina, where state officials and Presidential electors had previously been chosen not by popular vote but by a legislature dominated by the coastal parishes. The convention provided for the popular election of the governor, abolished property qualifications for membership in the legislature, and adjusted the system of representation so as to "give the power to the upper counties almost entirely." In Alabama, too, the convention adopted the "white basis" of legislative apportionment, a victory for the upcountry in its campaign to reduce the political power of the plantation region. These debates revealed that long-standing divisions in the Southern polity had survived the Civil War. Yet when it came to the status of the freedmen, there appeared to be little difference between the views of upcountry and lowcountry, Democrat and Whig. Even among unconditional Unionists, the demand for democratic reform meant enhancing the political power of those counties where whites predominated, a goal that would be fatally subverted were blacks included in the electorate. A Mississippi delegate expressed the prevailing opinion: " 'tis nature's law that the superior race must rule and rule they will."

With Johnson's requirements fulfilled, the South in the fall of 1865 proceeded to elect legislators, governors, and members of Congress. In a majority of the states, former Whigs who had opposed secession swept to victory. Of seven Southern governors elected in 1865, six had been antisecessionist Whigs, and the same group dominated the new legislatures and Congressional delegations. Southerners believed they had met the last prerequisite for reunion, choosing loyal men to direct their state governments and represent them in Washington. A closer look at the 1865 elections, however, discloses a striking difference between the results in the Upper South states where wartime Reconstruction governments had survived into 1865 and those that had experienced only Presidential Reconstruction. Of twenty-five men sent to Congress from Arkansas, Tennessee, and Virginia, five had served in the Union Army, many others had aided the federal war effort, and nearly all could take the Ironclad Oath. Farther south, despite the victories of former Whigs, Confederate service emerged as a prerequisite for success. The vast majority of the new Senators and Congressmen had opposed secession, yet nearly all had followed their states into the rebellion. Active Unionists were resoundingly defeated. Probably the most closely watched contest occurred in North Carolina, where Jonathan Worth, a Unionist Whig and Confederate state treasurer, defeated Governor Holden. Once in office, Worth quickly restored the old elite, whose power Holden had to some extent challenged, to control of local affairs. The result confirmed the power of wartime political leadership in a state with a large population of nonslaveholding yeomen.

All in all, the 1865 elections threw into question the future of Presidential Reconstruction. Johnson himself sensed that something had gone awry: "There seems, in many of the elections," he wrote at the end of November, "something like defiance, which is all out of place at this time." The stark truth was that outside the Unionist mountains, Johnson's policies had failed to create a new political leadership to replace the prewar slaveocracy. If the architects of secession had been repudiated, the South's affairs would still be directed by men who, while Unionist in 1860, formed part of the antebellum political establishment. Their actions would do much to determine the fate of Johnson's Reconstruction experiment.

The Anatomy of Presidential Reconstruction

One problem took precedence as the new Southern legislatures assembled. As William H. Trescot explained to South Carolina's governor in December 1865, "you will find that this question of the control of labor underlies every other question of state interest." The ferment in the countryside and ideologies and prejudices inherited from slavery together convinced the white South that coerced labor was necessary to resume the production of plantation staples. With their personal authority over blacks destroyed, planters turned to the state to reestablish labor discipline. Laws regarding labor, property rights, taxation, the administration of justice, and education all formed part of a broad effort to employ state power to shape the new social relations that would succeed slavery.

As the new legislatures prepared to convene, the Southern press and the private correspondence of planters resounded with calls for what a New Orleans newspaper called "a new labor system . . . prescribed and enforced by the State." The initial response to these demands was embodied in the Black Codes, a series of state laws crucial to the undoing of Presidential Reconstruction. Intended to define the freedmen's new rights and responsibilities, the codes authorized blacks to acquire and own property, marry, make contracts, sue and be sued, and testify in court in cases involving persons of their own color. But these provisions were secondary to the attempt to stabilize the black work force and limit its economic options. Henceforth, the state would enforce labor agreements and plantation discipline, punish those who refused to contract, and prevent whites from competing for black workers.

Mississippi and South Carolina enacted the first and most severe Black Codes toward the end of 1865. Mississippi required all blacks to possess, each January, written evidence of employment for the coming year. Laborers leaving their jobs before the contract expired would forfeit wages already earned, and, as under slavery, be subject to arrest by any white citizen. A person offering work to a laborer under contract risked imprisonment or a fine of $500. To limit the freedmen's economic opportunities, they were forbidden to rent land in urban areas. Vagrancy—a crime whose definition included the idle, disorderly, and those who "misspend what they earn"—could be punished by fines or involuntary plantation labor; other criminal offenses included "insulting" gestures or language, "malicious mischief," and preaching the Gospel without a license. South Carolina's Code required blacks to pay an annual tax from $10 to $100 if they wished to follow any occupation other than farmer or servant (a severe blow to the free black community of Charleston and to former slave artisans).

The Northern uproar caused by these laws led other Southern states to modify the language, if not the underlying purpose, of early legislation regarding the freedmen. Virginia included within the definition of vagrancy those who refused to work for "the usual and common wages given to other laborers." Louisiana and Texas, seeking to counteract the withdrawal of black women from field labor, mandated that contracts "shall embrace the labor of all the members of the family able to work." Louisiana empowered the employer to settle all labor disputes. Unlike the Mississippi and South Carolina codes, many subsequent laws made no reference to race. But, as Alabama planter and Democratic politico John W. DuBose later remarked, everyone understood that "the vagrant contemplated was the plantation negro."

Although blacks protested all these measures, their most bitter complaints centered on apprenticeship laws that obliged black minors to work without pay for planters. These laws allowed judges to bind to white employers black orphans and those whose parents were deemed unable to support them. The former owner usually had preference, and the consent of the parents was not required. Blacks pleaded with the Freedmen's Bureau for help in releasing their own children or those of deceased relatives. "I think very hard of the former oners," declared one freedman, "for Trying to keep My blood when I kno that Slavery is dead." As late as the end of 1867, Bureau agents and local justices of the peace were still releasing black children from court-ordered apprenticeships.

The statutes regulating labor and apprenticeship, as Northern reporter Sidney Andrews noted, "acknowledge the overthrow of the special servitude of man to man, but seek . . . to establish the general servitude of man to the commonwealth." The same was true of new criminal laws designed to enforce the property rights of landowners. Legislators sharply increased the penalty for petty larceny. Virginia and Georgia in 1866 made the theft of a horse or mule a capital crime. South Carolina required blacks employed in agriculture to present written authorization from their "masters" before selling farm produce. And North Carolina, at the urging of former Gov. William A. Graham, made "the *intent* to steal" a crime.

Simultaneously, Southern lawmakers moved to limit rights such as hunting, fishing, and the free grazing of livestock, which whites took for granted and many blacks had enjoyed as slaves. Planters opposed hunting and fishing because they allowed blacks to subsist while avoiding plantation labor; they also often involved trespass, thus flouting whites' property rights. Several states made it illegal for blacks to own weapons, or imposed taxes on their dogs and guns. Meanwhile, efforts were made to restrict livestock from ranging freely on unfenced land, a tradition deeply valued by both upcountry yeomen and the freedmen. Laws required livestock owners to fence in their animals, making it impossible for the landless to own pigs or cattle. Many of these "fence laws" applied only to black belt counties.

The entire complex of labor regulations and criminal laws was enforced by an all-white police and judicial system. Although disorder was hardly confined to blacks, virtually all the South's militiamen patrolled plantation counties. Often composed of Confederate veterans still wearing their gray uniforms, they frequently terrorized the black population, ransacking their homes to seize shotguns and other property and abusing those who refused to sign plantation labor contracts. Nor did the courts offer impartial justice. By mid-1866, most of the Southern states allowed blacks to testify on the same terms as whites, although not to serve on juries. The result, one British barrister noted after observing Richmond's courts early in 1867, was that "the verdicts are always for the white man and against the colored man."

Sheriffs, justices of the peace, and other local officials rarely prosecuted whites accused of crimes against blacks. When civil authorities or Bureau agents brought such cases to court, "it seldom results in anything but the acquittal of the criminal," complained South Carolina Bureau head Robert K. Scott. If convictions did follow, judges imposed sentences far more lenient than blacks received for the same crimes. Texas courts indicted some 500 white men for the murder of blacks in 1865 and 1866, but not one was convicted. "No white man in that state has been punished for murder since it revolted from Mexico," commented a Northern visitor. "Murder is considered one of their inalienable state rights." Arrested by white sheriffs and tried before white judges and juries, blacks understandably had little confidence in the courts of the Johnson governments. Blacks, a Bureau official concluded, "would be *just as well* off with no law at all or no Government," as with the legal system of Presidential Reconstruction.

Taxation provided yet another example of the inequitable turn

taken by public policy. Before the war, landed property in most
Southern states had gone virtually untaxed, while poll taxes and
levies on slaves, luxuries, commercial activities, and professions
provided the bulk of revenue. As a result, white yeomen paid few
taxes, planters paid more, although rarely an amount commensurate
with their wealth and income, and urban and commercial interests
bore an excessive tax burden. In Presidential Reconstruction, tax
policy was intended, in part, to reinforce the planter's position
vis-à-vis labor. Freedmen faced heavy poll taxes, while those unable
to pay were deemed vagrants, who could be hired out to anyone
meeting the tax bill. Meanwhile, minuscule levies on landed
property (one-tenth of one percent in Mississippi, for example)
shielded planters and yeomen from the burden of rising government
expenditures. As a result, "the man with his two thousand acres paid
less tax than any one of the scores of hands he may have had in his
employ who owned not a dollar's worth of property." In addition,
localities added poll taxes of their own. Mobile levied a special tax
of $5 on every adult male "and if the tax is not paid," reported the
city's black newspaper, "the chain-gang is the punishment."

Not surprisingly, blacks resented a highly regressive revenue
system from whose proceeds, as a North Carolina Bureau agent
reported, "they state, and with truth, that they derive no benefit
whatever." Even though taxes on blacks as well as whites helped fill
their coffers, states and municipalities barred blacks from poor
relief, orphanages, parks, schools, and other public facilities, insisting that the Freedmen's Bureau provide blacks with the services
they required. The few state efforts to provide for the freedmen's
needs were funded by special taxes levied on blacks, rather than
from general revenues.

The fate of public education in North Carolina illustrates the
astonishing lengths to which the leaders of Presidential Reconstruction went to avoid recognizing blacks as part of their common
constituency. Gov. Jonathan Worth, elected in 1865, had earlier in
his career sponsored the bill establishing public education in North
Carolina, but he now persuaded the legislature to abolish the state
school system. The governor feared that if white children were
educated at public expense, "we will be required to educate the
negroes in like manner." Instead, Worth and his legislature authorized localities to establish tax-supported private academies, destroying the South's only extensive system of public education.

These efforts to bar blacks from equal access to the courts and full participation in the marketplace flagrantly violated the free labor ideology. For this reason, many Southern laws never went into effect. Gen. Daniel E. Sickles, who insisted "all laws shall be applicable alike to all inhabitants," suspended South Carolina's Black Code, and Gen. Alfred H. Terry overturned Virginia's vagrancy law as an attempt to reestablish "slavery in all but its name." By the end of 1866, most Southern states had repealed those laws applying only to blacks. Yet Southern courts continued to enforce vagrancy, breach of contract, and apprenticeship statutes that made no direct reference to race, and tax policies, the militia system, and the all-white judiciary remained unchanged.

No one can claim that the legal structure erected in 1865 and 1866 succeeded fully in controlling the black laborer or shaping the evolution of the Southern economy. The "labor shortage" persisted, as did black efforts to resist plantation discipline. The law is an inefficient mechanism for compelling people to work in a disciplined manner. As a South Carolina plantation physician put it, "they can be forced by law *to contract*, but how to enforce their labor is not yet determined." Nonetheless, the legal system of Presidential Reconstruction had profound consequences, limiting blacks' options, reinforcing whites' privileged access to economic resources, shielding planters from the full implications of emancipation, and inhibiting the development of a free market in land and labor.

The aim of resurrecting as nearly as possible the old order governing black labor, moreover, contradicted a second purpose of the new governments: reshaping the economy to create a New South. With abolition accomplished and King Cotton apparently dethroned, the prospect beckoned of a South more fully attuned to nineteenth-century "progress." Northern investment would spur the growth of railroads and factories, immigration would introduce a new spirit of enterprise, and farmers would no longer see their capital frozen in the labor force. The Southern press extolled the idea of expanding the small prewar textile industry to utilize cotton locally and employ those widowed and orphaned by the war. "Our large plantations," declared a South Carolina newspaper in 1866, "must be carved up into respectable farms; our water power must be made available in the erection of manufactories; . . . our young men must learn to work."

This vision of economic change never commanded majority

support during Presidential Reconstruction. But governors like James L. Orr, James Johnson, and Robert Patton preached the virtues of a New South and found a receptive audience among the former Whigs who dominated politics. A "railroad fever" swept the region. Cities like Charleston and Vicksburg saw railroads as panaceas for economic stagnation, while upcountry towns hailed them as a means of bypassing older port cities and trading directly with the North. Railroads, declared a Mississippi newspaper, would "revive the energies of the people, open up the resources of the State, and put us in the way of growth and general prosperity."

Although the policy of lending the state's credit to promote railroad construction is usually associated with Radical Reconstruction, it in fact originated under the Johnson governments. Simultaneously, legislatures chartered manufacturing, mining, banking, and insurance corporations. And to promote investment in agriculture, states gave the force of law to credit arrangements guaranteeing a first lien on crops to persons advancing loans or supplies for farming. But the economic policies of Presidential Reconstruction failed. Programs of railroad aid accomplished virtually nothing—in the 11 states of the Confederacy, only 422 miles of track were laid in 1866 and 1867. The appointment of commissioners of immigration failed to divert immigrants southward—the number of foreign-born residents of the Confederate states was lower in 1870 than in 1860. Industrial development remained insignificant. A few establishments, like Richmond's Tredegar Iron Works, attracted enough Northern investment to resume production, but most Southern entrepreneurs seeking capital returned home empty-handed. With lucrative opportunities available in the West, investors declined to risk their funds in the South's unstable political climate.

The stillbirth of this early New South program had many causes, some far beyond the power of Southern politicians to affect. The disastrous economic consequences of the Civil War and the legacy of decades of plantation dominance could not be erased in two short years. But the failure also reflected the divided mind and contradictory aims of those advocating economic change. Genuine postwar modernization required an assault on the plantation. Throughout the world, plantation societies are characterized by persistent economic backwardness. Geared to producing agricultural staples for the world market, they have weak internal markets, and planter classes use their political power to prevent the emergence of alternative economic enterprises that might threaten their control of the labor force. The leaders of Presidential Reconstruction failed to come to grips with the plantation system. They wanted economic development but would not accept its full implications—an agrarian revolution and a free labor market. Newspapers that called for breaking up the plantations in the same breath demanded strict laws immobilizing the plantation labor force. Taxes on property remained so low that the establishment of public schools or other forward-looking social services became impossible.

At least the planter class possessed the virtue of consistency: It had no intention of presiding over its own dissolution. It wanted railroads, factories, and Northern investment so long as these supplemented and invigorated the plantation and did not threaten the stability of the black labor force. Those who spoke of dismantling the plantations had no idea what to do with the black population. The entire New South program, in fact, assumed that substitutes would replace black labor. Scientific agriculture and the introduction of machinery would enable large estates to "dispense with the services of freedmen." Family labor would suffice for small farms. Reformers spoke of factories employing white laborers, and of small farms tilled by white newcomers replacing black belt plantations, without making any provision for the former slaves, apart from morbid predictions that they would conveniently "die out." Certainly, spokesmen for a New South had no intention of seeing the finest land in the region fall into black hands.

The experience of Presidential Reconstruction underscores how profoundly attitudes toward the place of the emancipated slaves in the new social order affected efforts to reshape the Southern polity and economy. Andrew Johnson's obsession with keeping blacks in order led inevitably to abandonment of the idea of destroying planters' economic and political hegemony. And the inability of the governments he created to conceive of blacks as anything but plantation laborers doomed any real economic reform. In the end, their policies envisioned less a New South than an improved version of the old.

The outcome typified the failure of vision that marked the South's attempt at "self-reconstruction" from beginning to end. As Presidential Reconstruction drew to a close, Southern whites recognized that an opportunity had slipped away. Lawmakers were castigated by the press in language later turned upon Radical governments:

They were inept, lazy, and unable to deal effectively with the region's problems. "Probably the best thing the Legislature can do," remarked a correspondent of South Carolina Governor Orr, "will be to *go home.*" Thoughtful observers would later acknowledge that the white South brought Radical Reconstruction upon itself. "We had, in 1865, a white man's government in Alabama . . . ," declared Johnson's Provisional Governor Lewis E. Parsons, "but we lost it." The "great blunder" was not to "have at once taken the negro right under the protection of the laws."

The North's Response

When first announced, Andrew Johnson's Reconstruction policy enjoyed overwhelming Northern support. Along with numerous Northerners who, for one reason or another, favored the rapid restoration of the Southern states to the Union, Presidential Reconstruction won the backing of Democrats who hoped to revive their party's fortunes after its "most disastrous epoch," Republicans of Democratic antecedents who shared Johnson's states' rights orientation and racial prejudices, and Republicans who hoped to enhance their position within the party by identifying themselves with the new President.

No less committed to the President's program were influential Northerners who believed the speedy revival of cotton production essential for the nation's economic health. King Cotton may have been dethroned, but as the nation's leading export it remained, as the *New York Times* put it, "a magnate of the very first rank." The trade in the "white gold" was crucial to the wealthy merchants who dominated the economic life of Boston, Philadelphia, New York, and other commercial centers, and to a wide range of businessmen and professionals such as lawyers, bankers, insurance brokers, and shipowners. Without a speedy revival of cotton production, they believed, Southerners could never repay their prewar debts, New England textile factories would have to close, and the nation would be unable to earn enough foreign exchange to resume specie payments and pay its overseas indebtedness. Without cotton, declared Rhode Island textile manufacturer and Republican Sen. William Sprague, America would be "bankrupt in every particular." Thus, powerful Northern economic interests had a stake in speedy reunion and the resumption of staple agriculture and believed

Johnson's policies could accomplish these goals. "If the entire interests of the colored race," declared the New York *Journal of Commerce*, "were remanded where they belong, to the several states, there would be . . . vastly more productive labor."

Against the natural tendency among Northerners to support the new President and the range of interests that united behind him, only one group openly opposed Johnson's program. Radical Republicans were stunned by the May proclamations, believing that on the question of black suffrage, Johnson had misled them. During the summer and fall of 1865, Radicals and abolitionists embarked on a campaign to convince the North that suffrage was "the logical sequence of negro emancipation." To some Radicals, black suffrage formed only one part of a broader program of federal intervention to remake Southern society; others found it appealing because it offered an alternative to permanent national responsibility for the freedmen. Once blacks had the vote, declared *Harper's Weekly*, "the 'Negro question' [would] take care of itself." These differences of emphasis portended later divisions over Reconstruction policy and the eventual breakup of the Radical coalition. In 1865, however, all Radicals could unite on the principle that without black suffrage there could be no Reconstruction.

Throughout these months letters passed back and forth among leading Radicals, lamenting Johnson's policies and promising to organize against them. But an unmistakable note of gloom pervaded this correspondence. "I hope you will do all that can be done for the protection of the poor negroes," Sen. Henry Wilson wrote Freedmen's Bureau Commissioner Howard, since "this nation seems about to abandon them to their disloyal masters."

The question of black suffrage, commented New York diarist George Templeton Strong, was "full of difficulties and conflicting rights. No statesman ever had a more knotty problem set him by destiny." Despite the easing of some racial proscriptions in 1864 and 1865 and the agitation of Northern blacks for the suffrage, only five states, all in New England, allowed blacks to vote on the same terms as whites. The majority of Republicans were not Radicals but moderates and conservatives who resented the "element that seem to have the negro on the brain all the time" and feared the issue of black rights would prove fatal to the party's electoral prospects.

The potential danger quickly became apparent in three referenda on constitutional amendments extending the franchise to the North's tiny black population. In Minnesota, where the Republican convention endorsed voting rights for the state's few hundred black residents, an amendment failed by 2,600 votes even though a Republican was elected governor. Wisconsin gubernatorial candidate Gen. Lucius Fairchild, who personally favored black voting, refused to commit himself on the issue until late in the campaign, preferring, as he put it privately, defeat on the suffrage question to "losing the ticket and the amendment." Fairchild won a 10,000-vote majority, but the amendment fell 9,000 votes short of passage. Equally disheartening for the Radicals was the outcome in Connecticut, where black suffrage was defeated by 6,000 votes.

If they gazed long enough, Radicals could discern a silver lining in these results. Black suffrage had attracted forty-three percent of the vote in Connecticut, forty-five in Minnesota, and forty-seven in Wisconsin. Moreover, while nearly all Democrats opposed the policy, most Republicans voted in favor, an indication that the party's attitude toward black rights had indeed changed during the Civil War. Yet the 1865 referenda helped convince the President's supporters that his critics formed a tiny "radical and fanatic element" and deepened Johnson's commitment to his own course. When Congress reassembled in December, the issue of black suffrage was, for the moment, politically dead.

Yet despite the apparent triumph of Johnson's policies, a certain uneasiness pervaded broad sectors of Northern public opinion and influential Republican leaders. News of violence against the freedmen and the passage of the Black Codes aroused an indignation that spread far beyond Radical circles. Virtually all Republicans agreed, as Edward Atkinson put it, that the Civil War had been "a war for the establishment of free labor, call it by whatever other name you will." Thus, efforts by state legislation to "restore all of slavery but its name" were anathema. Johnson never quite understood that to mainstream Republicans the freedmen had earned a claim upon the conscience of the nation. Many Northerners who did not share the Radicals' commitment to black political rights insisted that the freedmen's personal liberty and ability to compete as free laborers must be guaranteed or emancipation would be little more than a mockery.

Reports also circulated of hotels and restaurants refusing to serve Northerners and steamboats denying them passage. But probably the most damaging accounts were those describing a revival of "rebel" political power. "As for negro suffrage," declared Chicago editor Charles A. Dana in September, "the mass of the Union men in the Northwest do not care a great deal. What scares them is the idea that the rebels are all to be let back . . . and made a power in the government again, just as though there had been no rebellion." Slowly, Southern events reshaped the thinking of such influential moderates as Sen. Lyman Trumbull of Illinois, who had at first strongly supported Johnson's policies. Hardly an advocate of black suffrage, Trumbull became convinced that further federal measures to protect blacks' civil rights, encourage Southern Unionism, and suppress violence must precede the South's return to national life.

When the Thirty-Ninth Congress convened early in December, Johnson's position remained impressive. The President sincerely claimed to have created a new political order in the South, controlled by men loyal to the Union. He simply could not believe, one suspects, that Northern Republicans would jettison his program over so quixotic an issue as the freedmen's rights. The door stood open for Johnson to embrace the emerging Republican consensus that the freedmen were entitled to civil equality short of the suffrage and that wartime Unionists deserved a more prominent role in Southern politics.

Those close to Johnson, however, knew he was not prone to compromise. Indeed, they relished the prospect of a political battle over Reconstruction. "A fight between the Radicals and the Executive is inevitable," declared Harvey Watterson. "Let it come. The sooner the better for the whole country."

The Making of Radical Reconstruction

It was a peculiarity of nineteenth-century politics that more than a year elapsed between the election of a Congress and its initial meeting. The Thirty-Ninth Congress, elected in 1864 in the midst of war, assembled in December 1865 to confront the crucial issues of Reconstruction: Who would control the South? Who would rule the nation? What was to be the status of the emancipated slave? In both houses, Republicans outnumbered Democrats by better than three to one. The interaction between the Republican party's distinctive factions would effectively determine the contours of Congressional policy.

The Radical Republicans

On the party's left stood the Radical Republicans, a self-conscious political generation with shared experiences and commitments, a grass-roots constituency, a moral sensibility, and a program for Reconstruction. At the core of Congressional Radicalism were men whose careers had been shaped by the slavery controversy: Charles Sumner, Benjamin Wade, and Henry Wilson in the Senate; Thaddeus Stevens, George W. Julian, and James M. Ashley in the House. With the exception of Stevens they represented constituencies centered in New England and the belt of New England migration that stretched across the rural North through upstate New York, Ohio's Western Reserve, northern Illinois, and the upper Northwest. Here lay rapidly growing communities of family farms and small towns, where the superiority of the free labor system appeared self-evident, antebellum reform had flourished, and the Republican party commanded overwhelming majorities.

The preeminent Radical leaders, Thaddeus Stevens and Charles Sumner, differed in personality and political style. The recognized floor leader of House Republicans, Stevens was a master of Congressional infighting, parliamentary tactics, and blunt speaking. One contemporary called him "a rude jouster in political and personal warfare." Sumner, disliked by Senate colleagues for egotism, self-righteousness, and stubborn refusal to compromise, acted as the voice, the embodiment, of the New England conscience. Unconcerned with the details of committee work and legislative maneuvering, his forte lay in lengthy, erudite speeches in which he expounded the recurrent theme of his political career: equality before the law. Abolitionists considered him *their* politician. So too did ordinary blacks, North and South, who deluged him with requests for advice and accounts of their grievances. "Your name," wrote a black army veteran in 1869, "shall live in our hearts for ever."

Uniting Stevens, Sumner, and the other Radicals in 1865 was the conviction that the Civil War constituted a "golden moment" for far-reaching change. The driving force of Radical ideology was the utopian vision of a nation whose citizens enjoyed equality of civil and political rights secured by a powerful and beneficent national state. For decades, long before any conceivable political benefit derived from its advocacy, Stevens, Sumner, and other Radicals had defended the unpopular cause of black suffrage and castigated the idea that America was a "white man's government" (a doctrine, Stevens remarked, "that damned the late Chief Justice [Roger B. Taney] to everlasting fame; and, I fear, to everlasting fire"). There was no room for a legally and politically submerged class in the "perfect republic" that must emerge from the Civil War.

To Radical egalitarianism, the Civil War wedded a new conception of the powers and potentialities of the national state. More fully than other Republicans, the Radicals embraced the wartime expansion of national authority, determined not to allow federalism and states' rights to obstruct a sweeping national effort to define and protect the rights of citizens. For Stevens, the war had created its own logic and imperatives. "We are making a nation," he told the House: The vanquished Southern states had sacrificed their constitutional standing and could be treated by Congress as conquered provinces. Yet Stevens's disregard for constitutional niceties denied him broad support. Other Radicals turned to a different reservoir of federal power, the Constitution's clause guaranteeing to each state a republican form of government. Sumner called the provision "a sleeping giant . . . never until this recent war awakened, but now it comes forward with a giant's power. There is no clause in the Constitution like it. There is no other clause which gives to Congress such supreme power over the states." A government that denied any of its citizens equality before the law and did not rest fully on the consent of the governed, he insisted, ceased to be republican.

Reconstruction Radicalism was first and foremost a civic ideology, grounded in a definition of American citizenship. On the economic issues of the day no distinctive or unified Radical position existed. Stevens, himself a small iron manufacturer, favored an economic program geared to the needs of aspiring entrepreneurs, including tariff protection, low interest rates, plentiful greenback currency, and promotion of internal improvements. On the other hand, Radicals like Charles Sumner and *Nation* editor E. L. Godkin, men attuned to orthodox laissez-faire economic theory, favored a low tariff, the swift resumption of specie payments, and minimal government involvement in the economy. Generally, Congressional Radicals viewed economic issues as secondary to those of Reconstruction. "No question of finance, or banks, or currency, or tariffs," declared Illinois Sen. Richard Yates, "can obscure this mighty moral question of the age." Nor did capitalists agree among themselves on Reconstruction. Bostonian John Murray Forbes, a leading investor in Midwestern railroads, viewed black suffrage as essential to creating the political conditions necessary for Northern investment in a reconstructed South. Radicals also won support among manufacturers who saw upwardly mobile blacks as a new market for their products. But other businessmen, especially those with ties to the cotton trade or who hoped to invest in the South, feared Radical policies would "disrupt the cheap Southern labor force" and interfere with the resumption of cotton production.

Radical Republicanism did possess a social and economic vision, but one that derived from the free labor ideology rather than from any one set of business interests. The South, Radicals believed, should be reshaped in the image of the small-scale competitive capitalism of the North. "My dream," one explained in 1866, "is of a model republic, extending equal protection and rights to all men. . . . The wilderness shall vanish, the church and school-house will appear; . . . the whole land will revive under the magic touch of free labor." In such a society, the freedmen would enjoy the same economic opportunities as white laborers. A correspondent of Sumner's, describing how New York City hotels denied his black servant accommodations, strikingly articulated the Radical ideal of equal opportunity regardless of race:

> Is not this state of things a disgrace to America, as a land of liberty and freedom? Must the black man—as free—be insulted and humiliated at every step? . . . The white servant is deemed not on an equality with his employer—yet recognized in the right to rise to that equality. Neither is the black servant on an equality with his employer—yet has an equal right with the white servant to gain it.

The idea of remaking Southern society led a few Radicals to propose that the federal government overturn the plantation system and provide the former slaves with homesteads. In a speech to Pennsylvania's Republican convention in September 1865, Stevens called for the seizure of the 400 million acres belonging to the wealthiest ten percent of Southerners:

> The whole fabric of southern society *must* be changed, and never can it be done if this opportunity is lost. . . . How can republican institutions, free schools, free churches, free social intercourse exist in a mingled community of nabobs and serfs? If the South is ever to be made a safe republic let her lands be cultivated by the toil of the owners.

Confiscation, Stevens believed, would break the power of the South's traditional ruling class, transform the Southern social structure, and create a triumphant Southern Republican party composed of black and white yeomen and Northern purchasers of planter land.

Even among the Radicals, however, only a handful stressed the land question as uncompromisingly as did Stevens. Most deemed land for the freedmen, though commendable, not nearly as crucial to Reconstruction as black suffrage. In a free-labor South, with civil and political equality secured, black and white would find their own level, and, as Benjamin Wade put it, "finally occupy a platform according to their merits." The key was that all must be given "a perfectly fair chance."

Yet whatever Radicals' indecision as to the economic future of the postwar South, the core of their ideology—that a powerful national state must guarantee blacks equal political standing and equal opportunity in a free-labor economy—called for a striking departure in American public life. As Congress assembled, no one knew how many Republicans were ready to advance this far. The growing perception of white Southern intransigence, and President Johnson's indifference to the rights of blacks, helped propel the party's center of gravity to the left. Radicalism, however, possessed a dynamic of its own, based above all on the reality that in a time of crisis, Radicals alone seemed to have a coherent sense of purpose. The "one body of men who had any positive affirmative ideas," Texas Senator-elect Oran M. Roberts discovered upon arriving in Washington, was "the vanguard of the radical party. They knew exactly what they wanted to do, and were determined to do it." Repeatedly, Radicals had staked out unpopular positions, only to be vindicated by events. Uncompromising opposition to slavery's expansion; emancipation; the arming of black troops—all these had, at first, little support, yet all finally found their way into the mainstream of Republican opinion. "These are no times of ordinary politics," declared Wendell Phillips. "These are formative hours: the national purpose and thought grows and ripens in thirty days as much as ordinary years bring it forward."

Origins of Civil Rights

From the day the Thirty-Ninth Congress assembled, it was clear the Republican majority viewed Johnson's policies with misgivings. Clerk of the House Edward McPherson omitted the names of newly elected Southern Congressmen as he called the roll, and the two houses proceeded to establish a Joint Committee on Reconstruction to investigate conditions in the Southern states and report on whether any were entitled to representation.

Some of Johnson's supporters considered these steps a direct challenge to Presidential authority, but Johnson's annual message to Congress took a conciliatory approach. Essentially, the President insisted, "the work of restoration" was now complete—all that remained was for Congress to admit Southern representatives. On the other hand, he conceded that Congress had the right to determine the qualifications of its members, apparently offering it some role in judging Reconstruction's progress. Most Republicans appear to have accepted the message as an acceptable starting point for discussions of Reconstruction. Radical proposals to overturn the Johnson governments and commit Congress to black suffrage fell on deaf ears. "No party, however strong, could stand a year on this platform," one Republican newspaper commented.

With the Radical initiative in abeyance, political leadership in Congress passed to the moderates. Politically, ideologically, and temperamentally, moderate leaders like James G. Blaine and John A. Bingham in the House and Lyman Trumbull, John Sherman, and William Pitt Fessenden in the Senate differed markedly from their Radical colleagues. While fully embracing the changes brought about by the Civil War, moderate Republicans viewed Reconstruction as a practical problem, not an opportunity to impose an open-ended social revolution on the South. Nor did they believe a break with Johnson inevitable or desirable. If "Sumner and Stevens, and a few other such men do not embroil us with the President," Fessenden insisted, "matters can be satisfactorily arranged . . . to the great bulk of Union men throughout the States." Nor were moderates enthusiastic about the prospect of black suffrage, seeing it as a political liability in the North and less likely to provide a stable basis for a new Republican party in the South than a political alliance with forward-looking whites.

Nonetheless, moderate Republicans believed Johnson's Reconstruction policies required modification. Alarmed by the numerous "rebels" holding office in the South, they insisted on further guarantees of "loyalty" and hoped Johnson would repudiate talk of party realignment and stop meeting so openly with "obnoxious Democrats." Equally important, while rejecting black suffrage, mainstream Republicans had embraced civil equality for blacks. The moderates' dilemma was that most of the rights they sought to guarantee for blacks had always been state concerns. Federal action to protect these rights threatened an undue "centralization" of power. Rejecting talk of "conquered provinces" or states reverting to territories, moderates adopted a constitutional position not unlike the President's. While indestructible, the states had forfeited some of their rights by attempting secession; for the moment, they remained in the "grasp of war." Johnson had used similar reasoning

to appoint provisional governors and require states to ratify the
Thirteenth Amendment. Moderates believed the same logic empowered Congress to withhold representation from the South until
the essential rights of the freedmen had been guaranteed.

Two bills reported to the Senate in January 1866 by Lyman
Trumbull, chairman of the Judiciary Committee, defined the moderates' policy. The first extended the life of the Freedmen's Bureau
and authorized agents to take jurisdiction of cases involving blacks
and punish state officials denying blacks the "civil rights belonging
to white persons." The bill represented a radical departure from
traditional federal policy, but as Trumbull assured the Senate, the
Bureau was "not intended as a permanent institution." More
far-reaching was his second measure, the Civil Rights Bill, which
Henry J. Raymond, editor of the *New York Times* and a Congressman from New York, called "one of the most important bills ever
presented to this House for its action." This defined all persons born
in the United States (except Indians) as national citizens and spelled
out rights they were to enjoy equally without regard to race—
making contracts, bringing lawsuits, and enjoying the benefit of "all
laws and proceedings for the security of person and property." No
state law or custom could deprive any citizen of what Trumbull
called these "fundamental rights belonging to every man as a free
man."

In constitutional terms, the Civil Rights Bill represented the first
attempt to give meaning to the Thirteenth Amendment, to define in
legislative terms the essence of freedom. The bill proposed, one
Congressman declared, "to secure to a poor, weak class of laborers
the right to make contracts for their labor, the power to enforce the
payment of their wages, and the means of holding and enjoying the
proceeds of their toil." If states could deny blacks these rights,
another Republican remarked, "then I demand to know, of what
practical value is the amendment abolishing slavery?" But, beyond
these specific rights, moderates, like the Radicals, rejected the
entire idea of laws differentiating between black and white in access
to the courts and penalties for crimes. The shadow of the Black
Codes hung over these debates, and Trumbull declared his intention
"to destroy all these discriminations."

As the first statutory definition of the rights of American citizenship, the Civil Rights Bill embodied a profound change in federal–
state relations and reflected how Radical ideas had entered the

party's mainstream. Before the Civil War, James G. Blaine later remarked, only "the wildest fancy of a distempered brain" could envision an act of Congress conferring upon blacks "all the civil rights pertaining to a white man." And although primarily intended to benefit the freedman, the bill invalidated many discriminatory laws in the North. "I admit," said Maine Sen. Lot M. Morrill, "that this species of legislation is absolutely revolutionary. But are we not in the midst of a revolution?"

In fact, however, the bill combined elements of continuity and change, reflecting Republican opinion in early 1866. It honored the traditional presumption that the primary responsibility for law enforcement lay with the states, while creating a latent federal presence to be triggered by discriminatory state laws. Nor did Congress create a national police force or permanent military presence to protect the rights of citizens. Instead it placed the burden of enforcement on the federal courts. And despite its intriguing reference to the role "custom" played in depriving blacks of legal equality, the bill was primarily directed against public, not private, acts of injustice. Moderates perceived discriminatory state laws as the greatest threat to blacks' rights, a questionable assumption when the freedmen faced rampant violence as well as unequal treatment by sheriffs, judges, and juries, often under laws that made no mention of race. And, as Trumbull insisted, the bill contained nothing "about the political rights of the Negro."

Thus, by February 1866, Republicans had united on Trumbull's Freedmen's Bureau and Civil Rights Bills as necessary amendments to Presidential Reconstruction. Meanwhile, the persistent complaints of persecution forwarded to Washington by Southern blacks and white loyalists persuaded Congress that the Southern states could not be trusted to manage their own affairs without federal oversight. Particularly alarming was the testimony gathered by the Joint Committee on Reconstruction. Army officers, Bureau agents, freedmen, and Southern Unionists repeated tales of injustice. Early in February, North Carolina Senator-elect John Pool concluded that Southern members would not gain admission for some time and that the South faced "conditions that would never have been thought of, if a more prudent and wise course had been adopted" by the Johnson governments.

To the surprise and dismay of Congress, the President vetoed the Freedmen's Bureau Bill. Moreover, rejecting a conciliatory draft written by Secretary of State William H. Seward, which criticized the bill's specifics while acknowledging a federal responsibility for the freedmen, Johnson's message repudiated the Bureau entirely, deriding it as an "immense patronage" unwarranted by the Constitution and unaffordable given "the condition of our fiscal affairs." Congress, he pointed out, had never provided economic relief, established schools, or purchased land for "our own people"; such aid, moreover, threatened the "character" and "prospects" of the freedmen by implying that they did not have to work for a living. These matters, Johnson added, should not be decided while eleven states remained unrepresented, and at any rate the President—"chosen by the people of all the States"—had a broader view of the national interest than members of Congress, elected "from a single district."

This was a remarkable document. In appealing to fiscal conservatism, raising the specter of an immense federal bureaucracy overriding citizens' rights, and insisting self-help, not dependence on outside assistance, offered the surest road to economic advancement, Johnson voiced themes that to this day have sustained opposition to federal aid for blacks. At the same time, he falsely accused Congress of intending to make the Bureau "a permanent branch of the public administration" and showed no sympathy whatever for the freedmen's plight. As for Johnson's exalting himself above Congress, this, one Republican remarked, "is modest for a man . . . made President by an assassin." The veto ensured a bitter political struggle between Congress and the President, for, as Fessenden accurately predicted, "he will and must . . . veto every other bill we pass" concerning Reconstruction.

Why did Johnson choose this path? The President had been remarkably successful in retaining support among Northerners and Southerners, Republicans and Democrats, but the Freedmen's Bureau Bill forced him to begin choosing among his diverse allies. Johnson knew Southern whites disliked the Bureau and Northern Democrats clamored for its destruction. He seems to have interpreted moderate Republican efforts to avoid a split as evidence that they feared an open breach in the party. And he was convinced the Radicals were conspiring against him.

Johnson, reported William H. Trescot, hoped the Republican mainstream would "form a new party with the President," excluding the Radicals. Unfortunately for this strategy, Johnson's belief that only the Radicals were concerned about the freedmen's rights caused him to misconstrue divisions within Republican ranks. The Senate vote on overriding his veto ought to have given him pause, for although the bill fell two votes short of the necessary two-thirds, thirty of thirty-eight Republicans voted for repassage. Trescot now recognized that Republicans might well unite against the President, inaugurating "a fight this fall such as has never been seen." But Johnson refused to believe that the majority of Republicans would insist on federal protection for the freedmen. The day after the Senate vote, the President continued his assault upon the Radicals. In an impromptu Washington's Birthday speech, he equated Stevens, Sumner, and Wendell Phillips with Confederate leaders, since all were "opposed to the fundamental principles of this Government." He even implied that they were plotting his assassination.

Attention now turned to the Civil Rights Bill. Republican opinion, Johnson's supporters warned him, insisted that the freedmen must have "the same rights of property and person" as whites. But this premise Johnson rejected. His veto message repudiated both the specific terms of the Civil Rights Bill and its underlying principle. The assertion of national power to protect blacks' civil rights, he insisted, violated "all our experience as a people" and constituted a "stride towards centralization, and the concentration of all legislative powers in the national Government." Most striking was the message's blatant racism. Somehow, the President had decided that giving blacks full citizenship discriminated against whites—"the distinction of race and color is by the bill made to operate in favor of the colored and against the white race." Johnson even invoked the specter of racial intermarriage as the logical consequence of Congressional policy.

For Republican moderates, the Civil Rights veto ended all hope of cooperation with the President. In a biting speech, Trumbull dissected Johnson's logic, especially the notion that guaranteeing blacks civil equality impaired the rights of whites. Early in April, for the first time in American history, Congress enacted a major piece of legislation over a President's veto. A headline in one Republican newspaper summed up the political situation: "The Separation Complete."

Johnson's rejection of the Civil Rights Bill has always been viewed as the most disastrous miscalculation of his political career. If the President aimed to build a new political coalition without the Radicals, he could not have failed more miserably. Whatever their differences, all Republicans agreed with the editorial response of the Springfield *Republican*: Protection of the freedmen's civil rights "follows from the suppression of the rebellion. . . . The party is nothing, if it does not do this—the nation is dishonored if it hesitates in this."

Yet despite the veto's outcome, Johnson's course cannot be explained simply in terms of insensitivity to Northern public opinion. Given the Civil Rights Act's astonishing expansion of federal authority and blacks' rights, it is not surprising that Johnson considered it a Radical measure against which he could mobilize voters. When, during one April speech, Johnson asked rhetorically, "What does the veto mean?" a voice from the crowd shouted: "It is keeping the nigger down." Johnson chose the issue on which to fight—federal protection for blacks' civil rights—and it was an issue on which he did not expect to lose.

The Fourteenth Amendment

As the split with the President deepened, Republicans grappled with the task of embedding in the Constitution, beyond the reach of Presidential vetoes and shifting political majorities, the results of the Civil War. At one point in January, no fewer than seventy constitutional amendments had been introduced. Not until June, after seemingly endless debate and maneuvering, did the Fourteenth Amendment, the most important ever added to the Constitution, receive the approval of Congress. Its first clause prohibited the states from abridging equality before the law. The second provided for a reduction in a state's representation proportional to the number of male citizens denied suffrage. This aimed to prevent the South from benefiting politically from emancipation. Before the war, three-fifths of the slaves had been included in calculating Congressional representation; now, as free persons, all would be counted. Since Republicans were not prepared to force black suffrage upon the South, they offered white Southerners a choice— enfranchise the freedmen or sacrifice representation in Congress. The third clause barred from national and state office men who had sworn allegiance to the Constitution and subsequently aided the Confederacy. While not depriving "rebels" of the vote, this excluded from office most of the South's prewar political leadership, opening the door to power, Republicans hoped, for true Unionists.

The Amendment also prohibited payment of the Confederate debt and empowered Congress to enforce its provisions through "appropriate" legislation.

Because it implicitly acknowledged the right of states to limit voting because of race, Wendell Phillips denounced the amendment as a "fatal and total surrender." Susan B. Anthony, Elizabeth Cady Stanton, and others in the women's suffrage movement also felt betrayed, because the second clause introduced the word "male" into the Constitution. Alone among suffrage limitations, those founded on sex would not reduce a state's representation.

Ideologically and politically, nineteenth-century feminism had been tied to abolition. Feminists now turned Radical ideology back upon Congress. If "special claims for special classes" were illegitimate and unrepublican, how could the denial of women's rights be justified? Should not sex, like race, be rejected as an unacceptable basis for legal distinctions among citizens? Rather than defining Reconstruction as "the negro's hour," they called it, instead, the hour for change: Another generation might pass "ere the constitutional door will again be opened." The dispute over the Fourteenth Amendment marked a turning point in nineteenth-century reform. Leaving feminist leaders with a deep sense of betrayal, it convinced them, as Stanton put it, that woman "must not put her trust in man" in seeking her rights. Women's leaders now embarked on a course that severed their historic alliance with abolitionism and created a truly independent feminist movement.

The Fourteenth Amendment, one Republican newspaper observed, repudiated the two axioms on which the Radicals "started to make their fight last December: dead States and equal suffrage." Yet it clothed with constitutional authority the principle Radicals had fought to vindicate: equality before the law, overseen by the national government. For its heart was the first section, which declared all persons born or naturalized in the United States both national and state citizens and prohibited the states from abridging their "privileges and immunities," depriving any person of life, liberty, or property without "due process of law," or denying them "equal protection of the laws."

For more than a century, politicians, judges, lawyers, and scholars have debated the meaning of this elusive language. But the aims of the Fourteenth Amendment can be understood only within the political and ideological context of 1866: the break with the

President, the need to find a measure able to unify all Republicans, and the growing party consensus in favor of strong federal action to protect the freedmen's rights, short of the suffrage. During many drafts, changes, and deletions, the Amendment's central principle remained constant: a national guarantee of equality before the law. This was "so just," a moderate Congressman declared, "that no member of this House can seriously object to it." In language that transcended race and region, the Amendment challenged legal discrimination throughout the nation and changed and broadened the meaning of freedom for all Americans.

On the precise definition of equality before the law, Republicans differed among themselves. Even moderates, however, understood Reconstruction as a dynamic process, in which phrases like "privileges and immunities" were subject to changing interpretation. They preferred to allow both Congress and the federal courts maximum flexibility in implementing the Amendment's provisions and combating the injustices that confronted blacks in much of the South. Indeed, as in the Civil Rights Act, Congress looked to an activist federal judiciary to enforce civil rights—a mechanism preferable to maintaining indefinitely a standing army in the South or erecting a national bureaucracy empowered to oversee Reconstruction.

In establishing a national citizenship whose common rights no state could abridge, Republicans carried forward the nation-building process born of the Civil War. The states, declared Michigan Sen. Jacob Howard, who guided the Amendment through the Senate, could no longer infringe upon the liberties the Bill of Rights protected against federal violation; henceforth, states must respect "the personal rights guaranteed and secured by the first eight Amendments." The Freedmen's Bureau had already tried to protect such basic rights as freedom of speech, the right to bear arms, trial by impartial jury, and protection against cruel and unusual punishment and unreasonable search and seizure, and the Amendment was deemed necessary, in part, precisely because every one of these rights was being systematically violated in the South in 1866.

When Congress adjourned in July, two divisive questions remained unresolved. One was precisely how the Southern states would achieve readmission. Tennessee quickly ratified the Fourteenth Amendment and regained its right to representation, but without Congress explicitly acknowledging that this established a binding precedent. And, for the moment, the vexing question of black voting rights had been laid aside. Henry M. Turner, the black minister and political organizer who had been sent to Washington to lobby for black rights by Georgia's statewide black convention, reported: "Several Congressmen tell me, 'the negro must vote,' but the issue must be avoided now so as 'to keep up a two thirds power in Congress.'" Even conservative Republican Sen. John B. Henderson of Missouri believed black suffrage inevitable: "It will not be five years from today before this body will vote for it. You cannot get along with it."

The Campaign of 1866

On May 1, 1866, two horse-drawn hacks, one driven by a white man, the other by a black, collided on a street in Memphis. When police arrested the black driver, a group of recently discharged black veterans intervened, and a white crowd began to gather. From this incident followed three days of racial violence, with white mobs, composed in large part of the mostly Irish policemen and firemen, assaulting blacks on the streets and invading South Memphis, an area that included a shantytown housing families of black soldiers stationed in nearby Fort Pickering. Before the rioting subsided, at least forty-six blacks and two whites lay dead, five black women had been raped, and hundreds of black dwellings, churches, and schools were pillaged or destroyed by fire.

Twelve weeks later, a similar outbreak rocked New Orleans, although this time the violence arose directly from Reconstruction politics. The growing power of former Confederates under the administration of Gov. James M. Wells had long dismayed the city's Radicals and eventually alarmed Wells himself. Wells now endorsed a Radical plan to reconvene the Constitutional Convention of 1864 in order to enfranchise blacks, prohibit "rebels" from voting, and establish a new state government. On the appointed day, July 30, only twenty-five delegates assembled, soon joined by a procession of some 200 black supporters, mostly former soldiers. Fighting broke out in the streets, police converged on the area, and the scene quickly degenerated into what Gen. Philip H. Sheridan later called "an absolute massacre." By the time federal troops arrived, thirty-four blacks and three white Radicals had been killed, and well over 100 persons injured. Even more than the Memphis riot, the events in New Orleans discredited Presidential Reconstruction. Many

Northerners agreed with Gen. Joseph Holt that Johnson's leniency had unleashed "the barbarism of the rebellion in its renaissance."

The New Orleans riot could not have occurred at a worse time for the President—only two weeks before the National Union convention, a gathering of his supporters, was to assemble in Philadelphia. On the surface, harmony prevailed at the convention. The 7,000 spectators cheered wildly as South Carolina's massive Gov. James L. Orr marched down the main aisle arm-in-arm with the diminutive Gen. Darius N. Couch of Massachusetts, leading a procession of the delegates. Yet behind the scenes, dissension reigned. *New York Times* editor Henry J. Raymond had been persuaded to deliver the convention's main address, but his draft of the platform included guarded praise of the Fourteenth Amendment and oblique criticism of slavery. This proved too much for the Resolutions Committee, which omitted the offending passages. In the end, the convention did not try to establish a new national party, but called for the election of Congressmen who would support Johnson's policies.

The President now decided to take his case to the Northern people. On August 28, accompanied by Ulysses Grant, Adm. David Farragut, and other notables, he embarked on the "swing around the circle," an unprecedented speaking tour aimed at influencing the coming elections. At first things went well, for New York and Philadelphia men of commerce and finance welcomed him with enthusiasm. Then the party traveled through upstate New York and on to the West. When they reached Ohio, Johnson, interrupted by hecklers, responded in kind. At Cleveland, when a member of the audience yelled "hang Jeff Davis," the President replied, "Why not hang Thad Stevens and Wendell Phillips?" Johnson also indulged his unique blend of self-aggrandizement and self-pity. On one occasion, he intimated that Providence had removed Lincoln to elevate Johnson himself to the White House. At St. Louis, he blamed Congress for instigating the New Orleans riot and unleashed a "muddled tirade" against his opponents: "I have been traduced, I have been slandered, I have been maligned. I have been called Judas Iscariot. . . . Who has been my Christ that I have played the Judas with? Was it Thad Stevens?" Even Johnson's partisans were mortified. "Thoroughly reprehensible," exclaimed the New York *Journal of Commerce*. The President, former Georgia Gov. Herschel V. Johnson declared, had sacrificed "the moral power of his position, and done great damage to the cause of Constitutional reorganization." In mid-September, Andrew Johnson returned to Washington from what one admirer called "a tour it were better had never been made."

Johnson's supporters subsequently contended that a small band of fanatics secured Republican victory by demagogic attacks against "rebels" and "Copperheads" that obscured the real issues, such as the tariff, on which a pro-Johnson majority could ostensibly have been forged. Yet both parties remained divided on economic questions, and voters displayed little interest in them in 1866. More than anything else, the election became a referendum on the Fourteenth Amendment. Seldom, declared the *New York Times*, had a political contest been conducted "with so exclusive reference to a single issue." And the President's supporters went down to a disastrous defeat. In the next Congress, Republicans would possess well over the two-thirds majority required to override a veto.

"This is the most decisive and emphatic victory ever seen in American politics," exclaimed *The Nation*. In its aftermath, the course of prudence seemed plain. The South, warned the *Times*, must ratify and comply with the Fourteenth Amendment and the President must cease to oppose it; otherwise, black suffrage was inevitable. Johnson, however, refused to alter his opposition to the Amendment. Southern newspapers, moreover, consistently misinformed their readers about Northern politics, portraying Johnson's opponents as a band of Radical fanatics who lacked broad popular support and predicting Congress could not possibly do things it then proceeded to do. The election returns came as a shock, but produced no political reassessment. Between October 1866 and the following January, ten Southern legislatures overwhelmingly repudiated the Amendment. All told, only thirty-three Southern lawmakers braved public opposition to vote for ratification. Not for the first time, Southern intransigence played into the Radicals' hands. For, as Benjamin S. Hedrick of North Carolina had warned, "If the Northern people are forced by the South to follow Thad Stevens or the Copperheads, I believe they will prefer the former."

The Coming of Black Suffrage

The Republicans who gathered in December 1866 for the second session of the Thirty-Ninth Congress considered themselves "masters of the situation." Johnson's annual message, pleading for the immediate restoration of the "now unrepresented States," was ignored. The President, declared the New York *Herald*, his erstwhile supporter, "forgets that we have passed through the fiery ordeal of a mighty revolution, and that the pre-existing order of things is gone and can return no more—that a great work of reconstruction is before us, and that we cannot escape it."

Black suffrage, it soon became clear, was on the horizon. In mid-December, Trumbull told the Senate that Congress possessed the authority to "enter these States and hurl from power the disloyal element which controls and governs them," an important announcement that moderates intended to overturn the Johnson governments. In January 1867, a bill enfranchising blacks in the District of Columbia became law over the President's veto. Then, Congress extended manhood suffrage to the territories. Even more radical proposals were in the air, including widespread disenfranchisement, martial law for the South, confiscation, the impeachment of the President. A *Herald* editorial writer apologized to Johnson for the paper's advocacy of his removal: Its editor always went with the political tide, and the tide now flowed toward the Radicals.

Congress, however, found it difficult to agree on a program, a situation not all Republicans regretted. Late in January, George W. Julian warned against precipitous action. What the South needed was not "hasty restoration" or oaths that invited men to commit perjury, but "*government*, the strong arm of power, outstretched from the central authority here in Washington." Only a prolonged period of federal control would enable loyal public opinion to sink deep roots and permit "Northern capital and labor, Northern energy and enterprise" to venture south, there to establish "a Christian civilization and a living democracy." The South, he proposed, should be governed directly from Washington and readmitted only at "some indefinite future time" when its "political and social elements" had been thoroughly transformed.

Julian's speech struck a chord in Congress. The Joint Committee quickly approved a bill to impose military rule on the South. But even as moderates accepted military rule as a temporary expedient, they insisted on clearly specifying how the South could establish new civil governments and regain its standing within the Union. The military bill passed the House, but in the Senate the Republican caucus appointed a committee to lay down conditions of readmission for the entire South. The main point of dispute concerned black suffrage: All agreed it must operate in elections for constitutional conventions, but not on whether to require new constitutions to incorporate it as well. To Sumner, this was crucial, and when the committee failed to mandate black suffrage in the new documents, he appealed to the full caucus. The question of black voting, he said, must be settled, or "every State and village between here and the Rio Grande would be agitated by it." By a margin of two, the Republican caucus overturned the committee's decision. Exclaimed Radical Sen. Henry Wilson; "This is the greatest vote that has been taken on this continent."

And so Republicans decided that blacks must enter the South's body politic. But when the amended bill returned to the House, it touched off a storm of Radical protest. Rebels, charged George Boutwell, had been handed "the chief places in the work of reconstruction," for while establishing military rule, the bill failed to remove the Johnson governments immediately or disenfranchise former Confederates. Two amendments, intended to place the Reconstruction process in the hands of loyal men, made the bill more palatable to its critics. The first barred anyone disqualified from office under the Fourteenth Amendment from electing, or serving as, constitutional convention delegates. The second declared the Johnson governments subject to modification or abolition at any time and prohibited individuals disqualified under the Fourteenth Amendment from voting or holding office under them. No one knew how many "leading rebels" these eleventh-hour changes affected. But for Southern Unionists, they represented a major victory. The larger part of a political generation, men of local influence ranging from prewar postmasters and justices of the peace to legislators and Congressmen, had been temporarily excluded from office and voting. "This Amendment . . . will prove of vital importance in the work of reconstruction . . . ," declared the Raleigh *Standard*. "We rejoice that there is to be an end to rebel rule."

Throughout these deliberations, Johnson remained silent. Toward the end of February, New York *Evening Post* editor Charles Nordhoff visited the White House. He found the President "much excited," certain "the people of the South . . . were to be trodden under foot 'to protect niggers.' " Nordhoff had once admired the President; now he judged him a "pig-headed man" governed by one idea: "bitter opposition to universal suffrage." Gone was the vision of a reconstructed South controlled by loyal yeomen. "The old Southern leaders . . . ," declared the man who had once railed against the Slave Power, "must rule the South." When the Reconstruction bill reached his desk on March 2, Johnson returned it with a veto, which Congress promptly overrode. Maryland Sen. Reverdy Johnson was the only member to break party ranks. Whatever its flaws, he declared, the bill offered the South a path back into the Union, and the President should abandon his intransigence and accede to the plainly expressed will of the people. Reverdy Johnson's was the only Democratic vote in favor of any of the Reconstruction measures of 1866–67.

In its final form, the Reconstruction Act of 1867 divided the Confederate states, except Tennessee, into five military districts under commanders empowered to employ the army to protect life and property. And without immediately replacing the Johnson regimes, it laid out the steps by which new state governments could be created and recognized by Congress—the writing of new constitutions providing for manhood suffrage, their approval by a majority of registered voters, and ratification of the Fourteenth Amendment. Simultaneously, Congress passed the Habeas Corpus Act, which greatly expanded citizens' ability to remove cases to federal courts.

Like all the decisions of the Thirty-Ninth Congress, the Reconstruction Act contained a somewhat incongruous mixture of idealism and political expediency. The bill established military rule, but only as a temporary measure to keep the peace, with the states assured a relatively quick return to the Union. It looked to a new political order for the South, but failed to place Southern Unionists in immediate control. It made no economic provision for the freedmen. Even black suffrage derived from a variety of motives and calculations. For Radicals, it represented the culmination of a lifetime of reform. For others, it seemed less the fulfillment of an idealistic creed than an alternative to prolonged federal intervention in the South, a means of enabling blacks to defend themselves against abuse, while relieving the nation of that responsibility.

Despite all its limitations, Congressional Reconstruction was indeed a radical departure, a stunning and unprecedented experiment in interracial democracy. In America, the ballot not only identified who could vote, it defined a collective national identity. Democrats had fought black suffrage on precisely these grounds. "Without reference to the question of equality," declared Indiana

Sen. Thomas Hendricks, "I say we are not of the same race; we are so different that we ought not to compose one political community." Enfranchising blacks marked a powerful repudiation of such thinking. In some ways it was an astonishing leap of faith. Were the mass of freedmen truly prepared for political rights? Gen. E. O. C. Ord, federal commander in Arkansas, believed them "so servile and accustomed to submit" to white dictation that they would "not dare to present themselves at the polls." Even some Radicals harbored inner doubts, fearing that "demagogues" or their former masters would control the black vote, or that political rights would prove meaningless without economic independence.

In the course of Reconstruction, the freedmen disproved these somber forecasts. They demonstrated political shrewdness and independence in using the ballot to affect the conditions of their freedom. However inadequate as a response to the legacy of slavery, it remains a tragedy that the lofty goals of civil and political equality were not permanently achieved. And the end of Reconstruction came not because propertyless blacks succumbed to economic coercion, but because a tenacious black community, abandoned by the nation, fell victim to violence and fraud.

"We have cut loose from the whole dead past," wrote Wisconsin Sen. Timothy Howe, "and have cast our anchor out a hundred years." His colleague, Waitman T. Willey of West Virginia, adopted a more cautious tone: "The legislation of the last two years will mark a great page of history for good or evil—I hope the former. The crisis, however, is not yet past."

Blueprints for a Republican South

The Political Mobilization of the Black Community

Like emancipation, the passage of the Reconstruction Act inspired blacks with a millennial sense of living at the dawn of a new era. Former slaves now stood on an equal footing with whites, a black speaker told a Savannah mass meeting; before them lay "a field, too vast for contemplation." As in 1865, blacks found countless ways of pursuing aspirations for autonomy and equality, and seizing the opportunity to press for further change. Strikes broke out among black longshoremen in Charleston, Savannah, Mobile, Richmond, and New Orleans. Hundreds of South Carolina blacks refused to pay taxes to the existing state government, and crowds rescued companions arrested by the all-white Richmond police. Three blacks refused to leave a whites-only streetcar in Richmond, and scores rushed to the scene shouting, "Let's have our rights."

But in 1867, politics emerged as the principal focus of black aspirations. Itinerant lecturers, black and white, brought the Republican message into the heart of the rural South. Voting registrars instructed freedmen in American history and government and "the individual benefits of citizenship." In Monroe County, Alabama, where no black political meeting had occurred before 1867, freedmen crowded around the speaker shouting, "Bless God for this." On August 1, Richmond's tobacco factories were forced to close because so many black laborers attended the Republican state convention.

So great was the enthusiasm that, as one ex-slave minister later wrote, "Politics got in our midst and our . . . religious work for a while began to wane." More typically, the church, and indeed every other black institution, became politicized. Every African Methodist Episcopal preacher in Georgia was said to be actively engaged in Republican organizing, and political materials were read aloud at "churches, societies, leagues, clubs, balls, picnics, and all other gatherings." One plantation manager summed up the situation: "You never saw a people more excited on the subject of politics than are the negroes of the south. They are perfectly wild."

The meteoric rise of the Union League reflected and channeled this political mobilization. Even before 1867, blacks had organized Union Leagues in some parts of the South, and the order had spread rapidly during and after the war among Unionist whites in the Southern hill country. Now, as freedmen poured into the league, "the negro question" disrupted some upcountry branches, leading many white members to withdraw altogether or retreat into segregated branches. Many local leagues, however, achieved a remarkable degree of interracial harmony. In North Carolina, one racially mixed league composed of freedmen, white Unionists, and Confederate Army deserters met "in old fields, or in some out of the way house, and elect[ed] candidates to be received into their body."

By the end of 1867, it seemed, virtually every black voter in the South had enrolled in the Union League or some equivalent local political organization. Usually, a Bible, a copy of the Declaration of Independence, and an anvil or some other emblem of labor lay on a table, a minister opened the meeting with a prayer, and new members took an initiation oath and pledged to uphold the Republican party and the principle of equal rights. The detailed minute book of the Union League of Maryville, Tennessee, a mountain community with a longstanding antislavery tradition, offers a rare glimpse of the league's inner workings. It records frequent discussions of such issues as the national debt and the impeachment of President Johnson, as well as broader questions: "Is the education of the Female as important as that of the male?" "Should students pay corporation tax?" "Should East Tennessee be a separate state?" Although composed largely of white small farmers, agricultural laborers, and town businessmen, many of them Union Army veterans, and located in a county only one-tenth black, the Maryville league chose a number of black officers, called upon Tennessee to send at least one black to Congress, and in 1868 nominated and elected a black justice of the peace and four black city commissioners.

The local leagues' multifaceted activities, however, far transcended electoral politics. They promoted the building of schools and churches and collected funds "to see to the sick." In the Alabama black belt, league organizer George W. Cox found himself besieged by freedmen requesting information about suing their employers, avoiding fines for attending political meetings, and ensuring a fair division of crops at harvest time. Here and in South Carolina, local leagues struck for higher wages and encouraged members not to contract for less than half the crop, while some Texas leagues demanded back wages for blacks held in slavery after the Emancipation Proclamation.

This hothouse atmosphere of political mobilization made possible a vast expansion of the black political leadership that had emerged between 1864 and 1867. Many of the blacks who plunged into politics in 1867 had been born or raised in the North. One white participant in South Carolina's first Republican convention, "astonished" by "the amount of intelligence and ability shown by the colored men," singled out Ohio-born William N. Viney, a young veteran who had purchased land in the lowcountry and, after the passage of the Reconstruction Act, organized political meetings throughout the region. Many Northern blacks, like Viney, had come south with the army; others had served with the Freedmen's Bureau or as teachers and ministers employed by black churches and Northern missionary societies. Still others were fugitive slaves returning home or the children of well-to-do Southern free blacks who had been sent north for the education (often at Oberlin College) and economic opportunities denied them at home. Reconstruction was one of the few times in American history that the South offered black men of talent and ambition not only the prospect of serving their race, but also greater possibilities for personal advancement than existed in the North.

Even more remarkable than the prominence of Northern blacks was the rapid emergence of indigenous leadership in the black belt. Here, local leaders tended to be ex-slaves of modest circumstances. Many were teachers, preachers, or individuals who possessed other skills of use to the community. Former slave Thomas Allen, a Union League organizer who would soon win election to the Georgia legislature, was a propertyless Baptist preacher, shoemaker, and farmer. But what established him as a leader was literacy: "In my county the colored people came to me for instructions, and I gave them the best instructions I could. I took the New York Tribune and other papers, and in that way I found out a great deal, and I told them whatever I thought was right." In occupation, the largest number of local activists appear to have been artisans, men whose skill and independence set them apart from ordinary laborers, but who remained deeply embedded in the life of the freedmen's community.

In Union Leagues, Republican gatherings, and impromptu local meetings, ordinary blacks in 1867 and 1868 staked their claim to equal citizenship in the American republic. In insistent language far removed from the conciliatory tones of 1865, an Alabama convention affirmed its understanding of equal citizenship:

> We claim exactly *the same rights, privileges and immunities as are enjoyed by white men*—we ask nothing more and will be content with nothing less. . . . The law no longer knows white nor black, but simply men, and consequently we are entitled to ride in public conveyances, hold office, sit on juries and do everything else which we have in the past been prevented from doing solely on the ground of color.

At their most utopian, blacks in Reconstruction envisioned a society purged of all racial distinctions. They retained a sense of racial identity, finding pride in the accomplishments of black soldiers, and preferring black teachers for their children and black churches in which to worship. But in the polity, those who had so long been proscribed because of color defined equality as color-blind. "I heard a white man say," black teacher Robert G. Fitzgerald recorded in his diary, "today is the black man's day; tomorrow will be the white man's. I thought, poor man, those days of distinction between colors is about over in this (now) free country." Indeed, black politicians sometimes found their listeners unreceptive to the rhetoric of racial self-consciousness. Martin R. Delany, the "father of black nationalism" and a South Carolina Republican organizer, found it "dangerous to go into the country and speak of color in any manner whatever, without the angry rejoinder, 'we don't want to hear that; we are all one color now.'"

As was true throughout Reconstruction, politics in 1867 fused with the freedmen's economic aspirations. Many Northern blacks, to be sure, carried south the ideology of free labor, with its respect for private property and individual initiative. Such views were echoed by the Southern free black elite, many of whom opposed confiscation and insisted that political equality did not imply the end of class distinctions: "We do not ask that the ignorant and degraded shall be put on a social equality with the refined and intelligent." 1867, however, was an inopportune moment to preach individual self-help to black belt freedmen, for successive crop failures had left those on share contracts with little or no income. Drawing on widespread dissatisfaction with a contract system that appeared to consign them permanently to poverty and dependence, rural blacks raised, once again, the demand for land.

The land issue animated grass-roots black politics in 1867. Talk of confiscation, reported an American Missionary Association official from North Carolina, "has much greater prominence . . . here than our friends at the North seem to be aware. The expectations of the poor have been very generally excited." In Alabama, freedmen delivered "inflammatory" speeches asserting that "all the wealth of the white man had been made by negro labor, and that the negroes were entitled to their fair share of all these accumulations." Yet land was only one among the many goals blacks sought to achieve through Reconstruction politics. In a society marked by vast economic disparities and a growing racial separation in social and religious life, politics became the only arena where black and white encountered each other on a basis of equality. And although elective office and the vote remained male preserves, black women shared in the mobilization. They took part in rallies and parades and, to the consternation of some men, voted on resolutions at mass meetings. During the 1868 campaign, Yazoo, Mississippi, whites found their black maids and cooks defiantly wearing buttons depicting General Grant.

Throughout Reconstruction, blacks remained "irrepressible democrats." And the Republican party became an institution as central to the black community as the church and school. Long after they had been stripped of the franchise, blacks would recall the act of voting as a defiance of white superiority and regard "the loss of suffrage as . . . the loss of freedom."

Early in 1868, a Northerner reporting on Alabama's election day captured the soaring expectations with which Radical Reconstruction began. "In defiance of fatigue, hardship, hunger, and threats of employers," blacks had come en masse to the polls. Not one in fifty wore an "unpatched garment," few possessed a pair of shoes, yet for hours they stood on line in a "pitiless storm." Why? "The hunger to have the same chances as the white men. . . . That is what brings them here." Rarely has a community invested so many hopes in politics as did blacks during Radical Reconstruction.

The Republican Coalition

Throughout Reconstruction, blacks comprised a large majority of Southern Republicanism. But, one Northerner had observed in 1866, "a party sustained only by black votes will not grow old." Of the eleven states of the old Confederacy, only South Carolina, Mississippi, and Louisiana contained a black majority; blacks comprised roughly one-quarter of the population of Texas, Tennessee, and Arkansas, forty percent in Virginia and North Carolina, and a bit less than half in Alabama, Florida, and Georgia. Even in states with black majorities, however, Southern Republicanism needed white support. They found it among "carpetbaggers" from the North and "scalawag" native white Southerners, who, in turn, were subjected to a torrent of abuse by their Democratic opponents.

Political, regional, and class prejudices combined to produce the image of the carpetbagger as a member of "the lowest class" of the Northern population. Able to pack "all his earthly belongings" in his carpetbag, he supposedly journeyed south after the passage of the Reconstruction Act "to fatten on our misfortunes." In fact, carpetbaggers tended to be well educated and middle class in origin. Not a few had been lawyers, businessmen, newspaper editors, and other pillars of Northern communities. The majority were veterans of the Union Army, and their ranks also included teachers, Freedmen's Bureau agents, and men who had invested tens of thousands of dollars in cotton plantations. Nearly all had come south before 1867, when blacks lacked the franchise and the prospect of office appeared remote.

A variety of motives and experiences propelled these Northerners into Southern Republican politics in 1867. Some were typical nineteenth-century men on the make for whom politics offered the opportunity for a quick profit. Others entered politics because they had earned the freedmen's good will as Bureau agents. Still others, bankrupted in unsuccessful cotton planting, saw in politics a means of earning a living. Henry Warren, a Massachusetts-born Yale graduate, and Albert T. Morgan, a young army veteran from Ohio, had both failed in the Mississippi cotton fields. In 1867 Warren accepted the invitation of military authorities to serve as voter registrar, while local blacks pressured Morgan to run for the constitutional convention, beginning careers that led both men to the legislature. And some carpetbaggers were idealists who, like future Mississippi Gov. Adelbert Ames, became convinced that they "had a Mission with a large M" to assist the former slaves. Most carpetbaggers probably combined the desire for personal gain with a commitment to reforming the "unprogressive" South by "establishing free institutions, free schools, and the system of free labor."

Generally representing black belt constituencies, carpetbaggers garnered a major share of Reconstruction offices, especially in Florida, South Carolina, and Louisiana, states with relatively few native-born white Republicans. Northerners, however, could hardly provide a voting base for Southern Republicanism, for in no state did they comprise even two percent of the total population. Far more numerous were Southern-born white Republicans, or "scalawags." In no Southern state did Republicans attract a majority of the white vote. But given the twin legacies of slavery and defeat, and the opprobrium attached to those who attended "Negro conventions" and took unorthodox political positions, what is remarkable is not how few whites supported the party but, in some states, how many. "It costs nothing for a Northern man to be a Union man," wrote one Georgia Republican, "but the rebuff and persecution received here . . . tells a horrible tale." Yet for a time, scalawags dominated the governments of Alabama, Georgia, Tennessee, Texas, and North Carolina, and played a major role in Mississippi.

Castigated as "white negroes" who had betrayed their region in the quest for office, scalawags had even more diverse backgrounds and motivations than Northern-born Republicans. They included men of prominence and rank outsiders, wartime Unionists and advocates of secession, entrepreneurs advocating a modernized New South and yeomen seeking to preserve semisubsistence agriculture. Their common characteristic was the conviction that they stood a greater chance of advancing their interests in a Republican South than by joining with Reconstruction's opponents.

Many scalawags possessed considerable political experience; their ranks included prewar Congressmen, judges, and local officials. Most were former Whigs who viewed the Republican party as the "legitimate successor" to Whiggery. James L. Alcorn, owner of the largest plantation in the Yazoo-Mississippi delta, was probably the most prominent Old Whig scalawag. In 1867, Alcorn addressed some "blunt speaking" to Mississippi's whites. The black electoral majority was here to stay, and only if men like himself took the lead in Reconstruction could "a harnessed revolution" take place in which the freedmen's civil and political rights were guaranteed, but whites retained control of state government. Moreover, only the Republican Congress could provide the capital essential for the state's economic recovery. So long as blacks were content to be junior partners in a white-dominated coalition, these Old Whig scalawags remained, but when blacks refused to submit to white dictation, Alcorn and his followers abandoned the Republican party.

Yet another group of scalawags were modernizers who saw in Republicanism a "progressive party" that could bring a long-overdue social and economic revolution to the South. Prewar "ideas and feelings," declared Thomas Settle of North Carolina, must be buried "a thousand fathoms deep. . . . Yankees and Yankee notions are just what we want in this country. We want their capital to build factories and workshops. We want their intelligence, their energy and enterprise." Republicans also attracted a number of urban and small-town artisans and some support among the South's foreign-born urban workingmen. The Germans of southwestern Texas comprised the largest bloc of immigrant Southern Republicans, helping to send to Congress Edward Degener, a San Antonio grocer and refugee from the failed revolution of 1848.

The most extensive concentration of white Republicans, however, lay in the upcountry bastions of wartime Unionism. East Tennessee, southwestern Missouri, western North Carolina, northwestern Arkansas, and northern Alabama became party strongholds, and some counties, like Winston in Alabama, with only seventeen black residents in 1880, remained so into the twentieth century. In Rutherford County, North Carolina, in the foothills of the Blue Ridge Mountains, Republicans included "a large majority of the small farmers, tenants, laborers," and small-town artisans.

To upcountry Republicans the party represented, first and fore-most, the inheritor of wartime loyalism. Bitter memories of persecution cemented their attachment, and more than other Republicans, upcountry scalawags supported the sweeping proscription of "rebels." But if wartime Unionism was the seedbed of yeoman Republicanism, 1867 was a year of political and ideological mobilization. In meetings of Union Leagues and the Heroes of America, long-standing class antagonisms and intrastate sectional rivalries were transmuted into the coin of nineteenth-century radicalism. Traditional regional demands, like an end to property qualifications for members of the North Carolina legislature, now merged with a retrospective denunciation of slavery as the foundation of a social order that had held "poor whites . . . as much under bondage" as blacks. "Now is the time," wrote a resident of the Georgia mountains, "for every man to come out and speak his principles publickly and vote for liberty as we have been in bondage long enough."

To some upcountry scalawags, Reconstruction promised an end to state policies favoring plantation counties at the expense of their own. Economic boosters like Tennessee Gov. William G. Brownlow had long looked to a statewide railroad system and infusions of Northern capital to bring East Tennessee the benefits of capitalist development. Many small farmers, however, had more immediate economic concerns, especially in upcountry communities where wartime devastation had been succeeded by disastrous crop failures. In the early days of Radical Reconstruction, many Georgia and South Carolina yeomen stood "on the eve of starvation," and "scenes of the Irish famine" were reported in hill country Alabama. Families burdened with prewar debts or obliged to mortgage their farms to replace livestock and implements destroyed during the war now confronted the possibility of losing their homes to creditors. Many looked to the Republicans to rescue "the poor . . . from this great privation" by providing debtor relief.

Here lay the seeds of future conflict over Republican economic policy. Debt-ridden yeomen viewed skeptically ambitious economic programs that would inevitably raise taxes and offer creditors security so as to attract outside capital. The platform of J. M. Wilhite, a Republican sent by Winston County to the Alabama constitutional convention, called for disenfranchising Confederates, the establishment of a public school system, and "low taxes." A few upcountry scalawags even joined blacks in demanding a redistribution of planter land, a program economic boosters viewed as certain to antagonize potential Nothern investors.

Such genuine identification with blacks' aspirations remained rare in the upcountry, where, as one local party leader put it, "our people are more radical against rebels than in favor of negroes." Certainly, scalawags almost unanimously rejected the idea that black political rights implied "social equality" between the races. Most scalawags agreed with the North Carolinian who wrote, "There is not the slightest reason why blacks and whites should sit in the same benches, in Churches, school houses, or Hotels. Each can have the equal protection and benefits of the law without these."

For most scalawags, the alliance with blacks remained a marriage of convenience. Yet whatever its origins, this partnership carried with it a further commitment, unprecedented for men reared in a slave society, to defend blacks' political and civil equality. Unionists, declared a North Carolina Republican newspaper, must choose "between salvation at the hand of the negro or destruction at the hand of the rebels." It would certainly be inaccurate to suggest that the heritage of racism had suddenly vanished. But the fact that so many upcountry whites stood ready "to affiliate . . . politically with the negro element" underscored the extent of the political revolution that swept across the South in 1867.

Thus, Southern Republicanism attracted a broad coalition of supporters with overlapping but distinct political agendas. Providing unity and inspiration were the party's commitment to civil and political equality and its self-image as a "party of progress, and civilization" that would infuse the region with new social ideas and open "the avenues to success and promotion" to black and white, rich and poor. The sense of living in a new era of progress animated the party as its first statewide conventions gathered in the spring and summer of 1867. Yet these meetings also revealed the inner tensions that would plague Southern Republicanism throughout its brief and stormy career. Virtually every party convention found itself divided between "confiscation radicals" (generally blacks) and moderates committed to white control of the party and a policy of economic development that offered more to outside investors and native promoters than to impoverished freedmen and upcountry yeomen.

In South Carolina, radicalism was triumphant in 1867. In March, a Charleston Republican convention dominated by the city's free-born blacks adopted a program for sweeping change in nearly every aspect of the state's life. To a call for expanded internal improvements (with blacks and whites enjoying "an equal and fair share" in the awarding of contracts), the platform wedded demands for an integrated common school system, the abolition of corporal punishment and imprisonment for debt, protection of the "poor man's homestead" against seizure for debt, government responsibility for "the aged, infirm and helpless poor," and heavy taxation of uncultivated land to weaken "large land monopolies" and promote "the division and sale of unoccupied lands among the poorer classes." In July, the state convention adopted essentially the same platform.

Radicalism was also in the ascendancy among Virginia Republicans in 1867, as well as in Louisiana, although here a group of carpetbaggers seized control of the party, to the dismay of New Orleans's free black leaders. Georgia Republicans, by contrast, downplayed blacks' demands, in an attempt to appeal to upcountry yeomen on the issue of debtor relief. In Texas, moderate Republicans interested in reconciliation with former Confederates pushed a vigorous program of railroad building and a secondary role for blacks, but were challenged by Radicals demanding the proscription of rebels, an aggressive defense of black rights, and an "antimonopoly" system of internal improvements, with safeguards against abuses by government-aided railroads. Such factionalism was hardly unusual in American politics. Some contemporaries, however, wondered whether a new party confronted by opponents far superior in finances, education, and political experience could afford such conflict. More than the struggle for personal advantage explains these divisions. At stake were competing visions of the party's social composition and of the extent of change that would result from Reconstruction.

Even as Southern Republicans debated the character of their region's new social order, however, outside forces attempted to turn Reconstruction in a moderate direction. From the opening of the Fortieth Congress in March 1867, mainstream Republicans, while determined to defend what had been accomplished, showed no inclination for further change. When Charles Sumner introduced resolutions to broaden the scope of Reconstruction by immediately abolishing existing Southern governments, requiring the establishment of integrated public school systems, and providing the freedmen with homesteads, even Radical Henry Wilson objected, declaring "the terms we have made are hard enough." "That is more than we do for white men," declared William Pitt Fessenden in opposing the land proposal. (To which Sumner responded, "White men have never been in slavery.") In the House, Thaddeus Stevens moved a bill providing forty acres to freedmen from confiscated land.

Moderate Northern leaders had no intention of being "run over by the car of Revolution." A party consensus now existed in favor of civil and political rights for Southern blacks, but not on the land question, and a barrage of criticism greeted Stevens's proposal. The Springfield *Republican* insisted that for the government to give blacks land would be an act of "mistaken kindness" that would prevent them from learning "the habits of free workingmen." Even more threatening, in the view of the *New York Times*, was the prospect that the precedent set by confiscation "would not be confined to the South." The *Times* lambasted the Radicals for desiring "a war on property . . . to succeed the war on Slavery."

Clearly, whatever Southern Republicans desired, the party in the North remained unwilling to embrace the land question. And one reason was that Northern Republicans in 1867 faced problems of their own at home. For the first time, the party went before the voters united in support of black suffrage, at least for the South. And Democrats seized upon racial prejudice with a vengeance. In Ohio, where a measure enfranchising blacks was on the fall ballot, Democratic gubernatorial candidate Allan G. Thurman pledged to save the state from "the thralldom of niggerism." On the West Coast, Democrats added anti-Chinese appeals, arguing that the Republican doctrine of "universal equality for all races" would lead to an "Asiatic" influx and control of the state by an alliance of "the Mongolian and Indian and African."

For their part, many Republicans tried to sidestep the race issue. Yet the crisis that shifted national politics leftward had also affected grass-roots Republicans. A remarkable number of non-Radicals now endorsed political equality for Northern blacks. Even in conservative New Jersey, the party committed itself to black voting, and California gubernatorial candidate George C. Gorham repudiated the "anticoolie" movement, insisting "the same God created both Europeans and Asiatics."

Two sets of elections occurred in the fall of 1867, producing sharply divergent outcomes. In the South, where voters passed on calls for constitutional conventions and selected delegates, the result was a Republican triumph. "The negroes," declared a white

Republican in Alabama's Tennessee Valley, "voted their entire walking strength—no one staying at home that was able to come to the polls." Among whites, apathy and the hope that abstention would deny conventions the necessary majority of registered voters kept turnout far lower, and the Republican campaign to attract white voters achieved only partial success. In North Carolina, Georgia, Alabama, and Arkansas, more than one white voter in five voted for the calling of a convention, but in others, white Republicans remained a tiny minority. The party made encouraging inroads in the upcountry, but elsewhere the electorate remained polarized along racial lines.

Counterbalancing victory in the South was a serious setback in the North. From Maine to California, Democrats gained dramatically, sweeping New York by more than 50,000 votes, coming within 3,000 of electing Ohio's governor, carrying California, and, according to *The Nation*'s calculation, reducing by three-quarters the massive Republican majorities of 1866. "It would be vain to deny," declared *The Nation*, "that the fidelity of the Republican party to the cause of equal rights . . . has been one of the chief causes of its heavy losses."

The results shifted the balance of power within the party. Even in Massachusetts, reported one Republican editor, "extreme radical measures are becoming more and more unpopular." Although few Republicans considered abandoning Reconstruction, many agreed with the Ohio politico who observed, "the Negro will be less prominent for some time to come." Certainly, the election results marked the end of any hope that Northern Republicans would embrace a program of land distribution. Henceforth, it appeared certain, the party would strive to bring Reconstruction to a successful conclusion rather than press it forward.

The Constitutional Conventions

With most antebellum officials barred from membership and blacks and carpetbaggers representing the plantation belt, the Southern constitutional conventions of 1867–69, as a British visitor remarked, mirrored "the mighty revolution that had taken place in America." As the first large group of elected Southern Republicans, the delegates epitomized the party's social composition. About one-sixth were carpetbaggers. Generally veterans of the Union Army, they were the best-educated Republican delegates, numbering many lawyers, physicians, and other professionals. Talented, ambitious, and youthful, carpetbaggers usually chaired the key committees and drafted the most important provisions of the new constitutions. Southern white Republicans formed the largest group of delegates; they were especially numerous in North Carolina, Georgia, Arkansas, Alabama, and Texas. Those of established standing, like Benjamin F. Saffold, son of Alabama's former chief justice, were far outnumbered by upcountry farmers and small-town merchants, artisans, and professionals, few of whom had ever held political office. Nearly all had opposed secession, and many had served in the federal army or been imprisoned for Unionist sentiments.

Although accounting for a total of 265 delegates, blacks remained substantially underrepresented in most states. They formed a majority of the Louisiana and South Carolina conventions and nearly 40 percent in Florida, but only about one-fifth in Alabama, Georgia, Mississippi, and Virginia, and 10 percent in Arkansas, North Carolina, and Texas. Of those for whom biographical information is available, 107 had been born into slavery (of whom 19 had become free before the Civil War) and 81 free. Twenty-eight had spent all or most of their lives in the North or, in the case of two South Carolina delegates, the West Indies. At least 40 black delegates had served in the Union Army, and the largest occupational groups were ministers, artisans, farmers, and teachers. Only a handful were field hands or common laborers. A few black delegates owned substantial amounts of property, but most paid almost no state taxes. Nearly all subsequently held other Reconstruction offices, including 147 elected to state legislatures and nine to Congress.

These figures, however, obscure local patterns that reflected the nature of black politics and the structure of black society in different parts of the South. In Louisiana, the freeborn enjoyed a virtual monopoly of black positions. Georgia, with a small prewar free population and few black veterans, saw ministers account for seventeen of the twenty-two black delegates. In Virginia, reflecting the greater opportunity for manumission and escape enjoyed by Upper South slaves, over one-third of the delegates born as slaves had gained their freedom before 1860. Outside Louisiana and South Carolina, most black delegates, lacking formal education, found "agricultural degrees and brick yard diplomas" poor preparation for the complex proceedings of a constitutional convention. Yet while generally remaining silent, black delegates proved perfectly capable of judging political and constitutional questions and promoting the interests of their constituents. On issues of civil rights and access to education, blacks in every state formed a unified bloc; on disenfranchisement and economic policy, black delegates, like whites, divided, reflecting diverse interests within the black community.

Most of the conventions produced modern, democratic documents, "magnificent," wrote New Orleans *Tribune* editor Houzeau, for their "liberal principles." The constitutions established the South's first state-funded systems of free public education overseen by central commissioners of education, and in South Carolina and Texas made school attendance compulsory, a provision strongly supported by black delegates. Clauses mandating the establishment of penitentiaries, orphan asylums, homes for the insane, and, in some cases, the provision of poor relief further expanded public responsibilities.

All the constitutions guaranteed blacks' civil and political rights, completing, as a Texas newspaper put it, the "equal rights revolution." They abolished whipping as a punishment for crime, property qualifications for office and jury service, viva voce voting, and imprisonment for debt. The constitutions reduced the number of capital crimes and in three cases reorganized local government along the lines of the New England township, to overthrow local oligarchies centered in unelected county courts. Nine of the ten states recognized the right of married women to separate property. And South Carolina for the first time in its history authorized the granting of divorces. Antebellum bills of rights were rewritten to include language from the Declaration of Independence declaring all men created equal, and recognizing a citizen's paramount loyalty to the federal government.

Although the conventions clearly embodied Republicans' commitment to equal rights and a New South, they also revealed the party's inner divisions. Republicans achieved far greater agreement on general principles than their actual implementation: on public education but not on racially integrated schools; civil and political rights for blacks but not "social equality"; the expansion of democracy but not black domination of local or state governments; loyal rule but not the disenfranchisement of rebels; economic modernization but not how to balance the need for outside capital with white farmers' demands for debtor relief and blacks' for land. The outcome of these debates illuminated the balance of power within individual states and differing perceptions of whether the party should try to forge a political majority by striving to serve the interests of blacks and poorer whites or by making its main concerns the attraction of "respectable" whites to its ranks and outside capital to the South.

Among the issues that came before the conventions, none was more highly charged than integration in education. No state actually required separate schools, but only Louisiana and South Carolina explicitly forbade them. Most blacks appeared more concerned with educational opportunities for their children and employment for black teachers than with the remote prospect of racially mixed schools. Even in South Carolina, the same black delegates who praised the school integration clause as "laying the foundation of a new structure" of society acknowledged that both races preferred separate education. But in every state, blacks objected to constitutional language *requiring* racial segregation. James W. Hood, later North Carolina's assistant superintendent of education, favored separate schools because nearly all white teachers viewed black children as "naturally inferior." But he adamantly opposed writing segregation into the constitution: "Make this distinction in your organic law and in many places the white children will have good schools . . . while the colored people will have none." Only the threat of integration would force states to provide blacks with "good schools" of their own.

Republicans also differed among themselves over the extent, and implications, of democratizing Southern politics. Demands by black delegates and reform-minded whites for popular election of state and local officials were countered by fears of Democratic majorities in white counties and concern among Whiggish scalawags who hoped they, not blacks, would control local affairs in the plantation belt. Torn between the desire to expand popular control of government and uncertainty about the breadth of their white support, the conventions adopted contradictory policies, in some cases greatly enhancing democracy, in others actually limiting it.

In North Carolina, where upcountry resentment at the undemocratic structure of state and local politics had a long history and the Republican party's biracial coalition appeared secure, the convention produced what Henry Wilson called "the most republican constitution in the land." The delegates dismantled the old state Executive Council and replaced county courts appointed by the General Assembly with state and local officials chosen by popular vote. And they made all judges elective. At the other end of the political spectrum stood Georgia and Florida, whose conventions, dominated by moderate scalawags, contrived to make Reconstruction palatable to white voters by minimizing what Georgia's first Republican governor called "the danger of negro suffrage." Both based legislative representation on counties, not population, limiting the influence of geographically concentrated black voters, and made numerous local offices appointive rather than elective.

Another issue pitting commitment to democracy against party survival was the disenfranchisement of former Confederates. Many Republicans could not reconcile their party's democratic rhetoric with proposals to strip large numbers of "rebels" of the vote. Although upcountry scalawags, especially those who had suffered for their Unionist beliefs or hailed from areas devastated by the South's internal civil war, vehemently supported disenfranchisement, the issue followed no simple pattern, for it reflected Republican divisions on how to attract white voters. Five states disenfranchised few or no Confederates: Georgia, Florida, and Texas, where moderates committed to luring white Conservatives into the party controlled the proceedings; South Carolina, with its overwhelming black voting majority; and North Carolina, where the party's white base appeared firm. Alabama, Arkansas, Louisiana, Mississippi, and Virginia all barred considerable numbers of "rebels" from voting (although the disenfranchisement provisions in the last two states were subsequently defeated in popular referenda and never went into effect). A hallmark of upcountry Republicanism, disenfranchisement generated less interest among black delegates, many of whom seemed uncomfortable with a policy that appeared to undermine the party's commitment to manhood suffrage. "I have no desire to take away the rights of the white man," declared former slave Thomas Lee, an Alabama delegate. "All I want is equal rights in the court house and equal rights when I go to vote."

On economic matters, the developmental spirit prevailed. With a modern constitution, declared Mississippi Union League president Allston Mygatt, "large landed estates shall melt away into small divisions, . . . agriculture become scientific, internal improvements be pushed on." The constitutions allowed extensive public aid to railroads and other ventures, and some for the first time established limited liability for corporate stockholders. Many voided usury laws entirely or dramatically increased the legal ceiling on interest rates. In every state, carpetbaggers emerged as the strongest proponents of economic modernization; upcountry scalawags and blacks, especially former slaves, were more cautious.

When the constitutional conventions assembled, many Conservatives, in the words of a New Orleans newspaper, feared "unadulterated agrarianism"—that is, attacks on private property. In one form or another, the interrelated questions of land and labor came before a majority of the conventions, but the results hardly justified either the hopes or fears kindled in 1867. Several conventions awarded mechanics and laborers liens for wages on the property of their employers, and Texas outlawed the establishment of "any system of peonage," but free labor assumptions doomed other attempts to enhance the position of black workers.

Both black and white Radicals spoke of the need to provide freedmen with land and encourage the breakup of the plantation system. "I have gone through the country," reported Richard H. Cain in South Carolina, "and on every side I was besieged with questions: How are we to get homesteads?" A few constitutions took modest steps toward meeting this demand. Texas offered free homesteads to settlers on the state's vast public domain, and Mississippi provided that land seized by the state to satisfy tax claims would be sold in tracts of no more than 160 acres. The most substantial action was taken by South Carolina's convention, which authorized the legislature to establish a state commission to purchase land for resale on long-term credit.

With each state producing its own mixture of radical and moderate elements, the new constitutions, taken together, failed to satisfy the economic aspirations that had animated much of the grass-roots organizing of 1867. But they introduced changes in the region's political structure that appeared dangerously radical to those wedded to the traditions of the Old South and Presidential Reconstruction. Democrat and Whig alike, most established Southern leaders now mobilized in opposition. Other issues were "trivial" compared to one overriding question: "Shall this country be ruled by the whites or the niggers?" Racial appeals, however, often went hand in hand with revulsion at the prospect of governments controlled by what North Carolina Governor Jonathan Worth called "the dregs of society." Government by "mere *numbers* [universal suffrage]," Worth wrote, "I regard as undermining civilization." Civilization he defined as "the possession and protection of property." It was clear that such remarks did not apply to blacks alone.

With blacks all but unanimous for the constitutions, Republicans no less than Conservatives focused their attention on the white vote. And fear of alienating white voters kept blacks off every state ticket except in South Carolina and Louisiana. Already, blacks found that their very unanimity as Republicans meant their ballots could be taken for granted by party leaders seeking the white vote.

The elections of winter and spring 1868 to ratify the constitutions and select state officials brought mixed results for Southern Republicans. The black vote again held firm, but white voters often proved unresponsive. The party's most remarkable success occurred in North Carolina, where the cry of racial unity failed to deter over 20,000 white voters, about a quarter of the white electorate, from supporting the new constitution. William W. Holden finally won election as governor, and Republicans swept to a commanding majority in the state legislature. "In North Carolina at least," wrote one observer, "it cannot be attributed to foreign influence that the Constitution was adopted." The new constitutions were approved in every state but Alabama and Mississippi. In the former, a white boycott prevented approval by a majority of registered voters (a requirement Congress quickly changed to a majority of those actually voting). In Mississippi, the disenfranchisement clause alienated nearly all white voters.

Thus, three years after the death of the Confederacy, Republicans came to power in most of the South. "These constitutions and governments," a Democratic newspaper vowed, "will last just as long as the bayonets which ushered them into being, shall keep them in existence, and not one day longer." The fate of Reconstruction still depended on the national political contest of 1868.

Impeachment and the Election of Grant

To the many dramatic innovations Reconstruction brought to American politics, the spring of 1868 added yet another: the unprecedented spectacle of a President on trial before the Senate for "high crimes and misdemeanors." The roots of the impeachment of Andrew Johnson lay not only in the increasingly hostile relations between himself and Congress, but in a peculiar feature of Republican Reconstruction policy: Congress had enjoined the army to carry out a policy its commander in chief resolutely opposed. To shield its policy against Presidential interference, Congress in 1867 required that General Grant approve all orders to subordinate army commanders and, in the Tenure of Office Act, authorized officials appointed with the Senate's consent to remain in office until a successor had been approved. Intended primarily to protect lower-level patronage functionaries, the law also barred the removal, without Senate approval, of Cabinet members during the term of the President who had appointed them. It remained uncertain, however, whether this applied to Secretary of War Edwin M. Stanton, who had been named to his post by Lincoln.

Determined to obstruct the implementation of Congressional policy, Johnson waited until midsummer of 1867 to exploit a provision of the Tenure of Office Act allowing him to suspend Stanton while Congress was not in session, pending a vote on his permanent removal once the Senate reconvened. A few months later, emboldened by the fall elections, he set about actively encouraging Southern opponents of Reconstruction and removed several military commanders in favor of more conservative replacements. And when the Senate refused to concur in Stanton's removal, Johnson, on February 21, 1868, ousted him from office.

Having failed to "play the part of Moses for the colored people," commented *The Nation*, Johnson had succeeded in doing so "for the impeachers." With unanimous Republican support, the House voted to impeach the President. Yet from the outset, the case against the President was beset with weaknesses. Of the eleven articles of impeachment, nine hinged on either the removal of Stanton or an alleged attempt to induce Gen. Lorenzo Thomas to accept orders not channeled through Grant. Two others charged the President with denying the authority of Congress and attempting to bring it "into disgrace." Nowhere were the real reasons Republicans wished to dispose of Johnson mentioned—his political outlook, the way he had administered the Reconstruction Acts, and his sheer incompetence. Taken together, the articles implicitly accepted what emerged as the central premise of Johnson's defense: that only a clear violation of the law warranted a President's removal.

Other factors enhanced Johnson's chances for retaining office. Since the Vice Presidency remained vacant, his successor would be Benjamin Wade, president pro tem of the Senate and a man disliked by moderates for his radical views and by many businessmen and laissez-faire ideologues for his high tariff, soft-money, prolabor stance. "All the great Northern capitalists," a Radical editor observed, feared impeachment would shatter public confidence in the government and its securities. The defense case, however, had its own weaknesses, notably the fact that its arguments seemed patently contradictory. On the one hand, Johnson's attorneys argued that since the Tenure of Office Act did not apply to Stanton, his removal was perfectly legal, although in that case it was hard to explain why in 1867 the President had followed the letter of the law by suspending the Secretary and informing the Senate of his reasons. On the other hand, they contended that Johnson had violated the statute in order to allow the Supreme Court to rule on its constitutionality, an argument that empowered the President to determine which laws he was required to obey.

Whatever the merits of the case, it soon became apparent that an influential group of Senate Republicans feared both the damage to the separation of powers that would result from conviction and the political and economic policies that might characterize a Wade Presidency. Meanwhile, Johnson's attorneys quietly passed along assurances that the President, if acquitted, would no longer obstruct Republican Southern policy. When the decision finally came in mid-May, only thirty-five Senators voted for conviction, one short of the required two-thirds. The votes of seven Republicans supplied Johnson's narrow margin of victory, although a number of others stood ready to support the President if necessary. Contrary to later myth, Republicans did not read the "seven martyrs" out of the party, and all campaigned for Grant that fall.

Johnson's acquittal further weakened the Radicals' position within the party and made the nomination of Ulysses S. Grant inevitable. A career army officer except for an unhappy civilian interlude in the 1850s, Grant before the war had displayed little interest in politics, although what views he had inclined him toward the Democrats. During the war, he rose to prominence not only by virtue of his courage and military genius, but also by cooperating with Lincoln and Congress in implementing such policies as emancipation and the raising of black troops. He emerged from the conflict as the

"The First Vote." Note that the voters represent key sources of the black political leadership—the artisan carrying his tools, the well-dressed urbanite, and the soldier. (*Harper's Weekly*, November 16, 1867)

"Electioneering at the South." Women as well as men attended these early political gatherings. (*Harper's Weekly*, July 25, 1868)

BLACK POLITICAL LEADERS

(*Above left*) Benjamin Turner, Congressman from Alabama. (Library of Congress)

(*Above right*) P.B.S. Pinchback, Lieutenant Governor and Governor of Louisiana. (Library of Congress)

(*Left*) Blanche K. Bruce, Senator from Mississippi. (Library of Congress)

(*Below left*) Robert Smalls, Civil War hero and Congressman from South Carolina. (Library of Congress)

(*Below right*) Robert B. Elliott, Congressman from South Carolina. (Library of Congress)

(*Above left*) James L. Alcorn, Governor of Mississippi. (Library of Congress)

(*Above right*) William G. Brownlow, Governor of Tennessee. (Library of Congress)

(*Right*) Henry C. Warmoth, Governor of Louisiana. (Library of Congress)

(*Below left*) Albion W. Tourgee, North Carolina Jurist. (Library of Congress)

(*Below right*) Adelbert Ames, Governor of Mississippi. (Library of Congress)

OPPONENTS OF RECONSTRUCTION

(*Above left*) Democratic Campaign Badge, 1868. (New York Public Library, Schomburg Center for Research in Black Culture)

(*Above right*) Zebulon Vance, Redeemer Governor of North Carolina. (Library of Congress)

(*Left*) Wade Hampton, Redeemer Governor of South Carolina. (Library of Congress)

(*Below left*) John B. Gordon, Democratic candidate for governor and head of the Ku Klux Klan in Georgia. (Library of Congress)

(*Below right*) William H. Trescot, South Carolina Planter (Library of Congress)

Klan Warning: a graphic prediction of the fate of Ohio carpetbagger A. S. Lakin and scalawag Noah B. Cloud in the event of a Democratic victory in the 1868 presidential election. (Tuscaloosa *Independent Monitor*, September 1, 1868)

"Two Members of the Ku-Klux Klan in Their Disguises." (*Harper's Weekly*, December 19, 1868)

Klansmen Firing Into a Home. (Dorothy Sterling)

(*Top left*) Victoria Woodhull, Feminist (New-York Historical Society)

(*Top right*) Jay Gould, Financier (Library of Congress)

(*Left*) Roscoe Conkling, Senator from New York (Library of Congress)

(*Below left*) Crazy Horse, Conqueror of General George A. Custer at Little Big Horn (Chicago Historical Society)

(*Below right*) Susan B. Anthony, Feminist (Metropolitan Museum of Art)

ilroad Workers. (American Social History ject)

"Capital and Labor": from a cotton textile depicting scenes of labor and industry, ca. 1870. The harmony of interests of capital and labor was a central tenet of the free labor ideology. (Metropolitan Museum of Art)

e Corliss Engine, symbol of the new indus- ll age at the Philadelphia Centennial Ex- sition. (*Harper's Weekly*, May 27, 1876)

Ruins of Pittsburgh Round House, the "Great Strike," July 1877. (*Scribner's Magazine*, July 1895)

"And Not This Man?" (*Harper's Weekly*, August 5, 1865)

"This is a White Man's Government." (*Harper's Weekly*, September 5, 1868)

"Colored Rule in a Reconstructed (?) State." (*Harper's Weekly*, March 14, 1874)

Changes in graphic artist Thomas Nast's depiction of blacks mirrored the evolution of Republican sentiment in the North. Upper left, the black soldier as upstanding citizen deserving of the franchise; upper right, the former slave as innocent victim of Irish immigrants, Confederate veterans, and Wall Street financiers (ostensibly, the three pillars of the Democratic party); bottom, black legislators as travesties of democratic government.

preeminent Union military hero, and as early as 1866 was well aware that influential Republicans favored his nomination. By 1868 he had committed himself fully to Congressional policy. Nonetheless, as one Republican put it, his candidacy had a "conservative odor," both because he lacked strong ideological convictions and because his earliest promoters had been the "great conservative and commercial interests in New York." The city's business elite feared a Democratic victory would reopen the now settled Reconstruction question, while a Grant Presidency promised moderation, fiscal responsibility, and stable conditions for Southern investment. The Republicans prepared to campaign, proclaiming: Reconstruction for the South, respectability for the nation, all overseen by the man whose slogan was, "Let Us Have Peace."

As for the Democrats, after twenty-one inconclusive ballots, their convention drafted New York Gov. Horatio Seymour to run against Grant. The colorless Seymour seemed a most unsatisfactory choice; Democrats, commented Secretary of State Seward, "could have nominated no candidate who would have taken away fewer Republican votes." Seymour's conduct during the war (when he addressed New York draft rioters as "my friends") surrendered the loyalty issue to Republicans, and his close ties with New York financiers neutralized any hope of appealing to Western economic resentments.

Thus, Democrats were forced back to a single issue: opposition to Reconstruction. Francis P. Blair, Jr., Seymour's running mate, embarked on a speaking campaign as disastrous in its own way as Johnson's swing around the circle. In blatantly racist language, he excoriated Republicans for placing the South under the rule of "a semi-barbarous race of blacks who are worshippers of fetishes and poligamists" and longed to "subject the white women to their unbridled lust." Having read Darwin's *The Origin of Species*, Blair now asserted that racial intermixing would reverse evolution, produce a less advanced species incapable of reproducing itself, and destroy "the accumulated improvement of the centuries." These were the convictions of the Democratic candidate for Vice President of the United States.

An influential Democratic Congressman would blame Seymour's defeat on Blair's "stupid and indefensible" behavior. But Blair set the tone of the Democratic campaign, the last Presidential contest to center on white supremacy. Fearing the turmoil that would follow a Democratic victory, many Northern conservatives who had supported Johnson now endorsed Grant. And, more than in any previous election, Northern capitalists united behind the Republican party.

In the South, the prospect that a Seymour victory would undo Reconstruction dominated the Democratic campaign. The party unsheathed its "employing power," with merchants cutting off credit to blacks attending Republican meetings and landlords threatening to evict from plantations "any negro who will not swear never again to vote the Radical ticket." And violence, an intrinsic part of the process of social change since 1865, now directly entered electoral politics. Founded in 1866 as a Tennessee social club, the Ku Klux Klan spread into nearly every Southern state, launching a "reign of terror" against Republican leaders black and white. Those assassinated during the campaign included Arkansas Congressman James M. Hinds, three members of the South Carolina legislature, and several men who had served in constitutional conventions. In Louisiana, even moderate ex-Governor Hahn by October complained that "murder and intimidation are the order of the day in this state." White gangs roamed New Orleans, intimidating blacks and breaking up Republican meetings. In St. Landry Parish, a mob invaded the plantations, killing as many as 200 blacks. Commanding Gen. Lovell Rousseau, a friend and supporter of the President, refused to take action, urging blacks to stay away from the polls for self-protection and exulting that the "ascendance of the negro in this state is approaching its end."

As expected, Grant emerged victorious, although by a surprisingly close margin. Nationally, he won every state except eight, but received less than fifty-three percent of the vote. It is more than likely that Seymour carried a majority of the nation's white electorate. In the South, Seymour won Georgia and Louisiana, where violence had decimated the Republican organization and made it impossible for blacks to vote. Eleven Georgia counties with black majorities recorded no Republican votes at all. The Klan's effectiveness was also demonstrated in states Grant did carry, for the Republican vote fell off sharply in middle Tennessee, northern Alabama, and upcountry South Carolina.

In one respect, 1868 marked a startling reversal of the political traditions of the Civil War era. Republicans, for a generation the party of change, campaigned on a platform of order and stability, while Democrats, who had appealed to continuity with the past, cast themselves as virtual revolutionaries. And if Grant's election guaranteed that Reconstruction would continue, it also confirmed a change in the Republican leadership that would direct it. Gone from the scene was Thaddeus Stevens, who died in August, his body attracting a throng of mourners to the Capitol second only to Lincoln's. For one last time, Stevens challenged his countrymen to rise above their prejudices, for he was buried in an integrated Pennsylvania cemetery in order, according to the epitaph he had composed, "to illustrate in my death the principles which I advocated through a long life, Equality of Man before his Creator." The Radical generation was passing, eclipsed by politicos who believed the "struggle over the negro" must give way to economic concerns. Significantly, the first statute enacted after Grant's inauguration was the Public Credit Act, pledging to pay the national debt in gold. "I look to Grant's administration," wrote one federal official, "as the beginning of a real and true conservative era."

As Congressional Reconstruction began, a Georgia attorney voiced the fears of many white Southerners: "My chief alarm is for the formation of a party south which will be more radical than the Radical party north." By 1868, national events, together with the nature of its own coalition, had eliminated some of the more radical policy alternatives envisioned the year before. And yet, among those who voted in November, the dreams of 1867 survived. As one resident of upcountry South Carolina wrote the state's Republican governor four days after Grant's victory:

> I am . . . a native borned S. C. a poor man never owned a Negro in my life. . . . I am hated and despised for nothing else but my loyalty to the mother government. . . . But I rejoice to think that God almighty has given to the poor of S. C. a Gov. to hear to feel to protect the humble poor without distinction to race or color.

The new Reconstruction governments now turned to the task of fulfilling the aspirations of their humble constituents for a new and more just South.

Reconstruction: Political and Economic

Party and Government in the Reconstruction South

Unprecedented challenges confronted the Southern Republicans who came to power between 1868 and 1870. Bequeathed nearly empty treasuries by their predecessors, they faced the devastation of war, the new public responsibilities entailed by emancipation, and the task of consolidating an infant political organization. Most of all, both the party and its governments faced a crisis of legitimacy. Ordinarily, political parties take for granted the authority of government and the integrity of their foes. Reconstruction's opponents, however, viewed the new regimes as alien impositions and their black constituency as outside the body politic. For Southern Republicans, as a result, the give-and-take of "normal politics" was superseded by a desperate struggle for political survival.

Like beauty, political legitimacy resides in the eyes of the beholder. To blacks, these governments possessed a greater claim to authority than any in Southern history. But with the region's traditional leaders arrayed against them and Northern Republicans urging Southern counterparts to court white support, the new governors adopted a conciliatory stance toward their political foes. Their course fueled factional conflicts that weakened an already vulnerable organization and led blacks to demand a greater voice in party affairs.

In some states, Republicans wooed white support by removing voting disabilities. By 1871 only Arkansas retained suffrage restrictions based on Civil War loyalties. Republican governors also extended patronage appointments to established local leaders, seeking to project a moderate image and defuse fears of black or carpetbagger domination. Mississippi's Alcorn appointed nearly as many Democrats as Republicans. Even in South Carolina, Robert K. Scott, who appointed a significant number of black trial justices, soon replaced many with white Democrats.

Such policies won the party a few notable converts, including Presidential Reconstruction governors James L. Orr and Lewis Parsons. But placing Democrats in office produced deep disaffection among the Republican rank and file. Few blacks had confidence in appointees who "will not give us justis and . . . who has opposed us all through the conflict." After one shift in Louisiana patronage, five Republicans protested: "It is a shame to erase a Radical Republican off the School Board to take a dam rebel."

The conciliatory patronage policy contributed to Republican factionalism, but was hardly the only cause. Intraparty rivalries also fed upon policy differences, longstanding regional conflicts within the Southern states, and tensions between native and Northern Republicans and blacks and whites. Political factionalism, of course, was not confined to the South in these years, but it was a luxury Southern Republicans could scarcely afford. Nonetheless, walkouts and fistfights disrupted party conventions, members of some factions connived with Democrats to defeat their rivals, Republican legislatures impeached Republican governors, and Florida's lieutenant governor seized the state seal and claimed the right to rule. Since conflict usually centered on the spoils of office, one Republican faction, made up of state and local officeholders, generally coalesced around the governor, while another consisted of holders of federal patronage posts, who gave their allegiance to Senators and Congressmen. In Mississippi, Republicans disaffected from Gov. James L. Alcorn rallied around Sen. Adelbert Ames. By 1871, the state's Republican party resembled "an army of recruits" lacking organization and discipline and "fighting each for himself."

"Our party," observed a Republican newspaper in the waning days of Reconstruction, "[has been] disorganized, disrupted, and demoralized, . . . rent and torn by internal feuds." Behind this debilitating factionalism lay the reality of a party with leaders utterly dependent on political position for their livelihood. Republican legislators raised substantially the compensation of positions from governor down to justice of the peace, and party members pursued offices aggressively and clung to them tenaciously. Southern Democrats leaving office returned to careers as merchants, planters, and lawyers, but for Republicans losing an office often meant economic disaster.

Among blacks, party infighting was especially dismaying. Republicans, declared a Virginia freedman in 1868, "ought to combine all of their influence, and not fight one against the other." Others, inevitably, were drawn into the fray. Although a few black politicos, like Louisiana Lieutenant Governors Oscar J. Dunn and P. B. S. Pinchback, became independent power brokers, most coalesced around competing factions of white politicians. Since most black leaders opposed the white-oriented patronage policies of the early Reconstruction governors, the majority sided with factions headed by federal officeholders, generally carpetbaggers. Their opposition eventually forced the party to give fuller recognition to blacks' concerns and to push aside the early moderate governors.

Initially, however, blacks stood aside when the political "loaves and fishes" were divided up, because white Republicans so desperately coveted office and black leaders did not wish to embarrass their party, heighten internal contention, or lend credence to Democratic charges of "black supremacy." At all levels of government, blacks initially received a lower share of offices than their proportion of the party's electorate warranted. Sixteen blacks sat in Congress during Reconstruction, but of these only three served in the Forty-First Congress (which met from 1869 to 1871). Hiram Revels of Mississippi, a North Carolina–born minister and educator, in February 1870 entered the United States Senate. In the House sat freeborn South Carolina barber Joseph H. Rainey and Jefferson Long, a Georgia freedman.

Nor did many blacks reach high levels of state government. In Texas, North Carolina, Alabama, Georgia, and Virginia, none held a major office during Reconstruction. Only Philadelphia-born missionary and educator Jonathan C. Gibbs won a major post in Florida, serving as secretary of state from 1868 to 1872 and then as superintendent of education. Blacks exercised far greater power in Mississippi and South Carolina, but here, too, whites initially monopolized most state positions. In Mississippi, Secretary of State James Lynch was, at first, the only black state official, and until 1870 Secretary of State Francis L. Cardozo was his lone South Carolina counterpart. Only in Louisiana did blacks hold more than one major position from the beginning of Republican rule. In 1868 Oscar J. Dunn became lieutenant governor and wealthy free sugar planter Antoine Dubuclet state treasurer, a post he retained until 1877.

It did not take long for black leaders to become dissatisfied with the role of junior partners in the Republican coalition. The results were most dramatic in South Carolina, where in 1870 black leaders, as the result of a concerted campaign for greater power, received half the eight executive offices, elected three Congressmen, and placed Jonathan J. Wright on the state supreme court, the only black in any state to hold this position during Reconstruction. In Mississippi, they mobilized effectively against Governor Alcorn. Arkansas in 1872 elected its first black state officials: Superintendent of Education Joseph C. Corbin, a college-educated editor from Ohio, and Commissioner of Public Works James T. White, a minister from Indiana. All told, by the end of Reconstruction, eighteen blacks had served as lieutenant governor, treasurer, superintendent of education, or secretary of state. In December 1872 P. B. S. Pinchback became the only black governor in American history when he succeeded Henry C. Warmoth, who had been suspended as a result of Louisiana impeachment proceedings.

A similar pattern of growing black influence appeared in state legislatures. Only in South Carolina, however, did blacks come to dominate the legislative process. Throughout Reconstruction, they comprised a majority of the House of Representatives, controlled its key committees, and, beginning in 1872, elected black speakers. In 1874 blacks gained a majority in the state senate as well.

Although whites generally retained political control, the fact that well over six hundred blacks, the majority former slaves, served as legislators represented a stunning change in American politics. Moreover, because of the black population's geographical concentration and the reluctance of many scalawags to vote for black candidates, nearly all these lawmakers hailed from plantation counties, home of the wealthiest and, before the war, most powerful Southerners. The spectacle of former slaves representing the low-country rice kingdom or the domain of Natchez cotton nabobs epitomized the political revolution wrought by Reconstruction.

An equally remarkable transformation occurred at the local level, where the decisions of public officials directly affected daily life and the distribution of power. Although the largest number served in South Carolina, Louisiana, and Mississippi, and the fewest in

Florida, Georgia, and Alabama, no state lacked black local officials. A handful held the office of mayor, including Robert H. Wood of Natchez, member of one of that city's most respected free families. A far larger number served on city and town councils scattered from Richmond to Houston. Some of the South's most important cities, and many towns of lesser note, became centers of black political power during Reconstruction. Republicans controlled the major rail and industrial center of Petersburg from 1870 to 1874, and blacks held posts ranging from councilman to deputy customs collector and overseer of the poor. Nashville's council was about one-third black, and Little Rock's at times had a black majority.

In virtually every county with a sizable black population, blacks held some local office during Reconstruction. As time went on, black sheriffs appeared in plantation counties. Eventually, nineteen held the office in Louisiana, and fifteen in Mississippi. Numerous blacks also assumed such powerful offices as county supervisor and tax collector. By 1871 blacks controlled boards of supervisors throughout the Mississippi plantation belt.

As Reconstruction progressed, blacks also laid claim to a larger role in many local Republican organizations. This was the case in Edgefield County, located in South Carolina's Piedmont cotton belt. Although blacks comprised sixty percent of its population, white Republicans, native and carpetbagger, initially dominated local and county offices. But by the 1870s blacks held positions as sheriff, magistrate, school commissioner, and officer of the state militia. A similar situation developed in Beaufort, an antebellum center of the lowcountry aristocracy. "Here the revolution penetrated to the quick," commented reporter Edward King in 1873; the mayor, police force, and magistrates were all black, and the celebrated former slave Robert Smalls dominated local politics. Other enclaves of black political power emerged in the Mississippi and Louisiana plantation belts. Blanche K. Bruce created a powerful machine in Bolivar County, Mississippi, simultaneously holding the offices of sheriff, tax collector, and superintendent of education. In 1875, this organization provided the springboard from which Bruce reached the United States Senate.

Less frequently, blacks rose to similar positions in other states. Georgia's only real enclave of black political power lay in coastal McIntosh County. Here, Tunis G. Campbell, a New Jersey–born abolitionist who went south during the war to take part in the Sea

Island experiment, served as state senator and justice of the peace. Campbell insisted that trial juries include equal numbers of blacks and whites and used his power to defend the economic interests of local freedmen. One overseer considered himself "powerless" to enforce work rules, for in the event of a labor dispute, "I should only get myself into trouble, and have the negro sheriff sent over by Campbell to arrest me."

Among black local officials were veterans of the postwar black conventions and of the Union Leagues. But as Reconstruction progressed, new leaders, mostly former slaves, came to the fore. Many were remarkable for their precocity—most of Edgefield County's black politicians had not reached twenty-five when they assumed public office, John Gair served in Louisiana's legislature at twenty-one, and John R. Lynch was only twenty-four when he became speaker of Mississippi's House. But however young, and whether free or freedmen, a web of connections bound this first generation of black officials to the network of religious, fraternal, and educational institutions created after emancipation.

Not surprisingly, many black officials lacked the advantages of an education. Many were illiterate and relied on other blacks or white Republicans to conduct official business. But large numbers of black politicians, especially those born free, had managed to acquire an education. Virtually all the black carpetbaggers and Louisiana and South Carolina free blacks who held state and local office were literate, and some had completed college. Mifflin Gibbs (brother of Florida official Jonathan C. Gibbs) had been a Vancouver city councilman and had studied law at Oberlin before holding a Little Rock judgeship. By the 1870s, moreover, graduates of new black universities swelled the ranks of black politicians.

The black political leadership included a few men of substantial wealth. Among the Charleston and New Orleans free elite were planters and businessmen worth tens of thousands of dollars before the Civil War, some of whom assumed Reconstruction offices. Others, like their white counterparts North and South, translated office into financial gain. Florida Congressman Josiah Walls purchased a large estate formerly owned by Confederate Gen. James H. Harrison, and about one-third of Virginia's black legislators purchased land with their salaries. Some black leaders enjoyed an aristocratic life-style, like Louisiana Lieut. Gov. C. C. Antoine, owner of an expensive racehorse, and Blanche K. Bruce, who acquired both a fortune in real estate and "the manners of a Chesterfield."

Although some black politicians achieved bourgeois status and others aspired to it, few successfully translated political power into a share of the economic growth of their states. The fact is that black politicians' wealth, while impressive when compared to that of most freedmen, paled before that of Conservatives and white carpetbaggers. Even prominent leaders like Hiram Revels and Robert B. Elliott sometimes met day-to-day expenses with small loans from white politicians. Most really wealthy blacks avoided politics, either because their businesses took precedence or so as not to jeopardize the personal connections with wealthy whites on which their economic standing depended.

Indeed, for many blacks, political involvement led not to social mobility but to devastating loss. Former slave Henry Johnson, a South Carolina Union League organizer and state legislator, was a bricklayer and plasterer by trade. "I always had plenty of work before I went into politics," he remarked, "but I have never got a job since. I suppose they do it merely because they think they will break me down and keep me from interfering with politics." Indeed, blacks' clamor for a larger share of elective and patronage posts arose in part from the same economic pressures that produced the "politics of livelihood" among white Republicans.

The presence of sympathetic Republican officials, irrespective of color, profoundly affected the freedmen's daily lives. Many worked actively to improve black neighborhoods and to ensure a fair share of jobs on municipal construction projects. In Louisiana, the state employed blacks, whites, and Chinese, all at the same wages, to repair the levees. The chief engineer reported: "our 'Cadian friends were a little disgusted at not being allowed double (colored) wages, and the Chinamen were astonished at being allowed as much and the American citizens of African descent were delighted at being 'par.' "

To those familiar with the law as an instrument of oppression, moreover, it seemed particularly important that Republicans now controlled the machinery of Southern law enforcement. Tallahassee and Little Rock chose black chiefs of police, and Vicksburg had a black captain empowered to give orders to whites on the force. By 1870, scores of blacks were serving as city policemen and rural constables; they comprised half the police force in Montgomery and Vicksburg, and more than a quarter in New Orleans, Mobile, and

Petersburg. In the courts, defendants often faced black magistrates and justices of the peace and racially integrated juries.

Throughout Reconstruction, planters complained it was impossible to obtain convictions in cases of theft and that in contract disputes "justice is generally administered solely in the interest of the laborer." Nor could vagrancy laws any longer be used to coerce freedmen into signing labor contracts. Black criminals, in fact, did not commonly walk away from Reconstruction courts scot-free. Indeed, as frequent victims of violence, blacks had a vested interest in effective law enforcement; they demanded merely that officials, in the words of one petition, "rise above existing prejudices and administer justice with . . . an even hand." Yet this basic notion of equal justice challenged deeply rooted traditions of Southern jurisprudence. Republican jurors and magistrates now treated black testimony with respect, the state attempted to punish offenses by whites against blacks, and minor transgressions did not receive the harsh penalties of Presidential Reconstruction.

For these reasons and more, Republican officeholders found their constituents expecting far more from them than in normal times. John R. Lynch later recalled how, when he served as justice of the peace, freedmen "magnified" his office "far beyond its importance," bringing him cases ranging from disputes with their employers to family squabbles. Most of all, ordinary Republicans of both races deluged the new governors with letters detailing their grievances and aspirations, requesting financial assistance, and seeking advice about all kinds of public and private matters. As one family, protesting their eviction for voting Republican, explained to Governor Holden, "we consider our selves under your protection [and] care." Such letters flowed from an understanding that the utopian hopes invested in Reconstruction now depended on the policies undertaken by the new Southern governments.

Southern Republicans in Power

As in so many other aspects of life, the combined effects of war, emancipation, and Reconstruction fundamentally altered the nature of Southern government. The task confronting Republicans, wrote North Carolina carpetbagger Albion W. Tourgée, was nothing less than to "make a state," and the Reconstruction state differed profoundly from anything the antebellum South had known. Slavery had sharply curtailed the scope of public authority. With planters enjoying a disproportionate share of political power, taxes and social welfare expenditures remained low and Southern education, as one Democrat admitted after the war, was a "disgrace." When Henry C. Warmoth became Louisiana's governor in 1868, the state lacked a hard-surfaced public road, and New Orleans, which contained only two hospitals, had a primitive water system that contributed to regular outbreaks of yellow fever and malaria.

Serving an expanded citizenry and embracing a new definition of public responsibility, Republican government affected virtually every facet of Southern life. Not only the scope of its activity but the interests it aspired to serve distinguished the Reconstruction state from its predecessors and successors. Public schools, hospitals, penitentiaries, and asylums for orphans and the insane were established for the first time or received increased funding. South Carolina funded medical care for poor citizens, and Alabama provided free legal counsel for indigent defendants. The law altered relations within the family, widening the grounds for divorce, expanding the property rights of married women, protecting minors from parental abuse, and obliging white fathers to support mulatto children. A parallel enhancement of government's scope occurred in many Republican-controlled localities. Under carpetbagger Mayor Augustus E. Alden, Nashville expanded its medical facilities and provided bread, soup, and firewood to the poor. Petersburg created a thriving school system, regulated hack rates, repaved the streets, and established a Board of Health that provided free medical care in the smallpox epidemic of 1873. All these activities entailed a dramatic growth in the cost of government. Charged with doubling the state budget between 1860 and 1873, South Carolina Republicans pointed out that much of the increase arose from support of the lunatic asylum, orphan house, state penitentiary, and public schools, none of which had existed before the war.

Four interrelated areas reveal the extent and limits of Republican efforts to reshape Southern society: education, race relations, the labor system, and economic development. All inspired disputes between those seeking to broaden the party's support and others intent on addressing the needs of its core constituents. All broke with the traditions of the prewar South, but in all, Republicans' achievements, while substantial, never truly fulfilled the lofty goals with which Reconstruction began.

Veterans of the Freedmen's Bureau and freedmen's aid movement, the new superintendents of education viewed schooling as the foundation of a new, egalitarian social order. If their goal of creating modern, centralized systems modeled on the most advanced educational thinking in the North proved unattainable, a public school system did take shape in the Reconstruction South. A Northern correspondent in 1873 found adults as well as children crowding Vicksburg schools and reported that "female negro-servants make it a condition before accepting a situation, that they should have permission to attend the night-schools." Whites, too, increasingly took advantage of the new educational system. Texas had 1500 schools by 1872, with a majority of the state's children attending classes. In Mississippi, Florida, and South Carolina, enrollment reached about half of all children by 1875. In many ways, educational progress must have appeared painfully slow; schooling continued to be far more available in towns and cities than in rural areas, and in 1880 seventy percent of blacks remained illiterate. Nonetheless, Republicans had established, for the first time in Southern history, the principle of state responsibility for public education.

Building schools was one thing; making them the cornerstone of an egalitarian society was quite another. White parents strongly resisted having their children sit alongside blacks in the classroom. A Texas board of education that attempted to integrate one school was removed by the Republican state superintendent. Only Louisiana, where the free black leadership had long opposed segregation, attempted to create an integrated system. Although schools in most rural parishes remained segregated, New Orleans witnessed an extraordinary experiment in interracial education. In its first year, white enrollment plummeted as new segregated private and parochial schools flourished. But many participants in this "white flight" soon returned, and by 1874 several thousand were attending integrated classes.

As for blacks, many believed with Edward Shaw, the militant Memphis political leader, that racial segregation attached a "stigma of inferiority to the black child." Few, however, seem to have believed integration practicable. Black parents focused their attention on an equitable division of school funds, and many believed all-black schools more open to parental control and more likely to hire black teachers than those enrolling whites. Indeed, as new teachers poured forth from black colleges, many staffed the new public schools. The number of black educators in South Carolina rose from fifty in 1869 to over 1,000 six years later.

Segregation also prevailed in public higher education, with the notable exception of the University of South Carolina. Henry E. Hayne, South Carolina's secretary of state, enrolled in the medical school in 1873 as the university's first black student, whereupon most of the white students withdrew, along with much of the faculty. In response, the legislature brought in professors from the North, abolished tuition, and established preparatory courses for those unable to meet admission requirements. Although mostly black, the "Radical University" managed to attract white students as well, and the two races, according to one undergraduate, "study together, visit each other's rooms, [and] play ball together."

If its role in education brought the Reconstruction state into line with an earlier expansion of public authority in the North, its effort to guarantee blacks equal treatment in transportation and places of public accommodation launched it into a realm all but unknown in American jurisprudence. But, as in the case of education, establishing a legal doctrine of equal citizenship proved easier than putting the principle into effect. Before the rise of a comprehensive system of legalized segregation, racial discrimination took a variety of forms. Many institutions, public and private, excluded blacks altogether; others provided separate and ostensibly equal facilities; still others offered blacks markedly inferior services. Railroads and steamboats generally refused to allow blacks, regardless of their ability to pay, access to first-class accommodations, relegating them to "smoking cars" or lower decks along with poor whites. Mississippi sheriff John M. Brown expressed vividly the resentment felt by prominent blacks over such treatment: "Education amounts to nothing, good behavior counts for nothing, even money cannot buy for a colored man or woman decent treatment and the comforts that white people claim and can obtain."

More than any other issue, demands by blacks, supported by many carpetbaggers, for the outlawing of racial discrimination exposed and sharpened Republicans' internal divisions. In states like Alabama and North Carolina, dominated by native white Republicans, bills by black legislators protecting equal rights on public conveyances failed to pass. But as blacks' influence and assertiveness grew, laws guaranteeing equal access to transportation and public accommodations were enacted throughout the Deep South. Mississippi, Louisiana, South Carolina, and Florida mandated stiff fines and prison terms for railroads, steamboats, inns, hotels, and theaters denying any citizen "full and equal rights." Generally the burden of enforcement rested with the injured party, but some states authorized their attorneys general to file damage suits and threatened common carriers and charted businesses with the loss of their license to operate.

Occasionally, aggrieved blacks launched successful suits under the new laws. Georgia legislator James Simms recovered nearly $2,000 from a Virginia railroad after being denied access to the first-class car, and P. B. S. Pinchback won an out-of-court settlement after being refused a Pullman berth. By and large, however, civil rights laws remained unenforced. State facilities like orphan asylums dealt separately with white and black children, railroads directed "colored ladies and gentlemen" to the smoking car, where, according to one complaint, "smoking, drinking, and obscene conversation were carried on continually by low whites," and few blacks thought it worth the effort to insist on equal privileges in theaters, hotels, and restaurants. Indeed, with the rise of independent black churches and fraternal societies, the establishment of separate schools, and the rapid expansion of black facilities from skating rinks to barrooms, separation, not integration, characterized Reconstruction social relations. Yet while most blacks valued these autonomous institutions and generally accepted voluntary racial separation, they insisted that the state remain color-blind. And in fact politics and government were the most integrated institutions in Southern life. Blacks and whites sat together on juries, school boards, and city councils, and the Republican party provided a rare meeting ground for like-minded men of both races. Thus, if Reconstruction did not create an integrated society, it did establish a standard of equal citizenship and a recognition of blacks' right to a share of state services that differed sharply from the heritage of slavery and Presidential Reconstruction, and from the state-imposed segregation that lay in the future.

Like education and race relations, economic legislation reflected the expanded scope and altered purposes of the Reconstruction state. The most dramatic transformation concerned labor relations. For the first time in Southern history, planters were unable to use public authority to control the black labor force, a change equally visible in the repeal of existing laws, the refusal to enact others, and new legislative departures. Southern lawmakers swept away the remnants of the Black Codes, with their limits on the freedmen's physical mobility and economic opportunities, required parental consent for apprenticeships, and rewrote vagrancy laws to narrow the crime's definition and prohibit the hiring out of offenders who could not pay their fines. Republicans humanized the harsh penal codes of Presidential Reconstruction, outlawing corporal punishment and sharply reducing the number of capital offenses and the penalties prescribed for theft. Equally significant was the consistent refusal of lawmakers to reinforce labor discipline. Throughout Reconstruction, planters pressed unsuccessfully for measures securing "the observance and performance of labor contracts," preventing an employer from "enticing" away another's workers, and barring the sale of farm produce at night so as to combat theft by laborers and restrict blacks' economic options.

Positive legislation also reflected the new aims of labor policy. During Presidential Reconstruction, anyone who advanced supplies to a planter or farmer was allowed to hold a lien on the crop, sometimes leaving unpaid a share worker whose employer fell into debt. Now the law gave workers a first lien on an employer's property, prohibited the discharge of laborers for political reasons, and required that evicted tenants be compensated for work performed. No wonder one planter complained in 1872, "under the laws of most of the Southern States, ample protection is afforded to tenants and very little to landlords."

Republican governments also shaped economic legislation to reach out to the white upcountry, where debt still rested "like an incubus upon the people." As state after state exempted specified amounts of land, personal property, mechanics' tools, and agricultural implements from seizure for debt, the majority of small property holders, and even some large ones, were protected against losing their property to creditors. In the upcountry, debtor relief for a time remained "a strong card in the party of Reconstruction."

Blacks, of course, had their own economic agenda. They saw in Republican governments a renewed chance at landownership. Given the importance of this issue, it is remarkable how little the Republican governments did. Again, South Carolina proved the exception, adopting a pathbreaking program of land distribution overseen by a land commission with the power to purchase real estate and resell it on long-term credit. Initially plagued by mismanagement and corruption, the commission accomplished little until Secretary of State Francis L. Cardozo reorganized its affairs in 1872. But by 1876 some 14,000 black families, about one-seventh of the state's black population, plus a handful of whites, had obtained homesteads. One Abbeville County tract, purchased from the commission by a group of black families, survives to this day as the community of Promised Land.

Rather than emulate South Carolina, Republicans in other states used taxation to weaken the plantation and promote black landownership. Rising state expenses and the fall in Southern property values necessitated an increase in rates, but the new tax system dramatically altered the burden borne by different groups of Southerners. In contrast to the prewar policy of low land taxes supplemented by levies on slaves and an array of licenses and fees, and the exorbitant poll taxes of Presidential Reconstruction, revenue now derived primarily from ad valorem taxation of landed and personal property. Moreover, while planters had previously been allowed to assess the value of their property for tax purposes, Republican officials, sometimes their own former slaves, now performed that task. Planters and white farmers, many for the first time, paid a significant portion of their income as taxes, while the law, complained an Alabama Democrat, " 'lets out,' as the phrase is, every negro," since a small amount of personal property, tools, and livestock was exempted from the levies.

Rising taxes quickly emerged as a rallying cry for Reconstruction's opponents, but many blacks hoped high levies would make extensive holdings of uncultivated land unprofitable and force real estate onto the market. And immense tracts did fall into the hands of state governments for nonpayment of taxes—in Mississippi alone over six million acres, one-fifth of the area of the state, was forfeited in this way. Yet relatively little land changed hands, for often the threat of sale led owners to satisfy their tax liabilities, and neighbors frequently conspired to prevent bids on lands placed at auction. Judged by the standard of basic equity, the Reconstruction tax system appeared to Republicans preferable to its predecessor, which had "borne so unjustly and unequally upon the people." But as a means of land distribution, it proved singularly ineffective.

Outside South Carolina, in fact, the same political and ideological barriers that had prevented constitutional conventions from resolving the land issue frustrated the freedmen's hopes. With Radicalism waning in the North, the national party seemed in no mood to countenance "agrarian" departures in economic policy, and the desire to attract the political support of progressive planters often stood at cross purposes to the aim of assisting the freedmen. Most white Republicans, and many freeborn blacks, moreover, while perfectly willing to guarantee the freedmen their rights as free laborers and equal citizens, opposed using the power of the state to redistribute property. Reconstruction, declared one Southern Republican newspaper, meant "protection and fair play," not "free gifts of land or money."

As the New Orleans *Tribune* repeatedly pointed out, the realities confronting the freedmen rendered free labor assumptions utterly unrealistic: lacking land and encountering not social harmony but the persistent hostility of planters and merchants, they "cannot rise, except in extraordinary cases. . . . They must be servants to others, with no hope of bettering their condition." But most Republican leaders preferred to await the freedmen's acquisition of property through the natural workings of the market. They invested their hopes for change not in a policy of economic redistribution, but in a program of regional development, with railroad construction as its centerpiece.

The Gospel of Prosperity

More than any other, the issue of economic development preoccupied Republican leaders in the first years of Reconstruction. With state aid, they believed, the backward South could be transformed into a society of booming factories, bustling towns, a diversified agriculture freed from the plantation's dominance, and abundant employment opportunities for black and white alike. The "gospel of prosperity" captivated the moderate leaders of early Republican rule, who hoped it would recast politics along nonracial lines and win legitimacy for the Reconstruction state. "The party that first completes the Internal Improvement System . . . ," wrote a follower of Gov. William W. Holden, "will hold the reins of power here for years to come."

In some respects, little in the program of railroad aid was new, for American government had long promoted entrepreneurial activity. The scope and purposes of Republican aid, however, differed substantially from those of their Southern predecessors, for Republicans saw railroads not as adjuncts of the plantation system, but as catalysts of a peaceful revolution that would dislodge the plantation from its economic throne.

In the first years of Republican rule, every Southern state extended generous aid to railroad corporations, either in direct payments to a particular company or in general laws authorizing the state's endorsement of a railroad's bonds once a specified number of track miles had been laid (thus assuring investors that the state would cover lapsed interest payments). County and local governments subscribed directly to railroad stock as well, from Mobile, which spent over $1 million, to tiny Spartanburg, South Carolina, which appropriated $50,000. Republican legislatures also chartered scores of banks and manufacturing companies, appropriated money to repair Mississippi levees and reclaim swamplands, and in several cases sought to encourage European and Northern immigration.

No matter how extensive, state aid alone could not bring capitalist development to the South. For this, private investment was indispensable, and the frantic effort to attract outside capital led Republican governments to act in ways that contradicted their professed concern for the black and white poor. In Mississippi, railroad companies, factories, and banks virtually escaped taxation. Some states authorized convict leasing to supply cheap labor to entrepreneurial allies of Republican governors like Rufus Bullock of Georgia, Harrison Reed of Florida, and Henry Clay Warmoth of Louisiana, although it involved far smaller numbers than under the Redeemers.

To some extent, the "gospel of prosperity" succeeded in bringing the two parties closer together. Democrats sat on the boards of railroads that received public aid and supported subsidy bills in many legislatures. In Alabama, the Republican-controlled Alabama & Chattanooga Railroad and the Louisville & Nashville, allied with the Democrats, vied for public assistance and access to the state's mineral resources. On the local level, leaders of the two parties often cooperated in railroad promotion. Charleston's Board of Trade, seeking to reverse the city's economic decline, lobbied black legislators for state aid to the Blue Ridge Railroad.

Nonetheless, railroad aid bills were generally drafted by Republican committees, passed by Republican legislatures, and implemented by Republican governors. Black lawmakers, like white, pressed for aid to enterprises that promised to enrich their communities. But the program of state-sponsored capitalist development, launched with grandiose hopes, proved in many ways the party's undoing. Vastly increasing the financial claims upon government, it produced spiraling state debts and taxes and drained resources from schools and other programs. Far from enhancing Republicans' respectability, it opened the door to widespread corruption. The state aid program alienated voters in the white upcountry, where many yeomen and artisans feared the railroad would subordinate their self-sufficient society to the tyranny of the marketplace. And the absence of tangible benefits for freedmen produced growing disillusionment with the leaders they had helped to place in power. What had begun in the hope of bolstering Republican government soon threatened to undermine the entire Reconstruction experiment.

Rising taxes, steadily increasing debts, and the declining value of state bonds vividly illustrated the new governments' financial problems. To a large extent, the fiscal crisis of the Reconstruction state arose from the war and emancipation and the circumstances under which Republicans assumed power. Without massive federal aid, the rebuilding of damaged facilities and the expansion of public services for a vastly enlarged citizenry required a dramatic rise in state expenditures, while property taxes rose sharply simply to compensate for the decline in Southern land values. The first Republican governors, moreover, inherited from their predecessors substantial public debts and empty treasuries. Upon taking office in Florida in 1868, Harrison Reed discovered that no account existed of how state monies had been spent between 1848 and 1860 or during Presidential Reconstruction. Reed had to dip into his own pocket to meet the government's initial expenses.

As the program of railroad aid took hold, bonds underwritten by Republican governments flooded the market. By 1872, North Carolina, where extravagant railroad aid had doubled state indebtedness, saw its credit virtually disappear, and South Carolina, whose bonds were selling at twenty-five cents on the dollar, could meet neither current expenses nor outstanding liabilities. Meanwhile, property taxes rose steadily. In Mississippi, where the rate had been 1 mill (one-tenth of one percent of assessed property values) before Republican rule, it reached nine mills in 1871, and over twelve two years later. To this were added rising local and county levies. Since the value of property had declined sharply, these figures exaggerate the actual increase in taxes paid, but the rise made tax rates a major political liability for Southern Republicans.

As the collapse of their credit reduced Southern governments' ability to finance the ambitious programs they had undertaken, widespread corruption undermined their political legitimacy. There was nothing unique about the corruption that cast a shadow over the conduct of public affairs in nearly every Reconstruction state. Ever since Capt. Samuel Argall, a deputy governor of early colonial Virginia, took advantage of the opportunity to "make hay whilst the sunne doth shine, however it may fare with the generality," bribery, fraud, and influence peddling have been endemic to American politics. Nor did the Tweed and Whiskey Rings in the Reconstruction North offer a model of government probity.

Corruption may be ubiquitous in American history, but it thrived in the Reconstruction South because of the specific circumstances of Republican rule. The expansion of public responsibilities and of captalist enterprise linked to the state dramatically increased both the size of budgets and the demands placed on them. Officials regularly handled unprecedented sums of money, corporations vied for the benefits of state aid, and communities concerned about their future prosperity competed for rail routes, offering numerous opportunities for bribery and plunder. The spirit of economic promotion fostered a get-rich-quick mentality, and many officials saw nothing wrong with taking a piece of the expanding economic pie for themselves. "Ten years from now," wrote an ally of one entrepreneur, "the people . . . will see so clearly the vast benefit of the present proposed Railroads that they will care very little how or by what means they were built." Many Republican officials, black and white, owning relatively little property and facing uncertain political and personal futures, determined to make the most of their tenure in office.

Corruption took many forms in the Reconstruction South. Bribery, either distributed voluntarily by railroads and other enterprises seeking state aid or demanded of them by state officials, became widespread in several states. South Carolina Gov. Robert K. Scott and state fiscal agent H. H. Kimpton speculated in state bonds, even as they issued and attempted to market far more securities than authorized by the legislature. Scott also joined the ring of officials who fraudulently acquired the state's shares in the Greenville & Columbia Railroad at a fraction of their true value. And he plunged into land-commission corruption, which involved the state's purchase at inflated prices of useless swamplands owned by well-connected individuals. Many legislators held directorships or stock in railroads receiving aid, as did officials like Louisiana's chief justice and Georgia's attorney general, who were called upon to rule on whether companies with which they were connected had fulfilled their legal obligations.

While political leaders often orchestrated corruption for their own gain, the largest schemes originated with economic buccaneers who looked to state aid to finance grandiose dreams of railroad empire. Most notorious was the ring headed by Milton S. Littlefield, a former Union general who had allegedly mustered in fictitious black soldiers and pocketed their bounty money, and George W. Swepson, a North Carolina entrepreneur who hoped to create a vast Southern transportation network. Disbursing $200,000 in bribes, loans, and lavish entertainments for the lawmakers, the ring succeeded in obtaining millions in appropriations for roads under its control. Instead of expending the money on construction, however, they bought up the stock of other railroads, speculated in state bonds, rewarded political friends with extravagant legal fees and bogus building contracts, and financed a European tour.

Although the charge of corruption did much to discredit Reconstruction, bribery, conflict of interest, and the misuse of public position for private gain transcended party lines. "The briber, my moral philosophy teaches, is just as bad as the bribed," commented a black Congressman, and Democratic lobbyists and railroad directors dispensed money as eagerly as Republican. "You are mistaken," a Louisiana Democrat wrote a Northern party leader, "if you suppose that all the evils . . . result from the carpetbaggers and negroes—the democrats are leagued with them when anything is proposed which promises to pay." In Georgia, leaders of the opposing parties joined forces to lease the state-owned Western & Atlantic Railroad under a remarkable arrangement by which "none need advance one dollar, and from which all will receive large dividends."

Black Republicans were hardly immune to the lure of illicit gain. Pinchback used his position on the New Orleans Park Commission to influence them to purchase, at an inflated price, land of which he was part owner. He also made a handsome profit speculating in state bonds. Inside information, he frankly admitted, allowed his operations to succeed: "I belonged to the General Assembly, and knew about what it would do. . . . My investments were made accordingly." The "politics of livelihood" weighed even more heavily on black officials than white. As a South Carolina legislator explained after selling his vote in an election for U.S. Senator, "I was pretty hard up, and I did not care who the candidate was if I got two hundred dollars." Overall, however, blacks hardly matched the share of the take of white governors like Warmoth and Scott, for few occupied political positions that allowed them access to plunder. And the going rate for bribing whites usually exceeded that for blacks.

Most important, corruption threatened to undermine the integrity of Reconstruction, not simply in the eyes of Southern opponents but in the court of Northern public opinion. It was true, but irrelevant, that corruption flourished outside the South, and that charges of malfeasance generally arose from hostile sources with a vested interest in exaggerating its scope. In normal times, corruption seemed an unfortunate but unavoidable aspect of political life, but for Southern Republicans it was an unmitigated disaster. "We cannot afford," one party newspaper remarked, "to bear the odium of profligates in office."

Along with rising taxes and swollen state debts, corruption not only handed the Democrats a potent issue, but contributed to the demise of the entire "gospel of prosperity." The high tide of state aid came between 1868 and 1871. Then disillusionment set in as a result of the program's high cost, corrupt practices, and meager results. The reaction coincided with growing opposition to the party's initial conciliatory policies and with blacks' increasing political assertiveness, for railroad aid epitomized the close working relationship the first Republican governors tried to forge with Democrats and their assumption that the party's future lay in appeasing its opponents rather than vigorously promoting the interests of its own constituents. Increasing numbers of Republicans demanded that corporations bear their fair share of the tax burden. Black legislators attacked the convict lease system, restricting its scope in Alabama and Georgia and abolishing it in South Carolina altogether. By the early 1870s the program of railroad aid ground to a halt.

Perhaps the reaction would have been less severe had the program of state-sponsored economic development come close to achieving its ambitious goals. Compared with the unsuccessful programs of Presidential Reconstruction, the Republicans could, in fact, claim real accomplishments. Between 1868 and 1872, Southern railroads had been rebuilt and some 3,300 miles added, an increase of nearly forty percent. But this progress was confined to Georgia, Alabama, Arkansas, and Texas; other states had little to show for their generosity except enormous debts. And throughout the South, railroads faced increasing economic difficulties as state aid proved insufficient to meet the enormous costs of construction and operation. By 1872, many were on the verge of bankruptcy. The number of workers employed in Southern manufacturing increased modestly, but mostly in small concerns processing agricultural goods. The real expansion of southern textile factories did not occur until the 1880s, nor was Alabama's industrial potential awakened until then.

Part of the problem was that despite the inducements offered by new laws, significant amounts of Northern and European capital failed to arrive. The prevailing "social discord," as New York diarist George Templeton Strong commented, made the South "the last region on earth in which . . . a Northern or European capitalist [would] invest a dollar." Indeed, one reason the South fell prey to buccaneers like Swepson was that more established entrepreneurs, except for New Yorkers with longstanding Southern connections, avoided the region.

Thus the gospel of prosperity failed in both its aims: It produced neither a stable Republican majority nor a modernizing economy. Within Southern society, nonetheless, profound changes were underway, affecting both the black and white communities and their relations with each other. Begun by the Civil War and emancipation, the transformation of Southern life was in some ways accelerated, in others redirected, by the years of Republican rule.

Patterns of Economic Change

Slowly, a new social order took shape in the Reconstruction South. While far from the modernizing economy envisioned by Republican policymakers, it differed in crucial respects from its antebellum predecessor. The demise of slavery and the rapid spread of market relations in the predominantly white upcountry produced new systems of labor and new class structures among both black and white Southerners. The burden of history weighed heavily upon the South's economic transformation, which took place in a war-torn, capital-scarce region that lacked the institutional base for sustained economic growth, faced a slowing world demand for its major export, and was excluded from a significant share of national political power. In retrospect, it was all but inevitable that the postwar South would descend into a classic pattern of underdevelopment, its rate of economic growth and per capita income lagging far behind the rest of the nation.

"One thing is perfectly certain," Kentucky Democrat Garrett Davis told the Senate in 1867: "[cotton] is to be made by negro labor." No aphorism could have been more misleading. The absorption of white farmers into the cotton economy took place at different speeds in different parts of the South. But where railroads penetrated already settled upcountry counties, as in South Carolina, Georgia, and Alabama, or opened new areas to cultivation in Texas, Arkansas, and Louisiana, the shift from subsistence to commercial farming proceeded apace. By the mid-1870s, both the geographical and racial locus of cotton production had been transformed. Nearly forty percent of the crop was raised west of the Mississippi River, mainly by white farmers, and in the older states production increasingly shifted to the upcountry. Black laborers, who cultivated nine-tenths of the South's cotton crop in 1860, grew only sixty percent in 1876.

At the close of the Civil War, Edward Atkinson predicted that the demise of slavery would cause a cotton boom among enterprising white farmers who, like their Northern counterparts, would prosper from an increasing involvement with the market. But things did not work out that way. Some yeomen found economic salvation in commercial agriculture, but for most, burdened by Civil War debts, postwar crop failures, rising Reconstruction taxes, and, during the 1870s, a precipitous decline in agricultural prices, cotton proved a recipe for disaster. Increasingly, upcountry farmers fell into new forms of dependency, their situation exacerbated by the South's new credit system. Because of the region's chronic capital shortage and scarcity of banking institutions, local merchants generally represented the only source of available credit. With land values having plummeted, merchants usually advanced loans only in exchange for a lien on the year's cotton crop, rather than take a mortgage on real estate, as was conventional in the North. The emergence of the crop lien as the South's major form of agricultural credit forced indebted farmers to concentrate on cotton, further expanding production and depressing prices. By 1880, one-third of the white farmers in the cotton states were tenants renting either for cash or a share of the crop, and a region self-sufficient before the Civil War was no longer able to feed itself.

The growth of tenancy, one journalist reported from North Carolina in 1871, "does not seem to be very popular with the poor whites." And many yeomen attributed its spread to the Republican program of railroad promotion, which brought market relations into the upcountry, and to rising taxes, which increased small farmers' need for ready cash. Indeed, these grievances proved almost as great a liability for Southern Republicans among white Piedmont voters as the party's identification with black political equality. It is significant that the white Republican vote remained most secure in the Southern mountains, for here not only had wartime Unionism sunk its deepest roots, but during Reconstruction the railroad had not yet penetrated, most farmers still tilled their own land, and the transition to cotton made little headway.

The rise of upcountry cotton farming represented only one part of a fundamental reorientation of Southern trading patterns and a wholesale shift in regional economic power. As railroad and telegraph lines worked their way into the interior, merchants in rapidly developing market towns for the first time found it possible to trade directly with the North, bypassing the coastal cities that had traditionally monopolized Southern commerce. Atlanta, whose rise was stimulated by its selection as state capital and the opening of rail connections to the North, was the quintessential upcountry boom city, serving as a gathering point for cotton grown in Georgia's Piedmont and a distribution center for Northern goods. Here a visitor in 1870 found "more of the life and stir of business than in all the other Southern cities, which I have seen, put together." The railroad also transformed smaller towns like Selma and Macon into commercial entrepôts. Meanwhile, older port cities languished. By 1880, Charleston was a minor seaport of little commercial significance. New Orleans found itself unable to compete with St. Louis for access to the expanding cotton trade of East Texas, and Richmond, Savannah, and Mobile, bypassed by the railroad, also stagnated economically.

The "economic reconstruction of the upcountry" laid the foundation for the rise of a bourgeoisie composed of merchants, railroad promoters, and bankers in interior towns. Nationally, this new class wielded little economic power, for it depended for credit and supplies on financiers and wholesale merchants in the North. But within the South, it reaped the benefit of the spread of cotton agriculture. Although some of these business leaders belonged to the old planter class, the economic importance of the new upcountry elite rested more on access to credit and ties with the North than on connections with the prewar aristocracy. By the end of Reconstruction an area dominated before the war by self-sufficient yeomen was being transformed into a commercial economy peopled by merchants, tenants, farm laborers, and commercially oriented farmers.

Towns and cities also exerted a growing influence on black life, although migration from the countryside slowed considerably after 1870. In urban centers were concentrated the schools, churches, newspapers, and fraternal societies that produced many of the articulate leaders of Reconstruction politics. And the variety of employment opportunities far outstripped those available in the countryside. But the black urban social structure was, compared with that of whites, truncated and heavily weighted toward the bottom. Nearly all urban blacks lived by manual labor, the vast majority as servants, porters, and unskilled day laborers. They received subsistence wages, faced much higher unemployment rates than whites, and enjoyed virtually no opportunities for the accumulation of property or upward mobility.

The black urban community contained no well-established elite of wealthy bankers and merchants and found most white-collar positions closed to it. Only a tiny minority achieved professional status during Reconstruction, although the number of lawyers and doctors increased in the 1870s thanks to the new black universities. Artisans, perhaps a quarter of employed blacks in most Southern towns and cities, comprised the largest group above the ranks of the unskilled. But instead of prospering, their economic position steadily worsened. Denied access to credit, threatened by an influx of Northern manufactured goods, and driven from many skilled crafts by white employers and competitors, black artisans were mostly confined to trades that required little capital, like carpenter, blacksmith, brickmason, and shoemaker, or to occupations like barber, traditionally avoided by whites.

At the apex of the urban community stood those few blacks able to escape manual labor for entrepreneurial occupations. In cities like Charleston, New Orleans, and Natchez, where wealthy free mulattoes brought skills and capital into the postwar years, color and class position overlapped well into the twentieth century. Yet in many ways Reconstruction was a time of crisis for the old free elite. Challenged for positions of political leadership by former slaves, they also faced severe economic difficulties because of the decline of the old port cities. Especially in growing inland cities like Atlanta and Montgomery, where newcomers did not have to contend with a preexisting black elite, a new business class arose, composed of enterprising freedmen who served a black clientele.

The essential fact about the black upper class, however, was its tiny size and negligible economic importance. Only in life-style and aspirations did this elite constitute a "black bourgeoisie," for it lacked capital and economic autonomy and did not own the banks, stores, and mills that could provide employment for other blacks. Black business was small business: grocery stores, restaurants, funeral parlors, and boardinghouses. Black proprietors formed no part of the national or regional bourgeoisie, and their businesses faced bleak prospects for long-term survival. When black business-men did acquire wealth, they tended to invest it in real estate rather than in economic enterprises. During Reconstruction, the black upper class remained too small and too weak to enjoy either political or cultural hegemony within its own community. Yet its future prominence was assured as the steady growth of separate black neighborhoods created the economic foundation for a black business class, while the declining position of black artisans and the port city free elite forecast their inevitable eclipse as leaders of black politics.

The black community, a white North Carolina Republican observed in 1879, was only beginning to divide into "classes or ranks of society." The distillation of a new system of social stratification to supersede prewar divisions between free and slave, mulatto and black, had only begun during Reconstruction, a fact that helps explain the black community's remarkable political unity. Yet, as in the cities and white upcountry, a new class structure in the plantation belt slowly replaced the shattered world of master and slave.

The planter still stood atop this new social pyramid. Slavery was gone, but in the absence of large-scale land distribution, the plantation system endured. The degree of "planter persistence" varied considerably among the South's crop regions. Louisiana sugar planters, unable to repair wartime destruction, saw themselves replaced by newcomers; by 1870, Northern investors owned half the estates. In the lowcountry rice kingdom, with its equally large capital requirements, continuing labor turmoil and the opening of new lands to rice cultivation west of the Mississippi discouraged outside investment. Many planters, unable to resume production, were reduced to penury. "I do not believe that the ruin of the French nobility at the first Revolution," commented a Northern reporter, "was more complete than . . . that of the proud, rich, and cultivated aristocracy of the low country of South Carolina." Elsewhere, however, the plantation South seemed at first glance to offer a remarkable example of social and economic continuity. No "revolution in land-titles" swept the tobacco and cotton belts; the majority of planter families managed to retain control of their land. Yet despite their uncanny capacity for survival, war, emancipation, and Reconstruction fundamentally altered the planters' world and their own role in it.

In the antebellum years, planters had dominated regional politics and enjoyed a significant share of national authority. Now they exerted little influence in Washington and in several states found themselves powerless on the state and local levels. Possession of a plantation no longer guaranteed wealth. "Although the owner of two of the best and largest cotton plantations in . . . South Carolina," lamented former Gov. Milledge Luke Bonham in 1874, "my life has been absorbed in trying to keep my head above water. The effect has been crushing." Many who had once seen planting as the only honorable calling now urged their sons to take up careers in business and the professions. Most of all, control of land no longer translated automatically into control of labor, a situation evident since the end of slavery but in many ways exacerbated by the advent of Reconstruction. In 1869, two Boston cotton brokers sent questionnaires to dozens of planters, inquiring about agricultural conditions. With virtually one voice, the respondents complained of a "labor problem." "Once we had reliable labor, controlled at will," commented a Georgia planter. "Now . . . it is both uncertain and unreliable; and our contracts must often be made at great disadvantage."

Republican rule subtly altered the balance of power in the rural South. The end of the state's efforts to bolster labor discipline and the coming to power of local officials sympathetic to the freedmen produced during Reconstruction a kind of stalemate on the plantations. "Capital is powerless and labor demoralized," wrote South Carolina agricultural reformer D. Wyatt Aiken in 1871. Labor was scarce not merely because fewer blacks were willing to work on plantations, but also because those who did were unmanageable. "The power to control [black labor]," the Selma *Southern Argus* agreed, "is gone."

As late as 1869, the *Annual Cyclopedia* commented on the "transitory state of the labor system in the Southern States." By then, however, new patterns of social relations had emerged in the different crop regions of the plantation South. Nowhere was the dialectic of continuity and change more evident than in the sugar districts of Louisiana, where the centralized plantation employing gang labor survived the end of slavery. An influx of Northern capital rescued the industry and, indeed, produced a concentration of landownership in the sugar parishes. Along with the liquidation of the old planter class and the new owners' access to cash, this situation helped produce the most rapid transition to capitalist labor relations. Blacks quickly became a wage-earning labor force, receiving daily or monthly wages considerably exceeding those elsewhere in the South and enjoying, as well, the traditional right to garden plots on which to raise vegetables and keep poultry and livestock. Yet the system did not end the conflict over labor discipline. Planters complained of a shortage of workers, especially at harvest time, and of blacks' demands for higher pay. Many estates lay idle, and production did not regain the level of 1861 until the 1890s.

An even more complex economic transition took place in the rice kingdom, where planter Ralph I. Middleton described labor relations as "a continuous struggle where the planter is all the time at a great disadvantage." Lowcountry rice output never regained its prewar levels. In 1874 Edward King found the region dotted with abandoned manorial houses, standing "like sorrowful ghosts lamenting the past." In the end, the great plantations fell to pieces, their lands rented or sold to blacks. In their place emerged a pattern of small-scale farming, with black families growing their own food and supplementing their income by marketing farm produce or seeking day labor in Charleston and Savannah. More than in any other region of the South, the lowcountry freedmen succeeded in shaping labor relations in accordance with their own aspirations.

Entirely different was the economic transition in the far larger plantation regions of the tobacco and cotton South. Here, where farming required less capital and a less coordinated labor force, the planter class by and large retained control of its land and resumed production. At the same time, Reconstruction reinforced what a Southern newspaper called blacks' "growing disposition to throw off all restraint and to assert the dignity of freedom by 'setting up' for themselves." Few blacks managed to fulfill this aspiration by acquiring homesteads of their own, for even those who possessed the necessary resources found most whites adamantly opposed to black landownership. In most of the cotton states, the commissioner of agriculture reported in 1876, only about one black family in twenty had managed to acquire land.

Like urban businessmen, landowners stood atop the emerging black class structure but had little impact on the economy at large. Compared to whites, they owned smaller farms, less machinery and livestock, and used fertilizer less frequently. Many black farmers, their tiny plots unable to provide a family with subsistence, found it necessary to engage in occasional plantation labor. Below landowners, although closest to them in independence from white control, stood those who rented for a fixed payment in cash or cotton. Renting seems to have involved as many as twenty percent of black farmers by the end of Reconstruction. At the bottom of the black social order were wage-earning farm laborers. But by the early 1870s, especially in the cotton belt, sharecropping had become the dominant form of black labor.

Sharecropping, according to a report of the Department of Agriculture, developed not as "a voluntary association from similarity of interests, but an unwilling concession to the freedman's desire to become a proprietor." Many planters continued to resist the system because it failed to allow for adequate supervision of the labor force. D. Wyatt Aiken railed against the inefficiency of sharecropping, but found himself forced to adopt it on his own plantation: "I had to yield, or lose my labor." The growing predominance of sharecropping had profound implications for the structure of rural black society. With the demise of the communal slave quarter, black families, living on isolated tenancies scattered across the length and breadth of the plantation, emerged as the basic units of social organization.

To some extent, sharecropping "solved" the plantation labor

shortage. Since each family had a vested interest in larger output, black women and children returned in large numbers to field work. In other ways, however, the system merely shifted the focus of labor conflict. Planters strongly resented the notion that sharecropping made the tenant "part owner of the crop" and entitled him to determine his family's pace of work. Republican laws awarding laborers a first lien on the crop reinforced blacks' belief that sharecroppers owned their share rather than receiving it as a wage from the planter. While sharecropping did not fulfill blacks' desire for full economic autonomy, the end of planters' coercive authority over the day-to-day lives of their tenants represented a fundamental shift in the balance of power in rural society and afforded blacks a degree of control over their time, labor, and family arrangements inconceivable under slavery.

For many blacks, however, the credit system that grew up alongside sharecropping quickly undermined its promise of autonomy. Although the black belt experienced little urban growth, tiny towns and crossroads stores spread across the region, offering a wide array of merchandise and serving as centers of political and social life. "We have stores at almost every crossroad," reported a South Carolina journalist, "and at the railway stations and villages they have multiplied beyond precedent." By 1880 the cotton South counted over 8,000 rural stores. Many landlords established stores on their own plantations, sometimes finding the business of supplying tenants "as lucrative, if not more so, than planting or renting."

Between black belt planters and the expanding merchant class, whose origins not infrequently lay in the North or Europe, tensions often ran high. Planters charged that the proliferation of country stores undermined good order by encouraging tenants to steal and sell growing cotton before the crop had been divided. They also objected to lien laws that failed to give a landowner's claim for rent priority over debts owed by the tenant to local merchants. Yet as planters and their children went into merchandising and storekeepers acquired land, the two groups tended to coalesce. Reconstruction witnessed the origin of a new landlord-merchant class that by the end of the century would dominate Southern rural life.

As for black tenants, the ability to seek supplies off the plantation enhanced their independence, since merchants rarely demanded the right to supervise day-to-day labor. On the other hand, interest rates for goods purchased on credit often exceeded fifty percent,

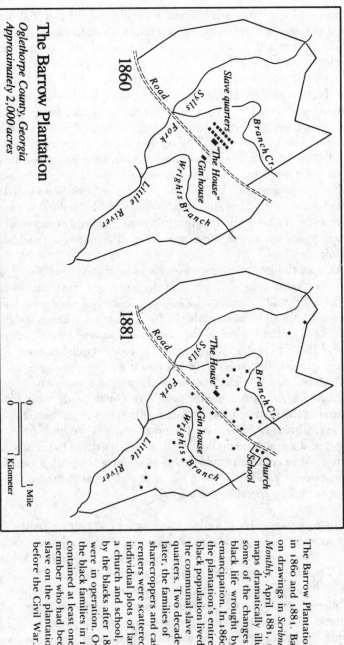

The Barrow Plantation

Oglethorpe County, Georgia
Approximately 2,000 acres

1860

Slave quarters

Stills

Branch Cr.

"The House"

■ Gin house

Wrights Branch

Little River

Road

1881

Road

Stills

"The House"

Branch Cr.

Fork

■ Gin house

Wrights Branch

Little River

Church

School

0

1 Mile

0

1 Kilometer

The Barrow Plantation in 1860 and 1881. Based on drawings in *Scribner's Monthly*, April 1881, these maps dramatically illustrate some of the changes in black life wrought by emancipation. In 1860, the plantation's entire black population lived in the communal slave quarters. Two decades later, the families of sharecroppers and cash renters were scattered on individual plots of land, and a church and school, built by the blacks after 1865, were in operation. Over half the black families in 1881 contained at least one member who had been a slave on the plantation before the Civil War.

reflecting both the South's capital shortage and the fact that many rural merchants faced no local competition. In many cases, too, they inflicted outright fraud on illiterate tenants. As cotton prices declined during the 1870s, many tenants, unable to settle their accounts at year's end, carried indebtedness over to the new season. To obtain additional credit, they were compelled to produce more and more cotton. For the region as a whole, the crop lien produced a growing overreliance on cotton and neglect of food, a pattern already clear by the 1870s. "The credit system," reported a resident of Mississippi, "has been pushed to such an extent that crops have been mortgaged for supplies before they have been planted. The culture of everything but cotton has either been abandoned or greatly curtailed." Thus, the credit system that helped reduce many upcountry whites from yeomen to tenants made it impossible for blacks to use sharecropping to accumulate the money with which to acquire land.

Like all the Reconstruction South's labor systems, sharecropping was not born fully formed, and its contours were continually reshaped by the ongoing conflict over control of plantation labor. Only after the depression of the 1870s and the end of Reconstruction combined to limit severely the bargaining power of black laborers would the exploitative implications of sharecropping become fully clear. Indeed, the early 1870s witnessed a partial economic recovery, stimulated by rising cotton production at a time when prices remained high. Although still unable to obtain land, many blacks shared in the relative prosperity. Reports spoke of increasing wages for agricultural laborers, rising deposits in the Freedman's Savings Bank, and a growing number of sharecroppers rising to the status of renter. "The colored people . . . ," claimed a Mississippi Republican newspaper in 1870, "were never so well off as at present. They have money to spend in the stores."

In 1872, newspapers recorded the passing of Maurice Jasper, the last surviving slave of George Washington. Born of parents brought from Africa over a century before, Jasper had lived, a black newspaper commented, to see the "second revolution." He died as the first period of Republican Reconstruction drew to a close. In political, economic, and social life, these years presented a complex pattern of achievement and disappointment. Compared with their predecessors, the accomplishments of the new governments were indeed impressive. Biracial democratic government, a thing unknown in American history, was functioning effectively in much of the South. Men only recently released from bondage cast ballots and sat on juries and, in the Deep South, enjoyed an increasing share of authority at the state level, while the conservative oligarchy that had dominated Southern government from colonial times to 1867 found itself largely excluded from power. Public facilities had been rebuilt and expanded, school systems established, and tax codes modernized. Occurring at a crucial juncture in the transition from slavery to freedom, Reconstruction had nipped in the bud the attempt to substitute a legalized system of labor discipline for the coercion of slavery and had enhanced blacks' bargaining power on the plantations. All in all, declared a white South Carolina lawyer in 1871, "we have gone through one of the most remarkable changes in our relations to each other, that has been known, perhaps, in the history of the world."

Most striking of all was the impact on the freedmen. For Reconstruction transformed their lives and aspirations in ways unmeasurable by statistics and in realms far beyond the reach of the law. A Northern correspondent, reporting from Vicksburg early in 1873, captured something of the change in blacks' conception of themselves: "One hardly realizes the fact that the many negroes one sees here . . . have been slaves a few short years ago, at least as far as their demeanor goes as individuals newly invested with all the rights and privileges of an American citizen. They appreciate their new condition thoroughly, and flaunt their independence." In many ways, of course, the "second revolution" was woefully incomplete. Blacks still suffered from dire poverty, and the old ruling class remained largely intact, implacably hostile to the new order of things. But as long as Reconstruction survived, so too did the possibility of further change.

"Nothing renders society more restless," Carl Schurz had written in 1865, "than a . . . revolution but half accomplished." If Reconstruction's failures betrayed the utopian aspirations with which Republican rule began, its successes persuaded those accustomed to controlling the South's destiny that the entire experiment must be brought to a violent, irrevocable end.

The Challenge of Enforcement

The New Departure and the First Redemption

If Southern Republicans suffered from factional, ideological, and racial strife, their opponents encountered difficulties of their own. In the aftermath of Grant's victory, with Reconstruction seemingly a fait accompli, Southern Democrats confronted their own legitimacy crisis—the need to convince the North that they stood for something other than simply a return to the old regime. A growing number of Democratic leaders saw little point in denying the reality that blacks were voting and holding office. These advocates of a New Departure argued that their party's return to power depended on putting the issues of Civil War and Reconstruction behind them. So began a period in which Democrats, like Republicans, proclaimed their realism and moderation and promised to ease racial tensions. But if, in political rhetoric, "convergence" reigned, in practice the New Departure only underscored the chasm separating the parties on fundamental issues and the limits of Democrats' willingness to accept the changes in Southern life intrinsic to Reconstruction.

Southern Democrats made their first attempts to seize the political center in 1869. Instead of running its own candidates for state office, the party threw support to disaffected Republicans and focused its campaigns on the restoration of voting rights to former Confederates rather than opposition to black suffrage. In Virginia and Tennessee, the strategy paid immediate dividends. The successful gubernatorial candidate in Virginia was Gilbert C. Walker, a Northern-born Republican banker, manufacturer, and railroad man.

In Tennessee, the Republican governor himself initiated the political realignment. Assuming office in February 1869 when "Parson"
Brownlow departed for the U.S. Senate, DeWitt Senter set out to
win election in his own right by conciliating the state's Democrats.
His policy split his already factionalized party, whose hold on power
rested on widespread disenfranchisement. Challenged for reelection by Congressman William B. Stokes, a Union Army veteran and
opponent of conciliation, the governor ignored the suffrage law and
allowed thousands of former Confederates to register, whereupon
the Democrats endorsed his candidacy. The result was an overwhelming victory for Senter, who carried the state by better than
two to one and even edged ahead in East Tennessee. The New
Departure gathered strength in 1870. As in Virginia and Tennessee,
Missouri's Democrats formed a victorious coalition with self-styled
Liberal Republicans, adopting a platform promising "universal
amnesty and universal suffrage."

In other states, Democrats accepted Reconstruction "as a finality," but retained their party identity rather than merge into new
organizations or endorse dissident Republicans. Alabama's successful Democratic gubernatorial candidate, Robert Lindsay, insisted
that his party had abandoned racial issues for economic ones, and
openly courted black voters. Benjamin H. Hill of Georgia, an
uncompromising opponent of black suffrage in 1867, now announced
his willingness to recognize blacks' right to the "free, full, and
unrestricted enjoyment" of the ballot. In place of racial issues,
Democratic leaders now devoted their energies to financial criticisms of Republican rule. In several states they organized Taxpayers'
Conventions, whose platforms denounced Reconstruction government for corruption and extravagance and demanded a reduction in
taxes and state expenditures. Complaints about rising taxes became
an effective rallying cry for opponents of Reconstruction. Asked if
his tax of four dollars on 100 acres of land seemed excessive, one
replied: "It appears so, sir, to what it was formerly, . . . next to
nothing."

Despite the potency of calls for tax reduction, the growing
prominence of the issue was something less than a transformation in
Reconstruction politics. Indeed, while accepting the "finality" of
Reconstruction and the principle of civil and political equality, the
Taxpayers' Conventions simultaneously exposed the limits of polit-
ical "convergence." Most Democrats objected not only to the

amount of state expenditures but to such new purposes of public spending as tax-supported schools. Democratic calls for a return to rule by "intelligent property-holders" meant the exclusion of many whites from government, while implicitly denying blacks any role in the South's public affairs except to vote for their social betters.

Even among its advocates, the New Departure smacked less of a genuine accommodation to the democratic implications of Reconstruction than a tactic for reassuring the North about their party's intentions. Indeed, there was always something grudging about Democrats' embrace of black civil and political rights. Publicly, Democratic leaders spoke of a new era in Southern politics; privately, many hoped to undo the "evil" of black suffrage "as early . . . as possible." And even centrist Democrats could not countenance independent black political organization. South Carolina's Taxpayers' Convention, for example, called for the dissolution of the Union Leagues.

Nor did official conduct in Democrat-controlled communities inspire confidence that a real shift in policy or ideology had occurred. Here, blacks complained of exclusion from juries, severe punishment for trifling crimes, the continued apprenticeship of their children against parental wishes, and a general inability to obtain justice. In one Democratic Alabama county in 1870, a black woman brutally beaten by a group of whites was ordered to raise $16.45 for court costs before her complaint was heard. After she did so, the judge released the offenders and instructed the injured woman to drop the matter or face a jail term.

Equally revealing were the statewide policies Democrats adopted in the border states and Upper South: Kentucky and Delaware, which Republicans never controlled; Maryland and West Virginia, "redeemed" by the Democrats, respectively, in 1867 and 1870; and Virginia, Tennessee, and Missouri, captured by "new movements" in 1869 and 1870. Having led the way in wartime Reconstruction, the border and Upper South now blazed the trail of Redemption. The threat of federal intervention restrained the most extreme proposals, and the diversity of the Democratic coalition ensured that specific policies varied from state to state, but it remained perfectly clear that the party was still devoted to white supremacy and labor control. As late as 1872, Kentucky still barred blacks from testifying in court. These states also pioneered in legal segregation, Delaware authorizing hotels, theaters, and common carriers to refuse admission to persons "offensive" to other customers, while Tennessee Democrats repealed the Republican law penalizing railroads for discriminating against blacks and drafted a new constitution requiring segregation in the public schools. This last provision appeared somewhat redundant, for the superintendent of public instruction elected in 1869 believed "it was not necessary to educate the farmer, mechanic, or laborer" at all, and the legislature repealed the state education law, leaving schooling a voluntary decision of each county and destroying public education for blacks except in Memphis and Nashville. Delaware, Kentucky, and Maryland Democrats initially made no provision at all for black education, then ordered that these schools be financed by taxes on black parents.

Despite the ratification in 1870 of the Fifteenth Amendment, prohibiting disenfranchisement because of race, border Democrats developed ingenious methods of limiting black voting power. Delaware, whose Democratic party insisted that the state was not "morally bound" by any of the postwar constitutional amendments, in 1873 made payment of a poll tax a requirement for voting, effectively disenfranchising the bulk of the black population and ensuring over twenty years of Democratic ascendancy in the state. Maryland's constitution of 1867 reoriented representation toward the plantation counties at the expense of Baltimore and the small farming regions to its north and west. "This they call a white man's Government," remarked one critic. "That is the right of a few white men, by counting the disfranchised blacks, to govern a great many white men. This is progress backwards."

The most comprehensive effort to undo Reconstruction, however, occurred in Georgia, whose legislature fell into Democratic hands in 1870, followed by the governorship a year later. A poll tax, coupled with new residency and registration requirements, sharply reduced the number of black voters, while a shift from ward to citywide elections eliminated Republicans from Atlanta's city council. To demolish the enclave of black political power in McIntosh County, the legislature ousted Tunis G. Campbell from his seat in favor of a white Democrat and appointed a board of commissioners to replace the elected local government. A state court subsequently sentenced Campbell to a year of hard labor on the flimsy pretext that as justice of the peace he had improperly arrested a white man. Measures now appeared on the statute book prohibiting the sale of farm products at night without the landlord's permission, making it a criminal offense to hire a laborer already under contract, making a laborer's lien on the crop inferior to that of the planter, restricting hunting and fishing, and facilitating changes in fence laws to the detriment of landless laborers. All in all, Georgia's Redeemers demonstrated the truth of Democratic Gov. James M. Smith's remark that the state could "hold inviolate every law of the United States and still so legislate upon our labor system as to retain our old plantation system."

Clearly, the First Redemption belied the idea that Southern Democrats acquiesced in the democratic and free labor revolutions embodied in Reconstruction. And in pursuit of power, the opponents of Reconstruction launched a campaign of violence that confronted Republican governments with a challenge to their very physical survival. It is a measure of how far change had progressed that the reaction against Reconstruction proved so extreme.

The Ku Klux Klan

Violence had been endemic in large parts of the South since 1865. But the advent of Radical Reconstruction stimulated its expansion. By 1870 the Ku Klux Klan and kindred organizations like the Knights of the White Camelia and the White Brotherhood were deeply entrenched in nearly every Southern state. The Klan, even in its heyday, did not possess a well-organized structure or clearly defined regional leadership. But the unity of purpose and common tactics of these local organizations make it possible to generalize about their goals and impact and the challenge they posed to the survival of Reconstruction. In effect, the Klan was a military force serving the interests of the Democratic party, the planter class, and all those who desired the restoration of white supremacy. Its purposes were political in the broadest sense, for it sought to affect power relations, both public and private, throughout Southern society. It aimed to destroy the Republican party's infrastructure, undermine the Reconstruction state, reestablish control of the black labor force, and restore racial subordination in every aspect of Southern life.

Violence was typically directed at Reconstruction's local leaders. As Emanuel Fortune, driven from Jackson County, Florida, by the Klan, explained: "The object of it is to kill out the leading men of the republican party . . . men who have taken a prominent stand." Jack

Dupree, victim of a particularly brutal murder in Monroe County, Mississippi—assailants cut his throat and disemboweled him, all within sight of his wife, who had just given birth to twins—was "president of a republican club" and known as a man who "would speak his mind." Countless other local leaders fled their homes after brutal whippings. And many blacks suffered merely for exercising their rights as citizens. Alabama freedman George Moore reported how, in 1869, Klansmen came to his home, administered a beating, "ravished a young girl who was visiting my wife," and wounded a neighbor. "The cause of this treatment, they said, was that we voted the radical ticket." Nor did white Republicans escape the violence. Klansmen murdered three scalawag members of the Georgia legislature and drove ten others from their homes. The Klan in western North Carolina settled old scores with wartime Unionists, burned the offices of the Rutherford *Star*, and brutally whipped Aaron Biggerstaff, a Hero of America and Republican organizer.

On occasion, violence escalated from the victimization of individuals to wholesale assaults on the Republican party and its leadership. In October 1870, after Republicans carried Laurens County, in South Carolina's Piedmont cotton belt, a racial altercation at Laurensville degenerated into a "negro chase" in which bands of whites drove 150 freedmen from their homes and committed 13 murders. The victims included the newly elected white probate judge, a black legislator, and others "known and prominent as connected with politics." In Meridian, a small Mississippi town to which many blacks had fled from centers of Klan activity in nearby western Alabama, three black leaders were arrested in March 1871 on charges of delivering "incendiary" speeches. Firing broke out at their court hearing, the Republican judge and two defendants were killed, and a day of rioting followed, which saw perhaps 30 blacks murdered in cold blood, including "all the leading colored men of the town with one or two exceptions."

The Klan's purposes, however, extended far beyond party politics. William Luke, an Irish-born teacher in a black school, suffered verbal abuse, saw shots fired into his home, and finally, in 1870, was lynched at Cross Plains, Alabama, along with four black men. Those blacks who managed to acquire an education were often singled out for attack. The Georgia Klan murdered freedman Washington Eager because, according to his brother, he was "too big a man . . . he can write and read and put it down himself."

Equally important as a goal of violence was the restoration of labor discipline on white-owned farms and plantations. Blacks who disputed the portion of the crop allotted them at year's end were frequently whipped, and, as in 1865 and 1866, violent bands drove freedmen off plantations after the harvest, to deprive them of their share. Blacks working on a South Carolina railroad construction gang were whipped and told to go "back to the farms to labor." The most "offensive" blacks of all seemed to be those who achieved a modicum of economic success, for, as a white Mississippi farmer commented, the Klan "do not like to see the negro go ahead."

Generally, Klan activity was concentrated in Piedmont counties where blacks comprised a minority or small majority of the population and the two parties were evenly divided. But no simple formula can explain the pattern of terror that engulfed parts of the South while leaving others relatively unscathed. Unknown in the overwhelmingly black South Carolina and Georgia lowcountry, the organization flourished in the western Alabama plantation belt. Scattered across the South lay counties particularly notorious for rampant brutality. Carpetbagger Judge Albion W. Tourgée counted 12 murders, 9 rapes, 14 cases of arson, and over 700 beatings in his judicial district in North Carolina's central Piedmont. An even more extensive "reign of terror" engulfed Jackson, a plantation county in Florida's panhandle. "That is where Satan has his seat," remarked a black clergyman; all told over 150 persons were killed, among them black leaders and Jewish merchant Samuel Fleischman, resented for his Republican views and for dealing fairly with black customers.

Nowhere did the Klan achieve greater power than in a group of Piedmont South Carolina counties where medium-size farms predominated and the races were about equal in number. An outbreak of terror followed the October 1870 elections, in which Republicans retained a tenuous hold on power in the region. In York County, nearly the entire white male population joined the Klan and committed at least eleven murders and hundreds of whippings; by February 1871 thousands of blacks had taken to the woods each night to avoid assault. The victims included a black militia leader, found hanging from a tree in March with a note pinned to his breast, "Jim Williams on his big muster."

Some historians attribute the Klan's sadistic campaign of terror to the fears and prejudices of poorer whites. The evidence, however, contradicts such an interpretation. Ordinary farmers and laborers comprised the bulk of the membership, and energetic "young bloods" were more likely to conduct midnight raids than middle-aged planters and lawyers, but "respectable citizens" chose the targets and often participated in the brutality. Among his sixty-five Klan assailants, Georgia black legislator Abram Colby identified men "not worth the bread they eat," but also some of the "first-class men in our town," including a lawyer and a physician.

Personal experience led blacks to blame the South's "aristocratic classes" for violence, and with good reason, for the Klan's leadership included planters, merchants, lawyers, and even ministers. When the Knights of the White Camelia initiated Samuel Chester in Arkansas, the pastor of his church administered the oath and the participants included Presbyterian deacons and elders "and every important member of the community." As the Rutherford *Star* remarked, the Klan was "not a gang of *poor trash*, as the leading Democrats would have us believe, but men of property . . . respectable citizens."

Many "respectable citizens," of course, had no connection with the violence, and a few spoke out manfully against it. When the son of former North Carolina Chief Justice Thomas Ruffin joined the Klan, his father dashed off a stinging rebuke: "I am satisfied that such associations [are] . . . dangerous to the community, and highly immoral. . . . It is wrong—all wrong, my son, and I beg you to have nothing to do with it." Yet even Ruffin said nothing in public. Indeed, the silence of the most prominent white Southerners spoke volumes of what Maj. Lewis Merrill, who investigated the Klan in York County, South Carolina, called "the demoralization of public opinion." Rather than dissociate themselves from the campaign of terror, prominent Democrats either minimized the Klan's activities or offered thinly disguised rationalizations for them. Some denied the organization's existence altogether, dismissing reports of violence as electoral propaganda from a Republican "slander mill." Others characterized the victims as thieves, adulterers, or men of "bad character" who deserved their fate.

Much Klan activity took place in those Democratic counties where local officials either belonged to the organization or protected it. Even in Republican areas, however, the law was paralyzed. When sheriffs overcame fear of violence and arrested suspects, witnesses proved reluctant to testify and Klansmen perjured themselves to provide one another with alibis. Community support extended far beyond the Klan's actual membership, embracing the numerous Southern women who sewed costumes and disguises for night riders, and those unconnected with the Klan who still seemed to view violence against blacks as something less than a crime.

Occasionally, organized groups successfully confronted the Klan. White Union Army veterans in mountainous Blount County, Alabama, organized "the anti–Ku Klux," which ended violence by threatening Klansmen with reprisal unless they stopped whipping Unionists and burning black churches and schools. Armed blacks patrolled the streets of Bennettsville, South Carolina, to prevent Klan assaults. The scale of violence, however, dwarfed these efforts at extralegal reprisal. Indeed, many Northerners wondered aloud, in an accusatory tone, how Republican communities allowed themselves to be terrorized by violent bands. Some found an answer in the legacy of slavery. "The colored men . . . ," declared Congressman Jeremiah Haralson, who had known bondage until 1865, "are afraid of the white men. He has been raised to be afraid of them."

It is indeed true that slavery, which gave rise to numerous forms of black resistance, did not produce a broad tradition of violent retaliation against abuse. But the failure of nerve, if such it was, extended up and down the Republican hierarchy and was not confined to one race. Perhaps the problem was that Republicans, black and white, took democratic processes more seriously than their opponents. No Republicans rode at night to murder their political foes, nor did armed bands seek to drive Democrats from the polls. "We could burn their churches and schoolhouses but we don't want to break the law or harm anybody," wrote one black from a violence-torn part of Georgia. "All we want is to live under the law."

The practical obstacles to armed resistance were immense. Many rural freedmen owned firearms, but these were generally shotguns, much inferior to the "first-class weapons" like Winchester rifles and six-shooters in the hands of the Klan. Although many had served in the Union Army, blacks with military experience were far outnumbered in a region where virtually every white male had been trained to bear arms. The specter of armed blacks taking the law into their own hands was certain to enrage the white community and produce a further escalation of violence. "It would be annihilation to the negroes if they should undertake such a thing," commented a white Republican official in Alabama. His appraisal was borne out in

Louisiana in 1873. The election of 1872 produced rival claimants for the governorship, a situation paralleled in localities throughout the state. In Grant Parish, freedmen who feared Democrats would seize the government cordoned off the county seat of Colfax and began drilling and digging trenches under the command of black veterans and militia officers. They held the tiny town for three weeks; on Easter Sunday, whites armed with rifles and a small cannon overpowered the defenders and an indiscriminate slaughter followed, including the massacre of some fifty blacks who laid down their arms under a white flag of surrender. Two whites also died. The Colfax Massacre was the bloodiest single instance of racial carnage in the Reconstruction era. Among blacks, it confirmed that in any large confrontation they stood at a fatal disadvantage.

Ultimately, of course, the responsibility for suppressing crime rests not with the victim, but with the state. "Put on your iron gloves," one Northerner advised Southern Republicans. And on paper, the new governments did take decisive steps, outlawing going about in disguise, raising the penalties for assault, murder, and conspiracy, authorizing ordinary citizens to arrest Klan members, sometimes even requiring counties to pay damages to citizens whose rights were abridged or property destroyed by a mob. Yet when it came to enforcing these laws, Republican leaders vacillated. Deep South governors had little confidence in the freedmen's prospects when confronting well-trained Confederate veterans and feared the arming of a black militia would inaugurate all-out racial warfare. Such a step, moreover, was certain to destroy efforts to attract white support and demonstrate the Republican party's moderation.

If Deep South governors sought stability through conciliation, those able to draw on large populations of white Republicans took decisive action. Gov. William G. Brownlow recruited a militia, manned largely by East Tennessee Unionists, and early in 1869 declared martial law in nine violence-plagued counties, a step that led to a drastic curtailment of Klan activities. Gov. Powell Clayton placed ten Arkansas counties under martial law at the end of 1868 and dispatched state militia units composed of blacks and scalawags. Scores of suspected Klansmen were arrested; three were executed after trials by military courts, and numerous others fled the state. By early 1869, order had been restored and the Klan destroyed. Texas Gov. Edmund J. Davis proved equally decisive, organizing a crack two-hundred-member state police, forty percent of whose members were black. Between 1870 and 1872, the police made over 6,000 arrests, effectively suppressing the Klan and providing freedmen with a real measure of protection in a state notorious for widespread violence.

As Clayton and Davis demonstrated, a government willing to suspend normal legal processes and employ armed force could mount an effective response to the Klan. But as many a modern government has discovered, the suspension of constitutional rights carries its own risks, especially the possibility of transforming perpetrators of violence from criminals into victims in the eyes of citizens who sympathize with their motives, if not their methods. Nowhere was this dilemma more apparent than in North Carolina, where Gov. William W. Holden's use of the militia provoked a reaction that brought down his administration. In 1870, the governor dispatched white militia units raised in the western North Carolina mountains to Caswell and Alamance counties, under the command of former Union Army officer George W. Kirk. About 100 men were arrested, and although the state constitution did not authorize the governor to declare martial law, Holden suspended the Klan-controlled local courts, ordered the prisoners tried before a military commission, and refused to honor a writ of habeas corpus issued by the state's chief justice. Ironically, Democrats then appealed to the federal courts under the Habeas Corpus Act of 1867, originally enacted to protect blacks and white Unionists. Holden was forced to release the captives, and the campaign against the Klan collapsed. The affair provided a bonanza for Holden's opponents, and in the 1870 legislative elections, which occurred amid the furor over habeas corpus, Democrats swept to victory. It was an inglorious end to his long, erratic political career and to Reconstruction in a state where its prospects had once appeared so bright.

In other ways as well, violence had a profound effect on Reconstruction politics. For the Klan devastated many local Republican organizations. By 1871, the party in numerous locales was "scattered and beaten and run out." No party, North or South, commented Adelbert Ames, could see hundreds of its "best and most reliable workers" murdered and still "retain its vigor." Indeed, the black community was more vulnerable to the destruction of its political infrastructure by violence than the white. Local leaders played such a variety of roles in schools, churches, and fraternal organizations that the killing or exiling of one man affected many institutions at once. And for a largely illiterate constituency in which political information circulated orally rather than through newspapers or pamphlets, local leaders were bridges to the larger world of politics, indispensable sources of political intelligence and guidance. Republican officials, black and white, epitomized the revolution that seemed to have put the bottom rail on top. Their murder or exile inevitably had a demoralizing impact on their communities.

The issue of violence transcended all divisions within the black community, uniting rich and poor, free and freed, in calls for drastic governmental action to restore order. To blacks, indeed, the violence seemed an irrefutable denial of the white South's much-trumpeted claims to superior morality and higher civilization. "Pray tell me," asked Robert B. Elliott, "who is the barbarian here?"

Most of all, violence raised in its starkest form the question of legitimacy that haunted the Reconstruction state. Indeed, as a former Confederate officer shrewdly observed, it was precisely the Klan's objective "to defy the reconstructed State Governments, to treat them with contempt, and show that they have no real existence." The effective exercise of power, of course, can command respect if not spontaneous loyalty. But only in a few instances had Republican governments found the will to exert this kind of force. As Klan activity escalated after the 1870 elections, Southern Republicans once again turned to Washington for salvation.

"Power from Without"

The President forced to cope with Southern violence had been elected on the slogan "Let Us Have Peace." While Ulysses S. Grant had clearly identified himself with Republican Reconstruction policies, no one could be certain what attitude toward the South would characterize his administration. For Grant's election both confirmed the "finality" of Southern Reconstruction and suggested that the slavery controversy had at last been settled. Even as he assumed office, what one Republican called "the vexed question of suffrage" appeared to have been laid to rest. In February 1869 Congress approved the Fifteenth Amendment, prohibiting the federal and state governments from depriving any citizen of the vote on racial grounds. A little over a year later, it became part of the Constitution.

To Democrats, the Fifteenth Amendment seemed "the most revolutionary measure" ever to receive Congressional sanction, the "crowning" act of a Radical conspiracy to promote black equality and transform America from a confederation of states into a centralized nation. Yet while clothing black suffrage with constitutional sanction, the Amendment said nothing about the right to hold office and did not forbid literacy, property, and educational tests that, while nonracial, might effectively exclude the majority of blacks from the polls. Unlike the Fourteenth Amendment, with its universalist language, the Fifteenth failed to expand the definition of citizenship for all Americans. Congress had rejected a far more sweeping proposal barring discrimination in suffrage and officeholding based on "race, color, nativity, property, education, or religious beliefs." "The whole question of suffrage," declared one Senator, "subject to the restriction that there shall be no discrimination on account of race, is left as it now is."

Thus, remarked Henry Adams, the Fifteenth Amendment was "more remarkable for what it does not than for what it does contain." The failure to guarantee blacks' right to hold office arose from fear that such a provision would jeopardize the prospects of ratification in the North. More significant, Congress rejected suffrage provisions that "covered the white man" as well as the black. Southern Republicans, joined by many Northern Radicals, feared that a blanket guarantee of the right to vote would void the disenfranchisement of "rebels." Equally important, Northern states wished to retain their own suffrage qualifications. In the West, the Chinese could not vote; if the Fifteenth Amendment altered this situation, noted California's Republican Sen. Cornelius Cole, it would "kill our party as dead as a stone." Pennsylvania demanded the payment of state taxes to vote; Rhode Island required foreign-born citizens to own $134 worth of real estate; Massachusetts and Connecticut insisted on literacy. Indeed, the Northern states during Reconstruction actually abridged the right to vote more extensively than did the Southern. Ironically, it was not a limited commitment to blacks' rights, but the desire to retain inequalities affecting whites, that produced a Fifteenth Amendment that opened the door to poll taxes, literacy tests, and property qualifications.

And, of course, proponents of both a "strong" and "weak" Fifteenth Amendment ignored the claims of women. To feminists like Elizabeth Cady Stanton and Susan B. Anthony, the Amendment added to the numerous "humiliations" Republicans had inflicted on their cause. Rejecting the idea that the Constitution should prohibit racial discrimination in voting while countenancing disabilities based on sex, they opposed ratification, dealing a final blow to the old abolitionist-feminist alliance. As her regard for her erstwhile allies waned, Stanton increasingly voiced racist and elitist arguments for rejecting the enfranchisement of black males while women of culture and wealth remained excluded. "Think of Patrick and Sambo and Hans and Ung Tung," she wrote, "who do not know the difference between a Monarchy and a Republic, who never read the Declaration of Independence . . . making laws for Lydia Maria Child, Lucretia Mott, or Fanny Kemble." In May 1869 the annual meeting of the Equal Rights Association, an organization devoted to both black and female suffrage, dissolved in acrimony. Out of the wreckage emerged rival national organizations: Stanton and Anthony's National Woman Suffrage Association, an embodiment of independent feminism, and the American Woman Suffrage Association, still linked to older reform traditions.

Most reformers, nonetheless, hailed the Fifteenth Amendment as a triumphant conclusion to four decades of agitation on behalf of the slave. "Nothing in all history," exulted William Lloyd Garrison, equaled "this wonderful, quiet, sudden transformation of four millions of human beings from . . . the auction-block to the ballot-box." In March 1870 the American Anti-Slavery Society disbanded, its work, members believed, now complete. Yet amid the blaze of celebration, a few voices of caution were raised. Wendell Phillips warned that the "long crusade" had not really ended, for as victims of "cruel prejudice" and "accumulated wrongs," the freedmen would continue to deserve the nation's "special sympathy." Even among reformers, however, this view came under attack. For their own benefit, said Thomas Wentworth Higginson, who had assisted John Brown and commanded black troops, the freedmen "should not continue to be kept wards of the nation."

Such opinions acquired increasing prominence in Republican circles. Even as they inscribed black suffrage in the Constitution, many party spokesmen believed the troublesome "Negro question" had at last been removed from national politics. With their civil and political equality assured, blacks no longer possessed a claim on the federal government; the competitive rules of the free market would determine their station in society. "The negro is now a voter and a citizen," declared an Illinois newspaper. "Let him hereafter take his chances in the battle of life."

Like all great social and political transformations, the Second American Revolution had arrived at a period of consolidation. Increasingly, Northern public opinion turned to other questions. Letters received by Republican Congressmen concentrated on economic issues like the currency, taxation, and internal improvements. Nor did the party's Southern wing inspire much fraternal concern in the North. Lacking strong support from the local business community, Southern Republicans were forced to rely on outside aid to finance newspapers and conduct campaigns. They found little forthcoming. Generally, the national party ignored Southern state organizations and local campaigns, and even when the Presidency was at stake, few experienced speakers ventured south and little money was dispatched by the Republican National Committee.

In Washington, Southern Republicans found themselves treated less as objects of special concern than as poor relations, an embarrassing presence. Northerners had grown "tired of this word reconstruction," one Senator told a South Carolina Congressman. Southerners received few important committee assignments and often found it difficult to obtain the floor to deliver speeches. Because Northerners controlled the key legislative posts and continued to view the South as a land of "rebels" undeserving of federal largesse, Southern Republicans could not obtain a fair share of spending. Of funds allocated for internal improvements by the Forty-First Congress, the entire South received only fifteen percent, mostly, complained Mississippi Congressman George McKee, aid to railroads controlled by "northern capitalists."

Nearly all Republicans still believed Reconstruction must be defended. But they showed little interest in promoting further change in the South. A bill establishing a national land commission, introduced by black Congressman Benjamin Turner with a moving speech about the plight of former slaves whose labor had enriched the nation but who "have consumed less of [its] substance . . . than any other class of people," never even came to a vote. Republicans also proved reluctant to promote the state's expansion into new realms. Measured by the magnitude of the federal budget, the size of the bureaucracy, and the number of bills brought before Congress, the scope of national authority far exceeded antebellum levels. Yet even among Republicans, doubts about the activist state persisted. Proposals for a national Bureau of Health, a federal railroad commission, a federal role in promoting public education, and the nationalization of the telegraph industry all died in Congress. As Georgia scalawag Amos T. Akerman shrewdly noted, while the postwar amendments had made the government "more national in theory," he had observed, "even among Republicans, a hesitation to exercise the powers to redress wrongs in the states." Yet just as the intransigence of Andrew Johnson and his Southern governments had helped to radicalize Congress in 1866, the Ku Klux Klan's campaign of terror propelled Republicans to intervene in Southern affairs. "If that is the only alternative," declared John Sherman, "I am willing to . . . again appeal to the power of the nation to crush, as we once before have done, this organized civil war."

In 1870 and 1871, Congress enacted a series of Enforcement Acts to counteract terrorist violence. They forbade state officials to discriminate among voters on the basis of race and authorized the President to appoint election supervisors with the power to bring to federal court cases of election fraud, the bribery or intimidation of voters, and conspiracies to prevent citizens from exercising their constitutional rights. The most sweeping measure, the Ku Klux Klan Act of April 1871, for the first time brought certain crimes committed by individuals under federal law. Conspiracies to deny citizens the right to vote, hold office, serve on juries, and enjoy the equal protection of the laws could now, if states failed to act effectively against them, be prosecuted by federal district attorneys and even lead to military intervention and the suspension of habeas corpus.

The Ku Klux Klan Act pushed Republicans to the outer limits of constitutional change. The Civil Rights Act and postwar amendments, designed largely to protect freedmen against hostile state actions, had left private criminal acts under the authority of local law enforcement officials. Now, in making violence infringing civil and political rights a federal crime punishable by the national state, Congress "moved tentatively into modern times." "These are momentous changes . . . ," observed *The Nation*. "They not only increase the power of the central government, but they arm it with jurisdiction over a class of cases of which it has never hitherto had, and never pretended to have, any jurisdiction whatever."

Republicans justified the Enforcement Acts by appealing to the vastly expanded national authority originating in the Civil War and embodied in the postwar amendments. "If the Federal Government," asked Benjamin F. Butler, "cannot pass laws to protect the rights, liberty, and lives of citizens of the United States in the States, why were guarantees of those fundamental rights put in the Constitution at all?" Democrats denounced the laws as Force Acts, dire threats to individual freedom. But one person's force may spell another's liberty. With terror rampant in large parts of the South, black Congressmen evinced little interest in abstract debates about the Constitution. "I desire that so broad and liberal a construction be placed upon its provisions," declared Joseph Rainey, "as will insure protection to the humblest citizen. Tell me nothing of a constitution which fails to shelter beneath its rightful power the people of a country."

Although, under the Enforcement Acts, aggrieved individuals could sue their assailants, it fell to the federal government to suppress violence. Overseeing enforcement were two representatives of Southern Republicanism: Amos T. Akerman, a New Hampshire–born lawyer long resident in Georgia, who had assumed the attorney generalship in mid-1870, and Solicitor General Benjamin H. Bristow, a Union Army veteran from Kentucky. Both insisted on vigorous implementation of the new laws. At their disposal stood the recently established Department of Justice and an array of federal marshals and district attorneys.

Despite a limited budget, difficulties in securing evidence, the reluctance of some victims to testify, and the fact that defendants employed talented and experienced lawyers to oppose the overworked district attorneys, the prosecution of accused Klansmen began in earnest in 1871. Hundreds of men were indicted in North Carolina, where federal troops helped apprehend suspects. Many ended up in prison, including Rutherford County Klan leader Randolph Shotwell, who served two years in an Albany, New York, penitentiary. United States Attorney G. Wiley Wells secured nearly 700 indictments in Mississippi. Only in South Carolina did the military provisions of the Enforcement Acts come into play. Grant in October 1871 proclaimed a "condition of lawlessness" in nine upcountry counties and suspended the writ of habeas corpus. Federal troops occupied the region, making hundreds of arrests, and perhaps 2,000 Klansmen fled the state. Personally directing the government's legal strategy, the Attorney General allowed those who confessed and identified the organization's leaders to escape without punishment, while trying a few dozen of the worst offenders before predominantly black juries. Most of those indicted eventually pleaded guilty and received prison sentences.

The trials of 1871, culminating in military action against the South Carolina Klan, represented a dramatic departure for the Grant administration, which had previously launched few initiatives in Southern policy. Much of the credit belongs to Akerman, who was deeply affected by the evidence that unfolded. "Though rejoiced at the suppression of KuKluxery even in one neighborhood," he wrote, "I feel greatly saddened by this business. It has revealed a perversion of moral sentiment among the Southern whites which bodes ill to that part of the country for this generation." Akerman embarked on a personal crusade to make known the full horror of Southern violence, lecturing in the North and unsettling Cabinet meetings with accounts of Klan atrocities. Not all of Grant's advisers shared his preoccupation. The Attorney General, complained Secretary of State Hamilton Fish, had the Klan "on the brain. . . . It has got to be a bore to listen twice a week to this thing."

Judged by the percentage of Klansmen actually indicted and convicted, the fruits of "enforcement" seem small indeed, a few hundred men among thousands guilty of heinous crimes. But in restoring order, reinvigorating the morale of Southern Republicans, and enabling blacks to exercise their rights as citizens, the policy proved a success. By 1872, the federal government's willingness to bring its legal and coercive authority to bear had broken the Klan's back and produced a dramatic decline in violence throughout the South.

So ended the Reconstruction career of the Ku Klux Klan, certainly one of the most ignoble chapters in all of American history. National power had achieved what most Southern governments had been unable, and Southern white public opinion unwilling, to accomplish: acquiescence in the rule of law. Yet the need for outside intervention was a humiliating confession of weakness for the Reconstruction regimes. "The Enforcement Act," wrote a Mississippi Republican, "has a potency derived alone from its source; no such law could be enforced by state authority, the local power being too weak." The outcome further reinforced Southern Republicans' tendency to look to Washington for protection. Only *"steady, unswerving power from without,*" believed carpetbagger Albert T. Morgan, could ensure the permanence of Reconstruction. Whether in the future such power would be forthcoming depended not only on events in the South, but on how the North responded to its own experience of Reconstruction.

The Reconstruction of the North

Like the South, the victorious North experienced a social transformation after the Civil War. And if the North's reconstruction proved less revolutionary than the South's, the process of change catalyzed by the war continued to accelerate in peacetime. Evidence abounded of the consolidation of the capitalist economy: a manufacturing boom, the spread of new forms of industrial organization, the completion of the railroad network, and the opening of the Trans-Mississippi West to mining, lumbering, ranching, and commercial farming. The North's social structure, like the South's, was altered in these years. An increasingly powerful class of industrialists and railroad entrepreneurs took its place alongside the older commercial elite; the number of professionals and white-collar workers grew dramatically; and the wage-earner irrevocably supplanted the independent craftsman as the typical worker. Returning from England in 1868, Charles Francis Adams and his family were stunned by the triumph of the new industrial economy over one centered on agriculture and artisanship: "Had they been Tyrian traders of the year B.C. 1000, landing from a galley fresh from Gibraltar, they could hardly have been stranger on the shore of a world, so changed from what it had been ten years before." As in the South, moreover, economic and social change produced new demands on the state and altered the terms of political debate and modes of party organization. From labor relations to party politics to attitudes toward the postwar South, no aspect of life remained unaffected by the reconstruction of the North.

The North and the Age of Capital

The war-inspired economic boom slackened only momentarily with the coming of peace, and manufacturing output quickly resumed its relentless upward course. By 1873, the nation's industrial production stood seventy-five percent above its 1865 level, a figure all the more remarkable in view of the South's economic stagnation. In the same eight years, three million immigrants entered the country, nearly all destined for the North and West, their labor fueling the rapid growth of metropolitan centers like New York and smaller industrial cities from Paterson to Milwaukee. By 1873, with the United States second only to Britain in manufacturing production and the number of farmers outstripped by nonagricultural workers, the North had irrevocably entered the industrial age.

If the cotton mill symbolized the early industrial revolution, the railroad epitomized the maturing capitalist order. Between 1865 and 1873, 35,000 miles of track were laid, a figure that exceeded the entire rail network of 1860. Railroads opened vast new areas to commercial farming and helped cities like Chicago and Kansas City extend their economic sway over agricultural hinterlands. Their voracious appetite for funds absorbed much of the nation's investment capital, contributed to the development of banking, and facilitated the further concentration of the nation's capital market in Wall Street. As significant as the completion of the railroad system, however, was its coordination and consolidation, as large trunk lines, controlled by Eastern capitalists, increasingly absorbed smaller companies. Under the aggressive leadership of Thomas A. Scott, the Pennsylvania Railroad, the nation's largest corporation, forged an economic empire that stretched across the continent and included coal mines and oceangoing steamships. Only two nations in the world, Britain and France, possessed more track than the Pennsylvania's 6,000 miles. For such freewheeling entrepreneurs as Collis P. Huntington, James J. Hill, and Jay Gould, railroads created opportunities for unheard-of wealth. For other Americans, the railroad acted as a nationalizing force, sharply reducing transportation costs and establishing a vast national market that, within a quarter century, helped make the United States the world's preeminent industrial nation.

Nowhere did capitalism penetrate more rapidly or dramatically than in the Trans-Mississippi West. At the close of the Civil War, the frontier of settlement was just across the Mississippi River. Beyond lay millions of acres of fertile and mineral-rich land roamed by immense buffalo herds that provided food, clothing, and shelter for a population of perhaps a quarter of a million Indians. By the time Grant left office, railroads traversed the Great Plains, farmers and cattlemen had replaced the buffalo, most Indians had been concentrated on reservations, and, although warfare did not end until the massacre of the Sioux at Wounded Knee in 1890, the world of the Plains Indians had come to an end. Even as the South struggled with the problems of recovery, a new agricultural empire arose in Minnesota, the Dakotas, Nebraska, and Kansas, whose population grew from 300,000 in 1860 to well over 2 million twenty years later.

The West, however, was more than an agrarian empire. Around the Great Lakes and in the Ohio Valley arose new mining and industrial complexes geared to processing the farmer's expanding output and meeting the railroad's enormous demand for machinery, coal, and iron products. The most startling growth occurred in Chicago, which dominated the region's grain, meat, and lumber trades and emerged as a major rail and industrial center, the home of iron and steel mills, farm machinery factories, and meat-packing plants. Throughout the West, highly capitalized corporate enterprises appeared with remarkable rapidity. The Wisconsin and Michigan lumber industry, dominated by small-scale producers in 1860, came under the control of Eastern-financed corporations that engrossed immense tracts of forest, constructed sawmills whose output far exceeded anything known before the war, and employed armies of loggers. Western mining increasingly fell under the sway of corporations that mobilized Eastern and European capital to introduce the most advanced technology and replace the independent prospector with wage-earning deep-shaft miners.

As in the South, the North's political structure was ill-equipped to deal with the enormous demands on the resources of the state and the new opportunities for corruption created by the soaring capitalist economy. "The galleries and lobbies of every Legislature . . . ," observed an Illinois Republican leader, "are thronged with men seeking to procure an advantage" for one corporation or another. But it was in the West that a "politics of development" akin to that of the Reconstruction South emerged most dramatically, with railroad, lumber, and mining companies exerting inordinate influence on government policy. Under Gov. Samuel J. Crawford, a lawyer associated with the Union Pacific, the Kansas legislature consigned hundreds of thousands of acres of public land to the state's railroads. In Wisconsin, many legislators held stock or directorships in state-aided lumber companies and railroads. Lobbyists thronged the statehouse; "the worst traits of the human character are brought out by them," observed Gov. Cadwallader C. Washburn, "and to see the majority of our legislators struggling for the grab . . . is humiliating."

The growing connection of Republican leaders with business corporations seemed even more apparent in Washington. Even officials of unimpeachable integrity felt comfortable with arrangements that today seem egregious conflicts of interest. Sen. Lyman Trumbull, for example, accepted an annual retainer from the Illinois Central Railroad. Less scrupulous lawmakers enriched themselves by serving companies allied with their party. The Central Pacific rewarded Sen. William M. Stewart of Nevada with 50,000 acres of land for his services on the Committee on the Pacific Railroad. Banker Jay Cooke, the "financier of the Civil War" and leading individual contributor to Grant's presidential campaigns, took a mortgage on Speaker of the House James G. Blaine's Washington home, sold a valuable piece of Duluth land to Ohio Gov. Rutherford B. Hayes at "a great bargain," and employed as lobbyists such out-of-office politicos as Benjamin Wade and Ignatius Donnelly.

Like the states, the federal government proved remarkably solicitous of the interests of the railroads and other corporations. The National Mineral Act of 1866 dispensed millions of acres of mineral-rich public land to mining companies free of charge. Between 1862 and 1872, the government awarded over 100 million acres of land and millions of dollars to support railroad construction, mostly to finance the transcontinental lines chartered during and after the Civil War. Blacks could not but note the contrast between such largesse and the failure to provide the freedmen with land. Why, asked freedman Anthony Wayne, "whilst Congress appropriated land by the million acres to pet railroad schemes . . . did they not aid poor Anthony and his people starving and in rags?" No one offered an answer.

As in the Reconstruction South, much of the Grant era's corruption stemmed from government promotion of railroad development. The most notorious example involved Crédit Mobilier, a dummy corporation formed by an inner ring of Union Pacific stockholders to build the government-assisted line at an exorbitant profit, an arrangement protected by distributing Crédit Mobilier shares to influential Congressmen. After a newspaper broke the story, a Congressional investigation resulted in the expulsion of two members and damaged the reputations of numerous other public officials, including House Speaker Blaine and Grant's Vice Presidents Schuyler Colfax and Henry Wilson.

It would be wrong, however, to accuse every lawmaker of malfeasance or to assume that corporate lobbying and political corruption fully explained the remarkable governmental generosity of what Mark Twain called America's Gilded Age. More significant was the widespread belief in the social benefits and political advantages of capitalist development. Despite their growing power, moreover, the new corporations joined many other groups struggling to use the state to advance their own interests. As in the South, social change profoundly affected Northern politics and government. The state became a battleground not only for entrepreneurs seeking economic advantage, but also for Radicals, blacks, and women hoping to extend northward government-promoted social and racial reconstruction, for farmers and workers bent on redressing inequities caused by capitalism's rapid expansion, and for a newly self-conscious intelligentsia determined to redefine the meaning of "reform."

The Transformation of Politics

In some respects, changes in Northern public authority paralleled those in the South. State governments assumed greater responsibility for public health, welfare, and education, and cities invested heavily in park construction and improved water and gas services. Government activism flourished where Republicans enjoyed secure majorities or Radicals dominated the party. Massachusetts, where a tight-knit cadre of Radicals controlled Republican politics throughout the 1860s, established state boards of public charities and public health and a state constabulary. Michigan Republicans expanded state facilities for homeless children and the insane, deaf, and blind; they established a board of health, made school attendance compulsory for the first time, outlawed cruelty to animals, and created a metropolitan police board for Democratic Detroit.

Under Radical Gov. Reuben Fenton, New York enacted the North's most ambitious reform program. Between 1865 and 1867, the legislature established eight new teacher-training colleges, created the state's first Board of Charities, eliminated fees for common schooling, and set minimum housing standards for New York City. A professional fire department replaced the city's notoriously inefficient volunteer companies, and the legislature created a new Board of Health, one of the few administrative agencies of the period with the power to enforce its regulations. Coupled with aid to corporations, such initiatives produced a rapid increase in state and city budgets, debts, and tax rates. But unlike the South, the North's ability to pay taxes—its aggregate wealth and per capita income—was also rising.

Republicans also took steps to improve the lot of Northern blacks. The party drew few benefits from efforts to combat racial discrimination, for white voters alienated by such a policy were likely to outnumber the tiny black population. Rather, the drive for civil and political equality arose from Radical ideology, the course of Reconstruction politics, and the agitation of black churches, newspapers, and state conventions that demanded the repeal of discriminatory laws, access to schools and streetcars, and an extension of Reconstruction's democratic revolution to the North.

A combination of Congressional measures and actions at the state and local level produced astonishing advances in the rights of Northern blacks. The Civil Rights Act of 1866 and postwar amendments voided laws barring blacks from entering Northern states, testifying in court, and voting, and were employed by individuals pressing damage claims against railroads and streetcars that denied them equal access. Pennsylvania's legislature prohibited streetcar segregation in 1867, and New York Republicans six years later enacted a pioneering civil rights law that outlawed discrimination in public accommodations. Blacks also gained access to public schools in states that had previously made no provision for their education. In a few states, integrated education now became the norm. Michigan's legislature outlawed school segregation in 1867, and the state university admitted its first black students in 1868. And Iowa's Supreme Court ruled separate schooling a violation of the Fourteenth Amendment.

Despite the toppling of these barriers, racial Reconstruction proved less far-reaching than in the South. Most Northern blacks remained trapped in inferior housing and menial and unskilled jobs (and even here their foothold, challenged by the continuing influx of European immigrants and discrimination by employers and unions alike, became increasingly precarious). An 1871 survey of New York City's black community identified some 400 waiters and 500 long-shoremen, but only two physicians and a handful of skilled crafts-men. Black politicians in the North lacked a viable strategy for addressing their community's economic plight. Perhaps this was inevitable for a group representing barely two percent of the North's population. Nonetheless, blacks now found public life open to them in ways inconceivable before the war. Their claim to political rights had become so much a part of what it meant to be a Republican that ninety percent of the party's voters in New York State supported equal suffrage in an unsuccessful 1869 referendum.

With blacks' enfranchisement, women remained "the only class of citizens wholly unrepresented in the government." And despite the disintegration of the abolitionist-feminist alliance in disputes over the postwar amendments, a broadly based movement pressed for an end to restrictions on women's social and legal rights. The vote remained central to feminist thinking, for it promised to give women equal standing in public life, overturn the ideology that defined the home as women's sphere, and empower them to address politically their other grievances.

"If I were to give free vent to all my pent-up wrath concerning the subordination of women," Lydia Maria Child wrote Charles Sumner in 1872, "I might frighten *you*. . . . Suffice it, therefore, to say, either the theory of our government is *false*, or women have a right to vote." Child's bitterness was not uncommon among nineteenth-century women, and her logic was irrefutable. But even in Radical Massachusetts, the issue split the party. Although Gov. William Claflin supported suffrage, the 1871 party convention sidestepped the question—noting only that it "deserves the most careful and respectful attention"—and a constitutional amendment failed in the legislature. The same fate befell proposals in Iowa and Maine, and when staunchly Republican Michigan held a referendum in 1874, women's suffrage suffered a decisive defeat.

If the women's suffrage agitation exposed Republicans' reluctance to carry equal rights to its logical conclusion, the political demands of economically aggrieved Northerners confronted the party with different problems. Especially in the West, railroad expansion provoked growing protest. Commercial farmers complained of exorbitant freight rates, favoritism for large shippers, and the high price of manufactured goods. River and lake ports resented being bypassed, and even Chicago merchants contended that they suffered discriminatory freight charges and high fees in railroad-controlled warehouses. To all these groups, the railroad increasingly seemed an alien, intrusive force that disrupted traditional economic arrangements and channels of commerce and threatened the independence of individuals and local communities. One response was the rapid spread in the upper Mississippi Valley of the Patrons of Husbandry, or Grange, which moved to establish cooperatives to circumvent exploitative middlemen and "*compel* the carriers to take our produce at a fair price." Although officially nonpartisan, Grange members quickly turned to politics, demanding that the activist state that had lavished aid upon corporations now redress the imbalances caused by the capitalist economy's rapid growth. The best-known and most controversial response, the Illinois Board of Railroad and Warehouse Commissioners, embodied a broad definition of state regulatory powers, for the legislature empowered it to eliminate rate discrimination, establish maximum charges, and enforce its decisions. A legal challenge by railroads and warehouse operators produced the landmark 1877 Supreme Court ruling in *Munn v. Illinois*, upholding the state's power to regulate businesses of a quasi-public character.

Even more thorny political and ideological questions arose from the North's revived labor movement. Although workers divided along lines of craft, skill, ethnicity, and religion, a sense of unity arose from aspects of economic life that nearly all laborers (and many other Americans) found alarming. Despite widespread prosperity, the unprecedented fortunes accumulated by the captains of commerce and industry helped produce unheard-of inequalities of income. The inexorable tendency toward the mechanization of industry and a larger scale of production transformed skilled craftsmen into "tenders of machinery" and threatened to entrench within American life what *The Nation* called "the great curse of the Old World—the division of society into classes." Massachusetts industry, Edward Atkinson had noted during the Civil War, stood "in a transition state, changing from transient help, farmer's daughters, etc. working for a few years and living in boarding houses, to a permanent factory population." By 1870, the same tendency was evident in the West. In Cincinnati, for example, a few large factories employed as many workers as the city's thousands of small shops. All this raised troubling questions about the continued validity of free labor axioms: that liberty rested on ownership of productive property, and that working for wages was merely a temporary resting place on the road to economic autonomy.

When the labor question entered the political arena, it produced alignments quite unlike those of Reconstruction. In Congress, George W. Julian's bill to establish an eight-hour day for federal employees brought together an unusual coalition of Northern Democrats, many representing urban working-class constituencies, and Radical Republicans accustomed to using the democratic state for reform purposes. The bill became law in 1868, after Radicals and Democrats defeated John Sherman's proposal for wage reductions to balance the cut in hours.

One Republican newspaper considered Radical support for the eight-hour bill perfectly natural, since labor and the Radicals shared a commitment to "the essential dignity of man" and "universal equality." At the state level, however, the issue proved more complicated, for while the federal law applied only to government-employed workers, state legislation would affect employees in private industry. The divisive potential of the labor question was strikingly illustrated in Massachusetts, the nation's most thoroughly industrialized state. Here, the labor movement and Radical Republicans shared common ground, for many union leaders had been influenced by abolitionism, and the Boston *Daily Evening Voice*, a labor journal, supported Congressional Reconstruction and urged unions to stop excluding blacks. For their part, many Massachusetts Radicals, including House Speaker James M. Stone, endorsed legislation to limit the working day, prohibit child labor, and ensure factory safety. Others, however, including Radical kingpin Francis W. Bird, insisted labor's demands violated the law of supply and demand and contradicted the very principle of free contract Republicans were attempting to introduce in the South. Dominated by Radicals, a succession of government commissions investigated the need for labor legislation, but all opposed state regulation of working hours as "subverting the right of individual property."

By questioning the equity of Northern labor relations, the labor movement raised fundamental questions for the free labor ideology. Like freedmen seeking land and Western farmers advocating regulation of the railroads, labor reformers pressured the Republican party to consider the realities of unequal economic power and widespread economic dependence and the state's responsibility for combating them. By itself, class conflict was not "the submerged shoal on which Radical dreams foundered"; Radical Republicanism, as we have seen, ran aground on the all too visible politics of race and Reconstruction. Yet what *The Nation* called the emerging "politics of class feeling" did weaken Radicalism by fostering a new kind of political leadership: nonideological power brokers in a contentious, pluralistic society.

The diversity of the claims upon postwar Northern state governments facilitated a shift within the Republican party from an ideological to an organizational politics. Especially after Grant's assumption of the Presidency defused the ideological crisis of the Johnson years and weakened Radical influence in Washington, state parties fell under the control of powerful Senators who saw government less as an instrument of reform than as a path to office and a vehicle for mediating the rival claims of the diverse economic and ethnic groups within Northern society. Although many of these Stalwarts had been active in the antislavery crusade, most had grown impatient with the ideological politics that had dominated the party. The organization, rather than the issues that had created it, commanded their highest loyalty.

Slowly, the political agenda shifted from Reconstruction to economic questions defined by shifting alliances along East-West, urban-rural, and occupational lines rather than Radical-moderate or even Democrat-Republican divisions. Nevertheless, the fact that Republicans divided on virtually every other question heightened the importance of the Civil War and Reconstruction as touchstones that served as a continuing definition of the party's identity. For some politicians, this meant cynically "waving the bloody shirt" at election time; for others, a genuine concern for the fate of Southern blacks endured. Thus, if the Southern question waned as an inspiration for far-reaching reform or a source of new policy initiatives, a commitment to Reconstruction remained a powerful rallying point for party leaders. Ironically, the rise of the Stalwarts did less to undermine Republican Southern policy than the emergence of an influential group of party reformers whose revolt against the new politics of the Grant era came to include the demand for an end to Reconstruction.

The Rise of Liberalism

By the end of Grant's first term, one disgruntled party leader complained, the "grand Republican organization" had "degenerated into thirty-seven Senatorial Cabals or 'Rings'," each monopolizing its state's share of federal patronage, and each unquestionably corrupt. And the new politics of the Gilded Age produced a growing call for reform. At reform's cutting edge stood a small but influential group of intellectuals, publicists, and professionals. Among their leading members were editors E. L. Godkin, Horace White, and Samuel Bowles, academic economists Francis Amasa Walker and David A. Wells, intellectually inclined businessmen Edward Atkinson and Isaac Sherman, and reform-minded politicians Carl Schurz and James A. Garfield. Mostly college graduates who resided in the urban Northeast or Western cities like Cincinnati and Chicago, these self-styled "best men" articulated a shared ideology and developed a sense of collective identity through organizations like the American Social Science Association and a network of influential journals, among them *The Nation, North American Review*, Springfield *Republican*, and Chicago *Tribune*. Their growing prominence reflected the coming of age of an American intelligentsia determined to make its mark on the politics of the Gilded Age.

Classical liberalism supplied the axioms of reformers' "financial science"—free trade, the law of supply and demand, and the gold standard. Limited government formed another pillar of reform faith, for state intervention in economic affairs fostered all the distasteful aspects of Gilded Age politics: bribery, high taxes, and public extravagance. "The Government," declared Godkin, "must get out of the 'protective' business and the 'subsidy' business and the 'improvement' and 'development' business. . . . It cannot touch them without breeding corruption."

In their own eyes, liberal reformers were disinterested spokesmen for the common good. Yet at the same time, the ideology of reform helped to crystallize a distinctive and increasingly conservative middle-class consciousness. "An ignorant proletariat and a half-taught plutocracy," wrote historian Francis Parkman, had "risen like spirits of darkness on our social and political horizon." Yet while the reformers railed against the railroad men and "iron and coal rings" whose actions distorted both marketplace and government, they seemed far more alarmed by a growing political danger from below. The "best men" responded to railroad regulation laws, strikes, and demands for eight-hour legislation with a violent counterattack. These "schemes for interference with property" violated the "eternal laws of political economy" by undermining the principle of supply and demand and employing government's coercive power in the interests of a single class of citizens.

Much of the degradation of Gilded Age politics, reformers believed, arose from the success of demagogues and spoilsmen who rose to power by playing upon the prejudices of working-class voters. New York's liberal reformers joined with a far larger number of businessmen, lawyers, financiers, and opposition politicians to overturn the Democratic machine of "Boss" William M. Tweed, which had plundered the city of tens of millions of dollars (the scale of its depredations dwarfed anything in the Reconstruction South). To the "best men," the Tweed Ring symbolized the symbiotic relationship among corruption, organizational politics, the political power of both railroad men and the urban working class, and the misuses of the state. For the Boss controlled city patronage, forged an alliance with railroad magnates Jim Fisk and Jay Gould, established close ties with labor unions, and fashioned an unofficial welfare system that used municipal funds to aid Catholic schools and provide food and fuel for the poor. To the reformers' annoyance, the exposure of Tweed's corruption failed to diminish his popularity among lower-class voters. Even more outrageous than Tweed, because he was a Republican, was Massachusetts Congressman Benjamin F. Butler, who flamboyantly supported causes that appalled reformers: the eight-hour day, inflation, and payment of the national debt in greenbacks. He further horrified respectable opinion by embracing women's suffrage, Irish nationalism, and the Paris Commune. "Butlerism" became a shorthand for a new kind of mass politics that had infused American public life with "the spirit of the European mob."

Clearly, liberal reform combined a moral creed, an emerging science of society, and the outcry of a middle-class intelligentsia alarmed by class conflict, the ascendancy of machine politics, and its own exclusion from power. Its emergence reflected a splintering of the Radical impulse that had flourished during the Civil War and early Reconstruction. Nearly all the reformers had been early advocates of emancipation and black suffrage. Yet if all Radicals agreed the state should embrace the principle of civil and political equality, liberals increasingly insisted it should do little else. As labor, farmers, and other groups of Northerners demanded new government-sponsored social and economic changes, the same liberal reformers who had once exalted the power of the activist state attacked "the fallacy of attempts to benefit humanity by legislation" and insisted that public authority was "by nature wasteful, corrupt, and dangerous." Many reformers abandoned democratic principles altogether, advocating educational and property qualifications for voting, especially in the nation's large cities, and an increase in the number of officials appointed rather than elected.

Civil service reform was the liberals' favored means of breaking the power of party machines and opening positions of responsibility to men like themselves. Beginning in 1865, Rhode Island Congressman Thomas Jenckes introduced proposals, modeled on British precedent, for a system of competitive examinations and permanent tenure in office for federal employees. Predictably, party leaders viewed the proposal as a threat to the lifeblood of their organizations. For their own reasons, they pointed out the antidemocratic implications of the plan. Life tenure, critics charged, would "establish an aristocracy of office-holders" insulated from the will of the people. The examination system, at a time when only a tiny percentage of Americans enjoyed access to a college education, would limit office to wealthy "dunce[s]" who had "crammed up to a diploma at Yale" but knew nothing of practical affairs.

Although they had supported, indeed helped to formulate, the Reconstruction Acts and postwar amendments, reformers became increasingly disenchanted with Reconstruction. Many saw the Southern question as an annoying distraction that enabled party spoilsmen to retain the allegiance of voters by waving the bloody shirt, while preventing tariff reduction, civil service reform, and good government from dominating political debate. Increasingly, Democratic criticisms of Southern government found a receptive audience among liberal reformers of the North. Like the Tweed Ring and Butlerism, Reconstruction underscored the dangers of unbridled democracy and the political incapacity of the lower orders. "Universal suffrage," wrote Charles Francis Adams, Jr., in 1869, "can only mean in plain English the government of ignorance and vice: —it means a European, and especially Celtic, proletariat on the Atlantic coast, an African proletariat on the shores of the

Gulf, and a Chinese proletariat on the Pacific." To reformers like Adams, egalitarian ideas seemed an anachronism, a throwback to the unscientific sentimentalism of an earlier era. Class and racial prejudices reinforced each other, as the reformers' concern with distancing themselves from the lower orders at home went hand in hand with a growing insensitivity to the egalitarian aspirations of the former slaves.

In addition to obvious parallels between Southern and Northern corruption, the economic and social policies of Reconstruction governments struck reformers as unbridled "class legislation." The complaints of taxpayers' conventions about extravagant expenditures by propertyless lawmakers won "the hearty sympathy of the best Northerners," partly because of increasing taxes and swollen public budgets in the North. More insistently than other Republicans, reformers argued that the nation had done all it could for blacks; it was now up to the freedmen to make their own way in the world. "The removal of white prejudice against the negro," declared *The Nation* in 1867, "depends almost entirely on the negro himself." Legislation could never counteract the "great burden" weighing upon the race: its "want of all the ordinary claims to social respectability." Many now viewed the goal of protecting blacks' equal rights as quixotic. "There are many social disorders," declared Schurz in the Senate, "which it is very difficult to cure by laws." And if local authorities proved unwilling or unable to put down violence? Blacks, said Godkin, should move to states where their rights were respected.

Nor, men like Godkin realized, were blacks likely to offer much support to "reform." To the freedmen, retrenchment and lower taxes meant fewer government services, and behind reformers' clamor against "class legislation" and admonitions to the freedmen to "work out their own destiny" they discerned a cruel indifference to their fate. "Does individual or national duty end," asked the *New National Era,* "where ceasing to do evil begins?" Blacks recognized, moreover, that civil service reform would effectively bar "the whole colored population" from office. As a Mississippi freedman eloquently explained after taking a federal examination for lighthouse keeper:

> It was not my good fortune to receive an education. I was in bondage from youth to manhood. . . . But I learned all that was practicable for

one in my situation. . . . I can navigate a vessel on our sound. Yet I cannot stand an examination in geometry, in scientific engineering, in mathematics, or even in artistic penmanship. . . . I think, without vanity, that I am qualified to keep a Light House. . . . If this test be the rule, you will exclude every colored man on this seaboard from position. You tell us that all the honors of the nation are open to us, yet you exclude us by ordeals that none of us can pass.

Fundamentally, reformers believed, Southern violence arose from the same cause as political corruption: the exclusion from office of men of "intelligence and culture." If in the North civil service reform offered a solution, in the South, reformers advocated the removal of political disabilities that barred prominent Confederates—the region's "natural leaders"—from office. Thus a remarkable reversal of sympathies took place, with Southern whites increasingly portrayed as the victims of injustice, blacks deemed unfit to exercise the suffrage, and carpetbaggers denounced as unprincipled thieves. Originating as a critique of social and political changes in the North, liberal reform had come to view Reconstruction as an expression of all the real and imagined evils of the Gilded Age. "Reconstruction," declared *The Nation*, "seems to be morally a more disastrous process than rebellion." As an experiment in government, it had "totally failed."

The Election of 1872

As Grant's first term drew to a close, the categories "moderate" and "Radical" no longer adequately described Republican factions. With the decline of Radicalism, the ascendancy of organizational politics, and the emergence of liberal reform, party alignments now focused on Grant himself and the new politics of the Gilded Age.

Conscious of their weakness within Republican ranks, reformers increasingly contemplated a new party. And nothing revealed more dramatically how the Republican organization had changed than the large number of party founders who rallied to the liberal cause. The list included numerous former Democrats, like Lyman Trumbull, who believed "old Whiggery dominated the [Republican] party." There were also antislavery pioneers such as George W. Julian, convinced that politics had degenerated into little more than "a struggle between the ins and outs for the loaves and fishes." But what united nearly all these disaffected politicians was the experience of having been pushed aside by the party's new leadership. Among them were three Civil War governors: New York's Reuben Fenton, his influence now eclipsed by Sen. Roscoe Conkling; Pennsylvania's Andrew Curtin, whose supporters had been ousted from power by Simon Cameron's ring; and Austin Blair, his ambition for a Michigan Senate seat frustrated by the Zachariah Chandler machine.

A heterogeneous collection of men alienated from the Grant regime assembled in Cincinnati in May 1872 for the Liberal Republican convention: reformers, free traders, antislavery veterans, and a considerable body of men who "had been turned out of office or expected to get in." In the end, to the astonishment of nearly everybody, New York *Tribune* editor Horace Greeley emerged as the nominee. The inability of reformers to unite on a single candidate, and Greeley's personal popularity among Republicans, explained this unexpected outcome. Yet the nominee was hostile to free trade and indifferent to civil service reform and other benchmarks of liberalism. As a result, the Greeley campaign came to focus on the one issue shared by the heterogeneous Liberal coalition: a new policy for the South.

On this question, Greeley possessed impeccable reform credentials. From the moment the war ended, he had opposed confiscation and treason trials and had called upon "gentlemen" of both sections to support a magnanimous Reconstruction based on "Universal Amnesty and Impartial Suffrage." In 1867 he had provided part of the bond that freed Jefferson Davis from prison. And while denouncing the Klan and supporting federal enforcement efforts, Greeley identified high taxes and the exclusion of the "best men" from office as barriers to regional development and national reconciliation. Meanwhile, this long-time defender of black rights increasingly echoed Democratic complaints about the freedmen. Blacks, Greeley insisted, must fend for themselves; his harsh injunction was "Root, Hog, or Die!" Having won the Cincinnati nomination in part because of strong support among Southern delegates, Greeley penned a letter of acceptance that stressed the issue of "local self-government" and called on Americans to "clasp hands across the bloody chasm" by putting the war and Reconstruction behind them.

Faced with this unexpected challenge, Republicans moved to steal their opponents' thunder. Within a month of Greeley's nomination, Congress cut tariff duties by ten percent and enacted an amnesty law restoring the right to hold office to nearly all former Confederates still excluded under the Fourteenth Amendment. As for the Democrats, the Liberal movement was a godsend to those who wished to demonstrate that their party had come to terms with the results of the Civil War. But the choice of Greeley fell on them "like a wet blanket." Could Democrats adopt as their candidate a man who had devoted his career to lambasting the party and everything it stood for? The party had no alternative if it hoped to defeat Grant. In July, the Democratic national convention endorsed the Liberal candidate and platform as its own. Whether Greeley won or lost, declared the *World*, was irrelevant; his nomination had "cut the party loose from the dead issues of an effete past."

Except for Georgia, whose Democratic administration did nothing to deter violence, 1872 witnessed the most peaceful election of the entire Reconstruction period. Greeley won only three ex-Confederate states, Georgia, Tennessee, and Texas, plus Kentucky, Maryland, and Missouri. Republicans made remarkable comebacks in states lost in 1869 and 1870, carrying West Virginia, electing a majority of the Congressmen in Tennessee and Virginia, and electing governors in North Carolina and Alabama. Although its legislature remained divided between the parties, Alabama became the only instance during Reconstruction in which Republicans regained control of a state administration previously "redeemed" by the Democrats. Redemption, it appeared, was neither inevitable nor irreversible, and Republicans, newly elected black Congressman John R. Lynch later recalled, seemed to be "the party of the future."

In the North, the Greeley campaign found itself beset with difficulties from the start, beginning with the candidate's own history. "I am curious to see the biography that his friends will put out," remarked one Democrat, and Greeley's supporters were forced to spend much of their time explaining his past references to Democrats as "murderers, adulterers, drunkards, cowards, liars, thieves."

For both parties, internally divided on other issues, Southern policy became the keynote of the fall campaign. The speeches of Greeley and his supporters focused almost exclusively on the evils of Reconstruction and the need to restore "local self-government." Thus the election of 1872 culminated the process by which opposition to Reconstruction became inextricably linked with the broader crusade for reform and good government. For their part, Republicans waved the bloody shirt, reinforced by references to "Ku Klux outrages and midnight murders and maraudings." But the party also defended blacks' rights to equal citizenship and protection against violent assault, concepts now deeply ingrained in the Republican electorate. "The cry that the liberties of the blacks are still in danger . . . ," concluded one Liberal editor, "has been the most potent weapon of the campaign." Grant carried every state north of the Mason-Dixon line. Nationally, the Republican total of over fifty-five percent of the vote represented the largest majority in any Presidential election between 1836 and 1892.

The election of 1872 reinforced the reign of organizational politics. For one thing, the fact that a significant number of former Radicals supported Greeley confirmed the death of Radicalism as both a political movement and a coherent ideology. The bolt of a group of prominent party leaders, moreover, only solidified the Stalwarts' hold on power. Individuals, it seemed, were dispensable; the party permanent.

Ironically, the election both demonstrated the Republican North's commitment to Reconstruction and strengthened tendencies within both parties that would soon set Southern policy on a course Liberals had pioneered. Northern Democrats, indeed, emerged from defeat strategically positioned to profit from the coming economic depression, for by abandoning explicit appeals to the race issue and absorbing a highly visible group of Liberal Republicans, they partially dissolved their old association with racism and disloyalty, while in no way altering their intention of undoing federal protection for blacks' rights. As for Republicans, the Democratic-Liberal call for "local self-government," an end to corruption, and sectional reconciliation found a more receptive audience than the returns appeared to indicate. Despite their espousal of black voting rights, few Northern Republicans actually defended the Reconstruction governments. More commonly, they seemed to accept the characterization of these regimes as inept and venal, adopting a tone of apology or embarrassment and falling back upon the hope that Grant's reelection would bring the South stability and good government. Henceforth, despite the President's sweeping victory, Reconstruction would be on the defensive in the North as well as the South.

The Politics of Depression

The Depression and Its Consequences

The intoxicating postwar economic expansion ended abruptly in 1873. In September, Jay Cooke and Company, a pillar of the nation's banking establishment, collapsed after being unable to market millions of dollars in bonds of the Northern Pacific Railroad. Within days, a financial panic engulfed the credit system. Banks and brokerage houses failed, the stock market temporarily suspended operation, and factories began laying off workers. The ensuing depression propelled the "labor question" to the forefront of social thought, undermined fundamental premises of the free labor ideology, and reshaped the political agenda and the balance of power between the parties.

In a way, it was fitting that the Northern Pacific's financial problems triggered the Panic of 1873, for if the railroad boom nourished postwar growth, the network's overexpansion, financed by unbridled speculative credit, erected a financial house of cards doomed to eventual collapse. By 1876 over half the nation's railroads had defaulted on their bonds and were in receivership. And as track construction halted, the industries dependent on railroad growth suffered disastrous reverses. By the end of 1874 nearly half the nation's iron furnaces had halted production. Meanwhile, a new generation of entrepreneurs drastically reorganized their concerns to increase productivity and lower costs. Depressions often provide the occasion for structural changes in capitalist production, and that of the 1870s was no exception. John D.

Rockefeller seized control of the oil industry, and Andrew Carnegie laid the foundations of his steel empire. While overall output dipped and the total number of establishments remained constant, the number of workers in manufacturing continued to rise, reflecting a growing concentration of capital and the triumph of large-scale mechanized production. The 1880 census reported four-fifths of manufacturing workers laboring "under the factory system."

For workers, the depression was a disaster, as unemployment spread in the major urban centers. One estimate found a quarter of New York City's labor force without jobs in 1874. So many men took to the roads in search of work that by mid-decade the "tramp" was "a fixed institution" on the social landscape. Never before, commented Pennsylvania's Bureau of Labor Statistics, had "so many of the working classes, skilled and unskilled, . . . been moving from place to place seeking employment that was not to be had."

Many mine and factory workers resisted wage cuts in militant, violent strikes. 1874 witnessed bitter labor disputes on the railroads and in Midwestern mines, and the following year 15,000 textile workers stayed out for two months in unsuccessful opposition to wage reductions. Also in 1875, the "long strike" in Pennsylvania's anthracite coalfields ended in defeat for the powerful Workingmen's Benevolent Association and produced the celebrated Molly Maguire trials, which culminated in the hanging of twenty militant miners. To one Boston newspaper, these strikes marked "a transition period" in the nation's history. The depression, it seemed, had brought European-style class conflict to America and, as a Pennsylvania official commented, "fearfully" deepened "the antagonism between rich and poor."

For farmers, too, the depression brought economic dislocation and galvanized new forms of protest. Farm population and output continued to increase throughout the decade, but as agricultural prices and land values tumbled, postwar prosperity gave way to hard times. Many responded by calling for increased railroad regulation and currency inflation, to raise agricultural prices and enable indebted farmers to meet their mortgage payments.

Rudely disrupting visions of social harmony, the depression of the 1870s marked a turning point in the North's ideological development. The widespread tension between labor and capital gave rise to a public discourse fractured along class lines. In small industrial centers throughout the North, striking workers found allies among local officials and small-town businessmen, many of whom shared labor's resentment against the disruptive impact of corporations controlled from outside the community. But in the larger cities, and among the leaders of both parties, older notions of equal rights and the dignity of labor gave way before a sense of irreducible barriers between the classes and the need to defend property, "political economy," and the economic status quo.

As the depression intensified, the Northern urban middle and upper classes embraced the critique of labor and farmers' movements and of the activist democratic state pioneered by Liberal reformers. Castigating labor leaders as "enemies of society" who believed "the world owes them a living," the urban press blamed poverty on laziness and extravagance and insisted that the laws of political economy dictated only one way out of the depression: "Things must regulate themselves." These beliefs quickly broadened to include a critique of both nongovernmental charity and workers' own collective efforts. A special report on "pauperism" for the American Social Science Association not only rejected public assistance outside workhouses, but blamed "indiscriminate" and "over-generous" private relief for exacerbating labor unrest by encouraging the unemployed to turn down jobs paying reduced wages. Indeed, many urban newspapers viewed the depression as "not an unmixed evil," since it promised to reduce wages, discipline labor, and curb the power of unions.

Such attitudes toward strikes and poverty had always comprised one strand of free labor thought. Now, cut loose from the more egalitarian aspects of that ideology, they formed part of a self-conscious bourgeois outlook whose emergence and consolidation liberal reformers directly encouraged. "All industries in our day stand or fall together," wrote Godkin in an appeal to businessmen to recognize their common class interests. During the 1870s, consciousness of being members of a distinct capitalist class spread within the business community. Many urban merchants previously critical of the railroads pulled back from the idea of regulation. The proliferation of trade associations also reflected the growth of bourgeois class consciousness, as did the formation of new political organizations among businessmen, such as the Citizens' Association in Chicago. Thus, faced with agrarian unrest and labor militancy, metropolitan capitalists united in defense of fiscal conservatism and the inviolability of property rights.

Although reformers failed to establish property qualifications for urban voters, the economic crisis strengthened their determination to insulate government from the vagaries of the popular will. New state constitutions of the 1870s, noted one commentator, represented "a wide departure from the theories of government so long and unquestioningly accepted among us," for they extended the terms of office of governors and judges, reduced the length of legislative sessions, and in a few cases even curtailed the jury system. As the depression battered the fiscal structure of state and city governments and threatened ever higher taxes, retrenchment became the order of the day. Several states prohibited public aid to railroads, limited budgets and tax rates, and armed governors with the item veto. State authorities, moreover, increasingly resorted to the courts and militia to assist capital, as Republican Gov. John Hartranft of Pennsylvania did in the miners' "long strike" of 1875, to the applause of newspapers of both parties. Perhaps most indicative of new tendencies in Northern public life was the proliferation of vagrancy laws designed to combat the perceived menace of tramps. Although intended more to clear towns of beggars than to establish a system of quasi-free labor, by making unemployment a crime the laws bore more than a passing resemblance to the Southern Black Codes of 1865–66. Indiana even directed that those who refused employment be put to work on city streets and leased out convicts to a manufacturer of railroad cars. Such policies illustrated how free labor principles seemed to have crumbled in the depression's wake.

The clash between demands for government intervention to ease the depression's impact and the growing clamor for law, order, and respectability quickly spilled over into national politics. The Forty-Third Congress, which assembled in December 1873, became embroiled in controversy over Iowa Republican George W. Mc-Crary's proposal for a national commission to establish "reasonable" railroad rates. The Republican party split along regional lines, as Westerners and Southerners favored the bill and most Easterners opposed it. Its supporters viewed federal railroad regulation as a legitimate exercise of expanded national authority. But Eastern Republicans denounced the bill as a form of "communism," appealing to the principle of states' rights—a doctrine, observed a Tennessee Congressman, "which now emanates from the North so suddenly and unexpectedly." By a five-vote margin, the bill passed the House, only to expire in the Senate.

The currency issue, which found members of both parties holding positions from "wild" inflation to the immediate resumption of specie payments, proved even more disruptive. Early in 1874 Congress enacted an "Inflation Bill" that proposed to add $64 million to the circulation of greenbacks and national bank notes. Although hardly an extravagant increase, the bill embodied the idea that the government could regulate the money supply to meet the economy's fluctuating needs. To the metropolitan bourgeoisie, it epitomized all the heretical impulses and dangerous social tendencies unleashed by the depression. "Nearly every man of intelligence and experience in commercial and financial matters," claimed *The Nation*, opposed the measure, and the reform press rallied respectable opinion against it. At the end of April, Grant vetoed the bill, and reformers lavished unaccustomed praise upon the President. The veto marked a milestone in the process by which what Henry L. Dawes called "the slow, conservative sentiment" gained ascendancy in Republican circles and economic respectability replaced equality of rights for black citizens as the essence of the party's self-image.

This appeal would serve Republicans well in years to come. But in 1874, as in 1896 and 1932, voters reacted to hard times by turning against the party in power. In the greatest reversal of partisan alignments in the entire nineteenth century, they erased the massive Congressional majority Republicans had enjoyed since 1861, transforming the party's 110-vote margin in the House into a Democratic majority of 60 seats. "The election is not merely a victory but a revolution," declared a newspaper in New York, where Democrat Samuel J. Tilden rolled up a 50,000-vote margin over Gov. John A. Dix. The political upheaval of 1874 inaugurated a national politics of stalemate. Only in 1896 would Republicans reestablish their electoral dominance; until then, the same party controlled both Houses only three times, and only twice the White House and Congress. Given the political impasse, Americans had to weather the economic crisis without leadership from Washington.

Although the depression far outweighed Reconstruction as a cause of Republican defeat, the implications for the party's Southern wing were indeed ominous. When Democrats assumed control of the House in 1875, the South received half the committee chairmanships. Southern Republicans feared the results portended the abandonment of national efforts to bolster their party and protect their rights. The election results, exulted the New York *Herald,* suggested that white Southerners were being welcomed back as "our brothers and our fellow-citizens." If the North had finally put the Civil War behind it, could Reconstruction long survive?

Retreat from Reconstruction

The election of 1874 offered only one indication of a pronounced shift in Northern attitudes toward the South during Grant's second term. In 1875 former Freedmen's Bureau agent and Georgia legislator John E. Bryant learned how profoundly Northern Republican thought had changed when he wrote for the *New York Times* a discussion of the political situation in his adopted state. Bryant's analysis rested on a classic free labor premise: "The laboring man should be as independent as the capitalist." Southern whites, he continued, in their heart of hearts, still believed workers "ought to be slaves." Although overstated, Bryant's analysis underscored the centrality of labor relations to Reconstruction politics. But on one point he appeared out of date. Did the Republican North still believe that the laborer should be "as independent as the capitalist"? As one of Bryant's Northern friends cautioned, "there was reason to believe" that the attitude toward "the labor question" and the "general view of society and government" held by the South's "old ruling class" were now "substantially shared by a large class in the North."

Only a few years earlier, Republicans had united to remake Southern society in accordance with the principles of free labor and legal and political equality. Now the erosion of the free labor ideology made possible a resurgence of overt racism that undermined support for Reconstruction. James S. Pike's influential book *The Prostrate State* depicted South Carolina as engulfed by political corruption and governmental extravagance and under the control of "a mass of black barbarism . . . the most ignorant democracy that mankind ever saw." Pike was hardly objective—he had long held racist views, acquired much of his information from interviews with white Democratic leaders, and seems to have spoken with only one black Carolinian. But despite its many inadequacies, *The Prostrate State* made South Carolina a byword for corrupt misrule and reinforced the idea that the cause lay in "negro government." In its wake, even newspapers friendly to Reconstruction joined in the condemnation of the state's black legislators, and a spate of articles appeared in middle-class journals like *Scribner's, Harper's,* and *The Atlantic Monthly,* echoing the conclusion that a return to "home rule" was necessary before good government and regional prosperity returned to the South. Meanwhile, these same journals expressed increasingly retrograde racial attitudes, reflected visually in a shift from engravings depicting the freedmen as upstanding citizens harassed by violent opponents to vicious caricatures presenting them as little more than unbridled animals. Ironically, even as racism waned as an explicit component of the Northern Democratic appeal, it gained a hold on respectable Republican opinion, as a convenient explanation for Reconstruction's "failure."

A "Counter-Revolution," Vice President Henry Wilson lamented to William Lloyd Garrison, was overtaking Reconstruction: "Men are beginning to hint at changing the condition of the negro . . . our Anti-slavery veterans must again speak out." But by the mid-1870s, with "reform" now suggesting rule by the "best men" rather than the desire to purge American life of racial inequality, survivors of the Radical generation seemed relics of a bygone era. The New England Freedmen's Aid Society disbanded in 1874, while the American Missionary Association, increasingly concerned with winning the good will of Southern whites, pronounced black suffrage a failure and blacks ungrateful for the organization's many efforts on their behalf.

Buffeted by the shifting tides of public opinion, preoccupied first with the depression and then with another wave of political scandals, the second Grant administration found it impossible to devise a coherent Southern policy. "*Radicalism* is dissolving—going to pieces," wrote a Democratic Senator, "but what is to take its place, does not clearly appear." Events lurched from crisis to crisis, with alternating moments of conciliation and firmness but no overriding sense of purpose. In retrospect, however, it is clear that, partly due to events outside his control, Grant in his second term presided over a broad retreat from the policies of Reconstruction.

Even had the will for an interventionist Southern policy survived in the White House, a series of Supreme Court decisions undercut the legal rationale for such action. Previously, the Court had proved reluctant to intervene in Reconstruction controversies. But during the 1870s it retreated from an expansive definition of federal power and moved a long way toward emasculating the postwar amendments—a crucial development in view of the fact that Congress had placed so much of the burden of enforcing blacks' civil and political rights on the federal judiciary.

The first pivotal decision, in the *Slaughterhouse* cases, was announced in 1873. Four years earlier, Louisiana had chartered a corporation to monopolize butchering in New Orleans. Butchers suddenly deprived of employment sued in federal court, contending that the monopoly violated their right to pursue a livelihood, guaranteed, they insisted, by the Fourteenth Amendment. In effect, they asked the Court to decide whether the Amendment had expanded the definition of national citizenship for all Americans, or simply accorded blacks certain rights already enjoyed by whites. Speaking for the five-man majority, Justice Samuel F. Miller rejected the butchers' plea, insisting Congress had intended primarily to enlarge the rights of the former slaves. Blacks might have been forgiven for thinking this construction would bolster federal action on their behalf, but Miller went on to distinguish sharply between national and state citizenship, and to insist that the Amendment protected only those rights that owed their existence to the federal government. What were these federal rights? Miller mentioned access to ports and navigable waterways and the ability to run for federal office, travel to the seat of government, and be protected on the high seas and abroad. Clearly, few of these rights were of any great concern to the majority of freedmen. The Fourteenth Amendment, Miller declared, had not fundamentally altered traditional federalism; most of the rights of citizens remained under state control, and with these the Amendment had "nothing to do." As Justice Stephen J. Field pointed out in a stinging dissent, if this were the Amendment's meaning, "it was a vain and idle enactment, which accomplished nothing and most unnecessarily excited Congress and the people on its passage."

Slaughterhouse at least affirmed the indisputable fact that the postwar amendments had been designed to protect black rights. Even more devastating was the 1876 decision in *U.S. v. Cruikshank*. This case arose from the Colfax Massacre, the bloodiest single act of terrorism in all of Reconstruction. Indictments were brought under the Enforcement Act of 1870, alleging a conspiracy to deprive the victims of their civil rights. The Supreme Court overturned the only three convictions the government had managed to obtain, arguing that the postwar amendments empowered the federal government to prohibit only violations of black rights by *states;* the responsibility for punishing crimes by individuals remained with local and state authorities. In the name of federalism, the decision rendered national prosecution of crimes committed against blacks virtually impossible and gave a green light to acts of terror where local officials were unable or unwilling to enforce the law.

Additional evidence of the nation's waning commitment to the freedmen abounded during the 1870s. Of greatest import to many blacks was the fate of the Freedman's Savings and Trust Company, one of the many financial institutions to succumb to the depression. Chartered in 1865, the bank had actively sought deposits from the freedmen, while at the same time instructing them in the importance of thrift. Blacks by the thousands came to the bank with tiny deposits—the majority of accounts were under fifty dollars and some amounted only to a few pennies—and used it to handle their financial affairs and remit funds to distant relatives. And organizations from churches to benevolent societies entrusted their modest treasuries to its vaults. Unfortunately, the bank's directors soon forgot their reforming zeal and prudent business practices and, joining the speculation of the early 1870s, invested heavily in Washington real estate and made unsecured loans to railroads and other companies. In June 1874, with only $31,000 on hand to cover obligations to its 61,000 depositors, the Freedman's Savings Bank suspended operations.

Although legally a private corporation rather than an arm of the government, the bank often shared offices with the Freedmen's Bureau, used army officers to solicit customers, and through newspaper advertisements and circulars festooned with images of Lincoln encouraged blacks to think the federal government stood behind its activities. Even a Kentucky Democrat hardly known as a friend of the freedmen told the House that the government was "as morally bound to see to it that not a dollar is lost . . . as it is possible to establish a moral obligation." But although a succession of Presidents and comptrollers of the currency urged that the freedmen be repaid with federal funds, Congress did little more than assist the bank in winding up its affairs. Eventually, half the depositors received compensation—an average of $18.51 per person—while the remainder received nothing. Well into the twentieth century, pathetic appeals arrived in Washington from depositors seeking the balance of their funds. "Mr. President," one wrote in 1921, "I pray you to consider us old People . . . our best life spent in slavery. . . . Just asking for what we worked for." Their letters now gather dust in the National Archives.

And then there was the Civil Rights Bill, mired in Congressional debate in 1874 despite the fact that Grant had, in his second inaugural address, publicly endorsed it. This measure made it illegal for places of public accommodation and entertainment to make any distinction between black and white patrons and outlawed racial discrimination in public schools, jury selection, churches, cemeteries, and transportation. That the bill survived was due to the tireless advocacy of Charles Sumner, and as he lay dying in March 1874, he whispered to a visitor: "You must take care of the civil-rights bill, . . . don't let it fail." Two months later, as a final tribute, his colleagues adopted Sumner's bill, shorn only of its church provision, even though many who voted for the bill believed it stood no chance of passage in the House. There, its manager was Benjamin Butler, who had introduced it earlier in the session with an eloquent account of how the wartime conduct of black soldiers had tempered his own racial prejudices. Over 500 blacks, Butler recalled, had died in one engagement on the James River: "As I looked on their bronzed faces upturned in the shining sun to heaven as if in mute appeal against the wrongs of the country for which they had given their lives . . . feeling I had wronged them in the past . . . I swore to myself a solemn oath . . . to defend the rights of these men who have given their blood for me and my country."

The seven blacks in the Forty-Third Congress spoke with vigor and eloquence on the Civil Rights Bill. Before galleries crowded with black spectators, their speeches invoked both personal experience and the black political ideology that had matured during Reconstruction. Several related their own "outrages and indignities." Joseph Rainey had been thrown from a Virginia streetcar, John R. Lynch forced to occupy a railroad smoking car with gamblers and drunkards, Richard H. Cain and Robert B. Elliott excluded from a North Carolina restaurant, James T. Rapier denied service by inns at every stopping point between Montgomery and Washington.

Especially in "redeemed" states, where "separate but equal" education was a mockery, Southern blacks considered the bill's schools clause its most important feature. The state's segregated education, declared a Tennessee black convention in April 1874, was "defective" and "anti-republican," teaching whites "the spirit of caste and hate" and blacks "their inferiority." But Butler came under tremendous pressure to bury the bill. Facing more than enough political liabilities, House Republicans put off consideration of the Civil Rights Bill until after the fall 1874 elections. Along with the shifting positions of the President and federal courts, Congress's handling of the bill suggested that Southern defenders of Reconstruction would face alone both the consequences of the depression and opponents again turning to violence.

The Waning of Southern Republicanism

The depression of the 1870s dealt the South an even more severe blow than the rest of the nation. Between 1872 and 1877, the price of cotton fell by nearly fifty percent, and tobacco, rice, and sugar also suffered precipitous declines. The effects rippled through the entire economy, plunging farmers into poverty and drying up the region's sources of credit. The depression disrupted commerce, bankrupted merchants, seriously undermined the economic situation of artisans, and all but eliminated prospects for social mobility among unskilled laborers of both races. It shattered hopes for the early emergence of a modernized, prosperous Southern economy and bankrupted even such long-established bulwarks of Southern industry as Richmond's Tredegar Iron Works. In 1880, with a per capita income only one-third that of the rest of the nation, the South lagged farther behind the North in the total value of its agricultural and industrial output than when the decade began.

As upcountry yeomen again found themselves engulfed by poverty and indebtedness, the trend toward cotton production and reliance on merchants for food and supplies rapidly accelerated. And along with cotton came the inexorable growth of tenancy. In one upcountry Georgia county, two-thirds of the white farmers were renting for cash or shares by 1880; in another, where the census found only 40 white families renting their farms in 1870, it reported nearly 250 a decade later.

In the black belt, many planters who had weathered the postwar years saw declining land prices sharply reduce the value of their holdings, while falling agricultural earnings made it impossible for them to discharge their debts to local merchants at the end of the year. In the rich cotton region surrounding Natchez, over 150 planters had forfeited all or part of their land by 1875 for debt or nonpayment of taxes. The trend toward outside control of Louisiana's sugar plantations continued apace, as many small planters lost their holdings to owners of larger estates. With most planters unable to pay money wages, the depression confirmed sharecropping as the nearly universal labor system in cotton agriculture.

If the spread of sharecropping fulfilled, in part, the freedmen's aspiration for day-to-day autonomy, in other ways the depression proved a disaster for blacks, severely limiting their power to influence working conditions. Where wage labor persisted, as in the Louisiana sugar fields and on diversified Upper South farms, monthly earnings plummeted. Except in the rice kingdom and parts of the Upper South, hard times arrested the modest spread of independent black farming and reduced many owners and cash renters to sharecroppers and laborers.

By a cruel irony, the depression hit just as blacks were increasing their political influence in states where Reconstruction still survived. Throughout the Republican South, the number of black officials rose significantly in the early 1870s. Black representation in Congress grew from five to seven in 1873 and reached a Reconstruction peak of eight in 1875. Florida and Arkansas in 1872 chose their first black state officials, and Louisiana and South Carolina each elected three. The number of black legislators rose dramatically in several states, and even where it did not, more blacks acquired committee chairmanships and seats in state senates. Local black officeholding also continued to increase. Traveling across the South in 1873 and 1874, reporter Edward King encountered black city councilmen in Petersburg, Houston, and Little Rock, parish jury members in Louisiana, and sheriffs scattered across the black belt. In Mississippi, black political leaders, alienated by the conservative policies of Governors James L. Alcorn and Ridgely Powers, helped engineer the 1873 gubernatorial nomination and election of Sen. Adelbert Ames, along with a six-man state ticket that included three black candidates. At the same time, blacks substantially increased their representation in the legislature and consolidated their hold on local offices throughout the black belt. When the lawmakers assembled, they chose a black speaker of the house and elected Blanche K. Bruce to the U.S. Senate. Blacks' growing assertiveness marked both a departure from their earlier willingness to step aside in favor of white candidates and a waning of the ideal of a polity in which color was irrelevant. The hard realities of Southern political life had taught black constituents that they needed black officials.

Under other circumstances, blacks might have used their enhanced political power to press for bold new political and economic programs. As 1873 began, however, Republicans enjoyed undisputed control of state government only in Arkansas, Louisiana, Mississippi, and South Carolina. Tennessee, Georgia, and Virginia had been "redeemed," while in Alabama, Florida, North Carolina, and Texas, Republican governors confronted hostile or divided legislatures. Blacks' political role waxed, moreover, precisely as the Northern outcry against corruption and "extravagance" reached its height. The depression, which devastated Southern credit, tax rolls, and budgets, added urgency to demands for retrenchment. Combined with the need to attract white voters, these developments left Southern Republicans with few policy options. Blacks found themselves helping to preside over a period of moderation and consolidation, rather than striking out in radical new directions.

Ironically, Reconstruction governments now took up their opponents' call for retrenchment and reform. Republican administrations strictly limited state debts and replaced outstanding bonds with new ones bearing a uniform interest rate and representing smaller amounts of principal. Retrenchment went farthest in Florida, which did away with special legislation by passing a general incorporation law and prohibited lending the state's credit to any corporation. By 1876, official salaries had been slashed, the legislature met only every other year, and the cost of state government barely exceeded that of Presidential Reconstruction.

Black Republicans reacted less enthusiastically than white to the lure of reform. The depression left many black leaders dependent on their official salaries for a livelihood, and both officeholders and ordinary freedmen feared that retrenchment meant cuts in state programs like education, of special concern to their community. Many blacks, moreover, continued to look to the activist state to ease their economic plight. "We will never be any good only to serve all the days of our lives if we don't get help from our government," wrote one freedman, calling for state aid for those seeking to acquire land. But such ideas lay far beyond the straitened resources of Southern governments and the view of the state's role held by national party leaders.

Nowhere was the need for change greater, or the conservative implications of "reform" more evident, than in South Carolina. Here the first Republican governor, Robert K. Scott, who served from 1868 to 1872, had an unenviable record of malfeasance in office, and his successor, scalawag Franklin J. Moses, Jr., proved to be "entirely devoid of moral sense." During the Moses administration, South Carolina joined the nationwide reaction against railroad aid and expensive government, reducing its public debt and state taxes. But the governor's extravagant life-style in the mansion he somehow managed to acquire in Columbia alienated much of the party. In 1874 carpetbagger Daniel H. Chamberlain was elected governor, promising reform.

An ardent Massachusetts abolitionist and wartime officer of a black regiment, Chamberlain had come to South Carolina in 1866 hoping to plant Sea Island cotton. Like other aspiring Northern planters, he failed and turned to politics for a living. For Chamberlain, reform offered a way to strengthen white control of the Republican party and woo respectable members of the Democracy. Earlier in the decade he had served as vice president of a Taxpayers' Convention and had once offered to run for governor "to keep the party from going over to *negroism*."

Chamberlain promised sweeping changes to ensure "economy and honesty in the administration of the government," and to a large extent, he succeeded. His administration reorganized state finances to consolidate and properly fund the debt, reduced taxes and equalized assessments, slashed public printing costs, and launched investigations into previous frauds. All these measures won the support of South Carolina's black-controlled legislature. But other "reform" proposals aroused widespread black opposition. To further curtail expenses and win the backing of white taxpayers, Chamberlain reduced the size of the state militia and removed many black trial justices and local school officials, frequently replacing them with white Democrats. He also proposed, unsuccessfully, to reinstitute the leasing of convicts and reduce appropriations for the insane asylum, state university, and public schools. By mid-1875 the governor had become the toast of upper-crust Democratic society, making the rounds of Charleston literary associations and openly allying himself with the Charleston *News and Courier*'s influential editor, Francis W. Dawson.

Chamberlain's policies demonstrated that blacks remained junior partners at the highest echelons of Southern politics. Together with frustration at Reconstruction's failure to improve radically black living conditions and a growing sense of foreboding as one state after another fell to the Redeemers, this reality inspired some black leaders to seek new strategies for community advancement. But they met with little success. Efforts at independent black politics during the 1870s collapsed as ordinary freedmen remained unwaveringly loyal to the Republican party. When Edward Shaw, a prominent Memphis black leader, ran for Congress against the white Republican incumbent, he received only 165 votes. With black votes taken for granted and political independence all but impossible, black politicos had little choice, as Frederick Douglass noted, but to act as "field hands" for the Republican party.

A number of black spokesmen urged their constituents to rely less on the state and more on individual self-help as a strategy for advancement. Such ideas, never entirely absent from black thought, gained increasing currency during the 1870s. Louisiana legislator and editor David Young declared there was "no use in keeping up the same old whine" about the denial of blacks' rights. In 1876 one delegate told the national black convention that recognition of their rights depended on proving themselves worthy of acceptance: "the educated colored man must be seen in the foundry, in the machine shop, in the carpenter shop."

Such talk of individual advancement that eschewed political action in favor of economic self-help anticipated the conservative ideology associated with Booker T. Washington that would emerge in the post-Redemption South. Like Washington, conservative blacks during Reconstruction urged their constituents to seek out political alliances with "the Independent-Conservative element of the South." And, like him, they dismissed demands for equal access to public facilities as unrealistic and counterproductive.

So long as Reconstruction survived, the new conservatism had little attraction for ordinary freedmen. But its appearance suggested the political implication of the growing class differentiation within the black community. Conservative ideas found their greatest support among the rising class of black businessmen who would later supply the principal base for Washington's ideology. After establishing a land and brokerage business in 1871, Martin R. Delany lectured blacks repeatedly on the harmony of interests between capital and labor and spoke out against carpetbaggers as representatives of "the lowest grade of northern society." His increasingly conservative outlook blended personal economic interests, disappointed political ambition, and pessimism about the future. Utopian hopes for a permanent change in Southern life, he counseled, should be abandoned; property was, as elsewhere, destined to rule in South Carolina, and blacks should strike a deal with leading whites while they still retained significant bargaining power.

Even as conservative blacks searched for a new political middle ground, however, Southern Democrats were abandoning the centrist rhetoric of the New Departure for the open racism of early Reconstruction. Various considerations facilitated the triumph of "white line" politics, including the 1872 Greeley debacle, the failure of the New Departure to attract black votes, and the candid judgment that white supremacy offered the best prospects for mobilizing the Democratic electorate and winning over remaining scalawags. The reassertion of the political color line had profound implications for the Democracy's political and economic strategies. Especially in the Deep South, where Democratic victory required the neutralization of part of the black electorate, it implied a revival of political violence. The depression also made retrenchment and tax reduction attractive to white voters who associated expensive government with new state programs that primarily benefited corporations and blacks and who feared that high taxes threatened both planters and yeomen with the loss of their land. And with Republicans proposing little more than a milder version of "reform," they had nothing to offer white voters to counteract Democrats' racist appeals.

The issues of white supremacy, low taxes, and control of the black labor force dominated the Democratic campaigns of the mid-1870s. And their appeal became evident in 1873 and 1874 as Democrats solidified their hold on states already under their control and "redeemed" new ones. Texas Democrat Richard Coke defeated Gov. Edmund J. Davis in 1873 by a margin of better than two to one. Meanwhile, Virginia Democrats jettisoned the moderate Republicans with whom they had cooperated in 1869 and carried the state with a "straight-out" ticket and a platform of "race against race." The 1874 Southern elections proved as disastrous for Republicans as those in the North. Democrats won over two-thirds of the region's House seats, redeemed Arkansas, and gained control of Florida's legislature.

In these campaigns, which mostly took place in states where blacks comprised a minority of the population, Democratic victories depended mainly on the party's success at drawing the political color line. In Louisiana and Alabama, however, the brutality of white-line politics came to the fore. Louisiana's White League, organized in 1874, was openly dedicated to the violent restoration of white supremacy. It targeted local Republican officeholders for assassination, disrupted court sessions, and drove black laborers from their homes. In Red River Parish, the campaign degenerated into a violent reign of terror, which culminated in August in the cold-blooded murder of six Republican officials. In September 1874 3,500 leaguers, mostly Civil War veterans, overwhelmed an equal number of black militiamen and Metropolitan Police under the command of Confederate Gen. James Longstreet and occupied the city hall, statehouse, and arsenal. They withdrew only upon the arrival of federal troops, ordered to the scene by the President. A similar campaign of violence helped "redeem" Alabama for the Democrats in the elections of 1874.

The Crisis of 1875

By the time the Forty-Third Congress reassembled in December, the political landscape had been transformed. As a result of the Democratic landslide, this session would be the last time for over a decade that Republicans controlled both the White House and Congress. With political violence erupting in many parts of the South, and their party's hegemony in Washington about to expire, Benjamin Butler and other Stalwarts devised a program to safeguard what remained of Reconstruction. Their proposals included the Civil Rights Bill, a new Enforcement Act expanding the President's power to suppress conspiracies aimed at intimidating voters, a two-year army appropriation (to prevent the incoming Democratic House from limiting the military's role in the South), a bill expanding the jurisdiction of the federal courts, and a subsidy for the Texas & Pacific Railroad. The package embodied the idealism, partisanship, and crass economic advantage typical of Republican politics. Civil rights was the program's spearhead, and to make it more palatable, Butler dropped the bill's controversial clause requiring integrated schools.

Events in Louisiana disrupted the already tenuous party unity necessary to enact such a program. Having suppressed the New Orleans insurrection of September 1874, Grant, newly determined to "protect the colored voter in his rights," ordered Gen. Philip H. Sheridan to use federal troops to counteract violence and sustain the administration of Gov. William P. Kellogg. On January 4, 1875, when Democrats attempted to seize control of the state assembly by forcibly installing party members in five disputed seats, a detachment of troops entered the legislative chambers and escorted out the five claimants.

If, for Reconstruction's critics, South Carolina epitomized the evils of corruption and "black rule," Louisiana now came to represent the dangers posed by excessive federal interference in local affairs. The spectacle of soldiers "marching into the Hall . . . and expelling members at the point of the bayonet" aroused more Northern opposition than any previous federal action in the South. In Boston a large body of "highly respectable citizens" gathered at Faneuil Hall to demand Sheridan's removal and compare the White League with the founding fathers as defenders of republican freedom. Wendell Phillips was among those present. Four decades earlier, Phillips had launched his abolitionist career in this very hall, when he reprimanded a speaker who praised the murderers of antislavery editor Elijah P. Lovejoy. Then, his eloquence converted the audience. Now, as he rebuked those who would "take from the President . . . the power to protect the millions" the nation had liberated from bondage, he heard only hisses, laughter, and cries of "played out, sit down." "Wendell Phillips and William Lloyd Garrison," commented the New York Times, "are not exactly extinct from American politics, but they represent ideas in regard to the South which the majority of the Republican party have outgrown." The uproar over Louisiana made Republicans extremely wary of further military intervention in the South.

The Civil Rights Bill became law shortly before Congress adjourned, as did the Jurisdiction and Removal Act, which facilitated the transfer from state to federal courts of suits asserting a citizen's rights under the Constitution or national law, a climax to the tremendous expansion of the federal judiciary's powers during Reconstruction. But the Enforcement, Texas-Pacific, and two-year army appropriation bills expired with the Forty-Third Congress. Even the Civil Rights Act reflected Republicans' divided mind. Despite having been shorn of its schools provision, the law represented an unprecedented exercise of national authority. Yet the law was more a broad assertion of principle than a blueprint for further coercive action by the federal government. It left the initiative for enforcement primarily with black litigants suing for their rights in the already overburdened federal courts. Only a handful of blacks chose to challenge acts of discrimination by hotels, theaters, and railroads, and well before the Supreme Court declared it unconstitutional in 1883, the law had become a dead letter.

For all their doubts about Reconstruction, Congressional Republicans found the will to reaffirm their party's image as the guardian of manufacturing and defender of fiscal responsibility. As the Forty-Third Congress drew to a close, it repealed the ten percent tariff reduction of 1872 and mandated the resumption of specie payments within four years. With Northern Republicans for the first time more united on economic and fiscal policy than on Reconstruction, and Democrats preparing to assume control of the House of Representatives, national politics, observed *The Nation,* had passed "out of the region of the Civil War."

The full implications of the "let alone policy" became clear in the 1875 political campaign in Mississippi. White Mississippians interpreted the 1874 elections as a national repudiation of Reconstruction. Although the Democratic state convention adopted a platform recognizing the civil and political rights of blacks, the campaign quickly became a violent crusade to destroy the Republican organization and prevent blacks from voting. Democratic rifle clubs paraded through the black belt, disrupting Republican meetings and assaulting local party leaders. Unlike crimes by the Ku Klux Klan's hooded riders, those of 1875 were committed in broad daylight by undisguised men, as if to underscore the impotence of local authorities and Democrats' lack of concern about federal intervention.

Two riots in late summer set the campaign's tone. On September 1, a Yazoo County white "military company" broke up a Republican rally, drove carpetbagger Sheriff Albert T. Morgan and other officials from the area, and murdered several prominent blacks, including a state legislator. A few days later, Democrats assaulted a Republican barbecue at Clinton, only fifteen miles from the state capital. A few individuals on each side were killed, and armed whites went on to scour the countryside, shooting down blacks "just the same as birds." They claimed perhaps thirty victims, among them schoolteachers, church leaders, and local Republican organizers.

Appeals for protection poured into the offices of Governor Ames. "They are going around the streets at night dressed in soldiers clothes and making colored people run for their lives . . . ," declared a petition by black residents of Vicksburg. "We are intimidated by the whites. . . . We will not vote at all, unless there are troops to protect us." Convinced "the power of the U.S. alone can give the security our citizens are entitled to," Ames early in September requested Grant to send troops to the state. From his summer home on the New Jersey shore, the President dispatched instructions to Attorney General Edwards Pierrepont. One widely quoted sentence came to epitomize the North's retreat from Reconstruction: "The whole public are tired out with these annual autumnal outbreaks in the South . . . [and] are ready now to condemn any interference on the part of the Government." Pierrepont sent an aide to the state, who in October arranged a "peace agreement" whereby the only two active militia companies were disbanded and whites promised to disarm. But Democrats, as black state senator Charles Caldwell reported, held the agreement "in utter contempt." On election eve, armed riders drove freedmen from their homes and threatened to kill them if they tried to vote. The next day, Democrats destroyed the ballot boxes or replaced Republican votes with their own. "The reports which come to me almost hourly are truly sickening . . . ," Ames reported to his wife. "The government of the U.S. does not interfere." The result was a Democratic landslide. Nor did this conclude Mississippi's "Redemption." In plantation counties where Republicans still held local positions, violence continued after the election, with officials forced to resign under threat of assassination and vigilante groups meting out punishment to blacks accused of theft and other violations of plantation discipline. On Christmas Day, Charles Caldwell, "as brave a man as I ever knew," according to one associate, was shot in the back in Clinton after being lured to take a drink with a white "friend." When the legislature assembled, it impeached and removed from office black Lieut. Gov. Alexander K. Davis and then compelled Gov. Ames to resign and leave the state rather than face impeachment charges himself.

Thus, in defiance of federal law and the national Constitution, Democrats gained control of Mississippi. As Ames had written in the midst of the election campaign, "a *revolution* has taken place— by force of arms—and a race are disfranchised—they are to be returned to a condition of serfdom—an era of second slavery."

Grant, who had sent troops to prop up the unstable and corrupt Republican regime in Louisiana, turned a deaf ear to pleas from the far stronger and more upright government of Mississippi. Could the postwar amendments be effectively nullified and the constitutional rights of American citizens be openly violated without provoking federal intervention? If so, remarked John R. Lynch, Mississippi's only Republican Congressman to survive the landslide, "then the war was fought in vain." Yet Northern Republicans now saw Reconstruction as a political liability. Lynch himself learned a political lesson when he asked the President in November why he had not sent troops. Northern party leaders, Grant replied, had pressured him not to act—there was no sense in trying to save Mississippi if the attempt to do so would lose Ohio, where a closely fought gubernatorial contest was simultaneously in progress.

All in all, from the inability of the Forty-Third Congress in its waning days to agree on a policy toward the South to Grant's failure to intervene in Mississippi, 1875 marked a milestone in the retreat from Reconstruction. As another Presidential election approached, it seemed certain that whoever emerged victorious, Reconstruction itself was doomed.

Redemption and After

The Centennial Election

To celebrate the anniversary of the nation's independence, Americans in 1876 flocked to Philadelphia for the Centennial Exposition, a monument to the "Progress of the Age." The attendance of nearly ten million represented over one-fifth of the population of the United States, and the fair's thousands of exhibits displayed everything from Siamese ivory to an animated wax replica of Cleopatra "in extreme dishabille." New inventions, harbingers of vast changes in American life, abounded: the telephone, typewriter, and electric light, packaged yeast, an internal combustion engine. But the focus of public interest was the mighty Corliss steam engine. Weighing 700 tons and rising forty feet into the air, it symbolized the exposition's theme: Machines were remaking the society, ushering in an era of technical progress and material abundance in which all Americans would share.

In the face of the continuing economic depression, with millions of workers unemployed and labor strife widespread, the mood of self-congratulation seemed somewhat incongruous. It was made possible only by ignoring the more sordid features of contemporary American life. Pennsylvania's exhibit did not mention the bitter Long Strike of 1875, and that of Massachusetts passed over conditions that had sparked the great walkout of Fall River textile workers, even as twenty-seven of the city's mills exhibited their wares. Nor were women offered a real opportunity to display their contributions to American society. A Woman's Pavilion exhibited the talents of female carpet and silk weavers, their power looms overseen by a "lady engineer." But the legal subordination of women received no attention, an oversight corrected when feminists led by Elizabeth Cady Stanton and Susan B. Anthony interrupted the exposition's July 4th celebration to read Woman's Declaration of Independence.

The Centennial Exposition barely touched on the nation's non-white population. Blacks were excluded from the construction crews that built the exhibition halls and largely absent from the displays. The exposition depicted American Indians as a harmless, "primitive" counterpoint to white civilization. In July, however, real Indians rudely interrupted the celebration when word reached Philadelphia of the massacre of Gen. George A. Custer and his command by Sioux warriors led by Sitting Bull and Crazy Horse. The Indians were defending lands reserved for them by an 1868 treaty. Although Custer's defeat only briefly halted the inexorable march of white soldiers, settlers, and prospectors, it said more of the twin realities of broken government promises and the Indians' tenacity in defending their way of life than all the exhibits at Philadelphia.

Like its economy, America's political health offered little cause for celebration in 1876, for even as workmen put the finishing touches on the exposition, new scandals engulfed the Grant administration. Secretary of War William Belknap resigned when it became known that he had taken kickbacks from the government-appointed Indian trader at Fort Sill. And an investigation exposed the Whiskey Rings, which had looted millions of dollars in federal internal revenue, and revealed that the President's private secretary, Orville E. Babcock, stood at the center of the frauds.

The crescendo of scandal strongly affected the scramble for the Republican Presidential nomination. Until early in the centennial year the choice of former House Speaker James G. Blaine, the party's most popular leader, seemed all but assured. But in April a newspaper revealed that Blaine had used his influence as Speaker to secure a land grant for an Arkansas railroad in which he owned stock and that the Union Pacific, another government-subsidized railroad, had accepted this stock as collateral for a loan that Blaine never repaid. After a search for a more upright candidate, the nomination went to Ohio Gov. Rutherford B. Hayes, a "third-rate nonentity" whose main claim to fame was having maintained cordial relations with all factions of the party while never being tainted with charges of corruption. In Congress in the 1860s Hayes had loyally supported Congressional Reconstruction. But he had later "come to doubt the ultra measures relating to the South," and his carefully worded letter of acceptance pledged to bring the region "the blessings of honest and capable local self government." His Democratic opponent was New York Gov. Samuel J. Tilden.

More than any other state, national attention in 1876 focused on South Carolina, whose political climate was transformed by an event in the tiny town of Hamburg. What came to be known as the Hamburg Massacre began with the black militia's celebration of the July 4th centennial. When the son and son-in-law of a local white farmer arrived on the scene and ordered the militiamen to move aside for their carriage, harsh words were exchanged, although militia commander Dock Adams eventually opened his company's ranks and the pair proceeded on their way. Four days later, the black militia again gathered in Hamburg, as did a large number of armed whites. After Adams refused a demand by Gen. Matthew C. Butler, the area's most prominent Democratic politician, to disarm his company, fighting broke out, about forty militiamen retreated to their armory, and Butler made for Augusta, returning with a cannon and hundreds of white reinforcements. As darkness fell, the outnumbered militiamen attempted to flee the scene. Hamburg's black marshal fell mortally wounded and twenty-five men were captured; of these, five were murdered in cold blood. After the killings, the mob ransacked the homes and shops of the town's blacks.

Among the affair's most appalling features was the conduct of Gen. Butler, who either selected the prisoners to be executed (according to black eyewitnesses) or left the scene when the crowd began "committing depredations" (his own, hardly more flattering, account). In either case, Butler's conduct underscored the utter collapse of a sense of paternalist obligation, not to mention common decency, among those who called themselves the region's "natural leaders." Certainly, no one could again claim that the South's "respectable" elite disdained such violence, for in one of its first actions, South Carolina's Redeemer legislature in 1877 elected Butler to the U.S. Senate.

During the killings, Dock Adams related, whites kept repeating: "This is the beginning of the redemption of South Carolina." In August Democrats chose a ticket headed by Gen. Wade Hampton, probably the state's most popular figure (at least among whites). Hampton pledged to strengthen the educational system, avoid "vindictive discrimination," and provide protection against violence. But among prominent blacks, Martin R. Delany alone campaigned on Hampton's behalf.

With so much at stake, the 1876 campaign became the most tumultuous in South Carolina's history and the one significant exception to the Reconstruction pattern that cast blacks as the victims of political violence and whites as the sole aggressors. In September, black Republicans assaulted Democrats of both races leaving a Charleston meeting; several were wounded and one white lost his life. A month later a group of blacks began firing at a "joint discussion" at Cainhoy, a village near the city, resulting in the deaths of five whites and one black.

But the campaign of intimidation launched by Hampton's supporters far overshadowed such incidents. Rifle clubs disrupted Republican rallies with "violent and abusive tirades." A reign of terror reminiscent of Ku Klux Klan days swept over Edgefield, Aiken, Barnwell, and other Piedmont counties, with freedmen driven from their homes and brutally whipped, and "leading men" murdered. The belief that they need not fear federal intervention gave Democrats a free hand. Former slave Jerry Thornton Moore, president of an Aiken County Republican club, was told by his white landlord that opponents of Reconstruction planned to carry the election "if we have to wade in blood knee-deep." "Mind what you are doing," Moore responded, "the United States is mighty strong." Replied the landlord: "but, Thornton, . . . the northern people is on our side."

South Carolina's election, a Democratic observer acknowledged, "was one of the grandest farces ever seen." Despite the campaign of intimidation, Chamberlain polled the largest Republican vote in the state's history. But Edgefield and Laurens County Democrats carried out instructions to vote "early and often" and prevent blacks from reaching the polls, thereby producing massive majorities that enabled their party to claim a narrow statewide victory.

Early returns on election night appeared to foretell a national Democratic victory. Tilden carried New York, New Jersey, Connecticut, and Indiana, more than enough, together with a solid South, to give him the Presidency. *New York Times* editor George F. Jones even wired Hayes announcing his defeat. But in the early hours of the morning, someone at Republican headquarters noticed that if Hayes carried South Carolina, Florida, and Louisiana, where the party controlled the voting machinery, he would have a one-vote Electoral College majority. Both Gen. Daniel E. Sickles and William E. Chandler later claimed to have made this discovery and to have sent telegrams, over the signature of the sleeping party chairman, Zachariah Chandler, urging Republican officials to hold their states for Hayes. Soon after he awakened, Chandler announced: "Hayes has 185 electoral votes and is elected."

The Electoral Crisis and the End of Reconstruction

Sixteen years after the secession crisis, Americans entered another winter of political confusion, constitutional uncertainty, and talk of civil war. Election boards in Florida, South Carolina, and Louisiana invalidated enough returns from violence-torn counties to make Hayes and the Republican candidate for governor victorious. Democrats challenged the results and dispatched rival electoral certificates to Washington.

"Everything now depends upon you · nerve and your leadership," Democratic editor Manton Marble wrote Tilden on December 10, but the Democratic aspirant, a man with an abiding fear of disorder, seems to have resigned himself to defeat almost from the moment the crisis began. Instead of putting his claim effectively before the public, Tilden retreated to his study, spending most of December drafting a lengthy examination of legal precedents concerning the counting of electoral ballots. In contrast to his rival's "annoying inactivity," Hayes at least gave tacit approval to a series of complex negotiations involving his close political associates, representatives of South Carolina and Louisiana Democrats, and a group of self-appointed schemers who hoped to promote their own vision of a New South. As an immediate objective, these efforts aimed, through assurances that the next administration would treat the South with "kind consideration," to detach enough Southern Democratic Congressmen from Tilden to insure Hayes's election. But many Northern Republicans also hoped to use the crisis to reduce the influence of carpetbaggers and blacks and attract the "better class" of local whites to Southern Republicanism. Meeting with a New Orleans editor who brought the message that Louisiana Democrats cared more about control of their own state than the

White House, Hayes remarked, "I believe, and I have always believed, that the intelligence of any country ought to govern it."

Meanwhile, a separate but overlapping set of negotiations was underway. These involved, among other individuals, William H. Smith, head of the Western Associated Press and a close friend of Hayes, and Memphis editor Andrew J. Kellar, a Tennessee railroad man eager to aid in "building up a Conservative Republican party in the South." To these men, a peaceful solution to the crisis, Hayes's inauguration, and a new era in Southern politics all hinged on Republican assurances of internal improvements subsidies for the South. They were particularly anxious for Hayes to pledge assistance to the Texas & Pacific Railroad. Rumors of backroom maneuvers abounded, and newspapers filled in the outlines of an embryonic deal. "There is undoubtedly danger of defection among southern Democrats," the New York *Sun*'s Washington correspondent reported in mid-December. "The friends of Hayes are certainly bidding high in that direction. . . . The subsidy for T[exas] P[acific] is part of the programme, as well as counting in of Hayes . . . and a new departure in Republican party policy is to date from Hayes' inauguration."

Things, however, did not work out quite this smoothly. For Republicans were deeply divided by the electoral crisis. Some Stalwarts opposed any deal at all, and others feared Hayes's "reform" inclinations. With neither party enjoying vigorous leadership or unity of purpose, Congress created an independent commission to decide the disputed returns. Enactment of the "plan of peace" reflected a growing desire within both parties for a settlement, the outgrowth, in part, of pressure from a "mercantile and business interest" thoroughly alarmed by extreme rhetoric among supporters of both candidates. Petitions advocating a peaceful solution flooded into Washington, signed mostly, one cynic noted, by "firms doing chiefly *southern* trade."

Enacted late in January, the Electoral Commission Law established a body with fifteen members: ten Congressmen, divided equally between the parties, and five Supreme Court justices. Four of the latter, two Democrats and two Republicans, were named in the bill and directed to select the fifth, who everyone assumed would be Justice David Davis, a political independent. But after unexpectedly being elected to the Senate from Illinois, Davis resigned from the commission, Republican Justice Joseph P. Bradley took his place, and by a series of 8–7 votes, the disputed votes were awarded to Hayes. "We have been cheated, shamefully cheated," protested one outraged Democrat.

Further turmoil, however, lay ahead before Hayes entered the White House. Tilden's supporters threatened to obstruct a final count of the electoral vote in the House, thereby preventing an inauguration on March 4. Hayes's Washington representatives initiated a new round of negotiations. A caucus of "conservative" Southerners proposed that Hayes agree to appoint to the Cabinet Tennessee Sen. David M. Key. There was also talk of Southern Democrats aiding the Republicans in organizing the closely divided House of Representatives in the next Congress, and lobbyists resumed their effort to make federal aid to the Texas & Pacific part of any deal. On February 26 four Southern Democrats met with five Ohio Republicans at Washington's Wormley House hotel. Hayes's confidant Stanley Matthews announced that the new President intended to recognize Democrat Francis T. Nicholls as Louisiana's governor and pursue a policy of noninterference in Southern affairs, while Nicholls's emissary, Col. Edward A. Burke, pledged to avoid reprisals against Republicans and respect the rights of blacks. Similar discussions with Wade Hampton's representatives followed. Throughout, the fate of Reconstruction remained the central issue in the bargaining. "It matters little to us who rules in Washington," commented an Abbeville newspaper at the end of February, "if South Carolina is allowed to have Hampton and Home Rule."

James A. Garfield, who left the meeting early, believed "a compact of some kind was mediated" at Wormley House, but the terms of the "Bargain of 1877" remain impossible to determine with any precision. Certainly, Hayes became President, and Key Postmaster General. The Texas & Pacific never did receive federal assistance, nor did a single Southern Democrat support Garfield's bid the following autumn to become Speaker of the House. No flood of former Whigs entered the Republican party, and peaceful, honest elections did not soon return to the South. But "home rule" quickly came to Louisiana and South Carolina. Within two months of taking office, Hayes ordered federal troops surrounding the South Carolina and Louisiana statehouses to return to their barracks. (Hayes did not, as legend has it, remove the last federal troops from the South.) Hampton and Nicholls peacefully assumed office, marking the final triumph of "Redemption." "The whole South—every state in the

South," lamented black Louisianan Henry Adams, "had got into the hands of the very men that held us as slaves."

"To think that Hayes could go back on us," commented one freedman, "when we had to wade through blood to help place him where he is now." But rather than an abrupt change in Northern policy, Hayes's actions, as the New York *Herald* pointed out, only confirmed in two states "what in the course of years has been done by his predecessor or by Congress" elsewhere in the South. Indeed, the abandonment of Reconstruction was as much a cause of the crisis of 1876–77 as a consequence, for had Republicans been willing to intervene in defense of black rights, Tilden would never have come close to carrying the entire South. Nonetheless, the "withdrawal" of troops marked a major turning point in national policy. "The negro," proclaimed *The Nation,* "will disappear from the field of national politics. Henceforth, the nation, as a nation, will have nothing more to do with him."

Among other things, 1877 marked a decisive retreat from the idea, born during the Civil War, of a powerful national state protecting the fundamental rights of all American citizens. Yet the federal government had been rendered impotent only in matters concerning blacks. Within three months of the end of Reconstruction, the Hayes administration confronted one of the bitterest explosions of class warfare in American history—the Great Strike of 1877. Beginning on July 16, when workers on the Baltimore & Ohio Railroad walked off their jobs at Martinsburg, West Virginia, to protest a wage cut, the strike spread westward along the great trunk lines, affecting every region of the country except New England and the Deep South and expanding to other industries. In Pittsburgh, traffic was halted on the Pennsylvania Railroad, and miners and steel workers organized sympathy strikes. Militiamen were brought in from Philadelphia to replace local units who refused to act against the strikers, and when they fired on crowds that had seized railroad switches, killing twenty people, outraged citizens set fire to the Pittsburgh railroad yards. Flames engulfed over 100 locomotives and 2,000 railroad cars. General strikes paralyzed Chicago and St. Louis, uniting skilled and unskilled workers in demands for an eight-hour day, a return to predepression wage levels, the nationalization of the railroads, and the repeal of "tramp ordinances" allowing the arrest of unemployed workers.

"The most extensive and deplorable workingmen's strike which ever took place in this, or indeed in any other country," as *The Nation* described it, the labor upheaval suggested how profoundly American class relations had been reshaped during the Civil War and Reconstruction. The strike exposed the deep hostility to railroads—symbols and creators of the new industrial order—that permeated many American communities. At the same time, the Great Strike revealed the political power and collective consciousness of the urban middle and upper classes, which joined with municipal authorities and veterans' organizations to form "citizen militias" to do battle with strikers. St. Louis's Committee of Public Safety organized a huge private army, commanded by one Union and one Confederate general, and effectively suppressed the city's general strike. Louisville's city hall was "converted virtually into an arsenal," from which "influential and wealthy citizens" received arms to augment the local police.

The response to the labor upheaval underscored the alliance of the new industrial bourgeoisie with the Republican party and national state. Where local authorities and middle-class citizens proved unable to restore order, federal troops stepped into the breach. Hayes had filled his Cabinet with party leaders who were also corporate attorneys and railroad directors. Thomas A. Scott, the Pennsylvania's president, had direct access to the White House during the strike. As frightened governors and beleaguered railroad executives frantically pressed for military action, Hayes neither investigated the need for troops nor set clear guidelines for their use. Thus, when soldiers were sent to cities from Buffalo to St. Louis, they acted less as impartial defenders of order than as strikebreakers, opening railroad lines, protecting nonstriking workers, and preventing union meetings. With the army suddenly overextended, units were hastily transferred from the South, including some who, until recently, had guarded the Louisiana statehouse. By July 29 the Great Strike had ended. Just as the era of Reconstruction had opened in 1863 with the promise of freedom to blacks, quickly followed by an explosion of class and racial antagonisms in the streets of New York City, the restoration of white supremacy in the South coincided with an even more powerful reminder of the conflicts that divided Northern society. The upheaval marked a fundamental shift in the nation's political agenda. "The Southern question," a Charleston newspaper declared, was "dead"—the railroad strike had propelled to the forefront of politics "the question of labor and capital, work and wages."

Enjoying a triumphal visit to Europe, former President Grant found the events of 1877 "a little queer." During his administration, he wrote, the entire Democratic party and the "morbidly honest and 'reformatory' portion of the Republican" had thought it "horrible" to employ federal troops "to protect the lives of negroes. Now, however, there is no hesitation about exhausting the whole power of the government to suppress a strike on the slightest intimation that danger threatens." Grant was not the only contemporary to note the ironic juxtaposition of home rule for the South and armed intervention in the North. "I wish Sheridan was at Pittsburgh," a neighbor told William Lloyd Garrison II. "Indeed," Garrison replied, "but remember how you denounced him at New Orleans."

All in all, 1877 confirmed the growing conservatism of the Republican party and portended a new role for the national state in the post-Reconstruction years. The federal courts, for example, used the greatly expanded jurisdiction born of Reconstruction primarily to protect corporations from local regulation. In 1883 the Supreme Court declared the Civil Rights Act of 1875 unconstitutional. Joseph P. Bradley, whose vote on the Electoral Commission had made Hayes President, wrote the majority opinion, which observed that blacks must cease "to be the special favorite of the laws." Only Kentucky's John Marshall Harlan dissented. The United States, he warned, had entered "an era of constitutional law, when the rights of freedom and American citizenship cannot receive from the nation that efficient protection which heretofore was unhesitatingly accorded to slavery." The general approval that greeted the decision, observed *The Nation*, revealed "how completely the extravagant expectations" aroused by the Civil War had "died out."

The Redeemers' New South

As a period when Republicans controlled Southern politics, blacks enjoyed extensive political power, and the federal government accepted responsibility for protecting the fundamental rights of black citizens, Reconstruction came to an irrevocable end with the inauguration of Hayes. Of course, the coming of "home rule" did not end the process of change or resolve the social conflicts unleashed by the Civil War. But these took place in a new context, in which the South's rulers enjoyed a free hand in managing the region's domestic affairs. Constrained only by the remote possibility of federal intervention, the survival of enclaves of Republican political power, and fear of divisions within the now dominant Democracy, the Redeemers moved in the final decades of the nineteenth century to put in place new systems of political, class, and race relations. A new social order did not come into being immediately, nor were the achievements of Reconstruction entirely undone. But Redeemer rule confirmed what a North Carolina Democrat had predicted as Reconstruction began: "When the bayonets shall depart . . . then look out for the reaction. Then the bottom rail will descend from the top of the fence."

No single generalization fully describes the social origins or political purposes of the South's Redeemers, whose ranks included secessionist Democrats and Union Whigs, veterans of the Confederacy and rising younger leaders, traditional planters and advocates of a modernized New South. They shared, however, a commitment to dismantling the Reconstruction state, reducing the political power of blacks, and reshaping the South's legal system in the interests of labor control and racial subordination. In a majority of Southern states, they moved, on assuming office, to replace Reconstruction constitutions with new documents severely restricting the scope and expense of government. Redeemer constitutions reduced the salaries of state officials, slashed state and local property taxes, and curtailed the government's authority to incur financial obligations.

Judged by their pledges to reduce the cost of government and the burden of property taxes, the Redeemers were a success. Tenants, however, received no benefit from the fall in taxation of landed property, and yeomen, although paying less, saw Reconstruction laws excluding a fixed amount of property from taxes replaced by exemptions only for specific items, such as machinery and implements utilized on a plantation. Laborers, tenants, and small farmers paid taxes on virtually everything they owned, while many planters had thousands of dollars in property excluded. The tax system became increasingly regressive, as those with the least property bore the heaviest proportional burden.

Fiscal retrenchment went hand in hand with a retreat from the idea of an activist state meeting broad social responsibilities. "Spend nothing unless absolutely necessary," Gov. George F. Drew advised the Florida legislature in 1877, and lawmakers took his advice to heart, abolishing the penitentiary and abandoning a nearly completed agricultural college, leaving the state without any institution of higher learning, public or private. Alabama's Redeemers closed public hospitals at Montgomery and Talladega, and Louisiana's were "so economical that . . . state services to the people almost disappeared." Public education, described as a "luxury" by one Redeemer governor, was especially hard hit, as some states all but dismantled the education systems established during Reconstruction. Louisiana spent so little on education that it became the only state in the Union that saw the percentage of native whites able to read or write actually decline between 1880 and 1900. Blacks suffered the most from educational retrenchment, for the gap between expenditures for black and white pupils steadily widened.

Simultaneously, the Redeemers tightened their hold on state and local government and curtailed Republicans' remaining political power. In the border and Upper South, white Republican voting persisted, and the advent of "home rule" had little immediate effect on the black franchise, keeping the party competitive into the 1890s. But in the Deep South, where electoral fraud and the threat of violence hung heavily over the black community, the Republican party crumbled after 1877. Here, long before their outright disenfranchisement around the turn of the century, black political rights progressively eroded. Small numbers of blacks remained in Southern legislatures, and a few even won election to Congress. Blacks still held seats on city councils and minor posts in some plantation counties, and enclaves of genuine black power persisted, from the "black second" Congressional district of eastern North Carolina to South Carolina's lowcountry and the Texas black belt. But the political context had changed profoundly since the days of Republican rule. Local officials confronted hostile state governments, and black lawmakers found themselves without influence in Democratic legislatures. Their ability to provide constituent services now depended on connections with influential white Republicans or the goodwill of prominent local Democrats, rather than on leadership of a politically mobilized community.

Thus, the New South saw a progressive narrowing of blacks' political and social options. In some realms, to be sure, change came slowly. Southern race relations remained for a time flexible and somewhat indeterminate. Blacks could still gain admission to theaters, bars, and a few hotels and obtain equal seating on some streetcars and railroads. A new etiquette of race relations slowly took shape under the Redeemers, as more reserved kinds of everyday behavior replaced the black assertiveness so evident during Reconstruction. But not until the 1890s did racial segregation become embedded in Southern law.

In other realms, however, change was immediate. Throughout the South, Democrats rewrote the statute books to reinforce planters' control over their labor force. Broad new vagrancy laws allowed the arrest of virtually any jobless person, and "antienticement" laws made it a criminal offense to offer employment to anyone already under contract or to leave a job before a contract had expired. Meanwhile, Southern criminal laws increased sharply the penalty for petty theft. South Carolina made arson a capital offense and mandated life imprisonment for burglary. Mississippi's famous "pig law" defined the theft of any cattle or swine as grand larceny punishable by five years in jail. "It looks to me," commented a black resident of the state, "that the white people are putting in prison all that they can get their hands on." One result was a vast expansion of the convict lease system. Within two months of Redemption, South Carolina's legislature authorized the hiring out of virtually every convict in the state, as did Florida after dismantling its penitentiary. Railroads, mining and lumber companies, and planters competed for this new form of involuntary labor, most of whom were blacks imprisoned for petty crimes.

New laws also gave the planter control of credit and property—the essence of economic power in the rural South. Lien laws gave precedence to a landlord's claim to his share of the crop over that of a laborer for wages or a merchant for supplies, thus shifting much of the risk of farming from employer to employee. North Carolina's notorious Landlord and Tenant Act of 1877 placed the entire crop in the planter's hands until rent had been paid and empowered him to decide when a tenant's obligation had been fulfilled, making the landlord "the court, sheriff, and jury," complained one former slave. A series of court decisions defined the sharecropper not as a partner in agriculture or a renter with a property right in the growing crop, but as a wage laborer possessing "only a right to go on the land to plant, work, and gather the crop."

Blacks, moreover, were all but excluded from the machinery of law enforcement. Few remained on local police forces or in state militias, whose budgets were exempted from the Redeemers' parsimony. Except in a few localities, blacks no longer served on Southern juries. And, if necessary, the Redeemer state employed brutal force to control labor. Throughout the 1880s and 1890s Southern sheriffs, backed by state militias, crushed efforts to organize farm workers.

Redeemer rule proved only partially successful in controlling the black labor force. Complaints about a "labor shortage" continued, and blacks clung to the autonomy they could wrest from the sharecropping system and the right to move from plantation to plantation. But the balance of power between social classes in the South had been transformed. "This year," reported a New York business journal at the end of 1877, "labor is under control for the first season since the war."

The policies of Redeemer governments not only reshaped Southern class relations, but also affected regional economic development in the last quarter of the nineteenth century. Partly because of Redeemer rule, the South emerged as a peculiar hybrid—a poverty-stricken colonial economy integrated into the national capitalist marketplace yet with its own distinctive system of repressive labor relations. While the region's new upper class of planters, merchants, and industrialists prospered, the majority of Southerners of both races sank deeper and deeper into poverty. For Southern yeomen, the restoration of white supremacy brought few economic rewards. As cotton prices fell and world demand stagnated, upcountry farmers were forced into indebtedness and tenancy. By 1890, owners cultivated less than half the farms in Upper Piedmont Georgia. The enhancement of rural labor control eliminated any incentive for the mechanization of agriculture. With much Northern investment going into extractive enterprises like mining and lumbering that made little contribution to regional development, and with the poverty of rural Southerners precluding a substantial home market, economic growth proved remarkably meager. The Deep South showed no increase at all in its per capita income between 1880 and 1900. As late as 1900, only six percent of the Southern labor force worked in manufacturing.

Blacks in the Redeemers' New South were enmeshed in a seamless web of economic, political, and social oppression. In illiteracy, malnutrition, inadequate housing, and a host of other burdens, blacks paid the highest price for the end of Reconstruction and the stagnation of the Southern economy. With politics eliminated as an avenue to power, and displays of militancy likely to be met by overwhelming force, ambitious and talented black men turned to education, business, the church, and the professions. Severed from any larger political purpose, economic self-help, especially among the emerging black middle class, became an alternative to involvement in public life. "All my politics, gentlemen," the black owner of a Raleigh livery stable told a Congressional committee, "is that if a man has got 25 cents I will take him uptown on my omnibus." In general, black activity turned inward. Assuming a defensive cast, it concentrated on strengthening the black community rather than on directly challenging the new status quo.

One index of the narrowed possibilities for change was the revival of interest, all but moribund during Reconstruction, in emigration to Africa or the West. The greatest attention centered on Kansas, which became the destination of tens of thousands of refugees from "oppression and bondage." Nationally prominent black leaders, including Frederick Douglass, opposed the Kansas migration, fearing it amounted to a tacit surrender of the struggle for citizenship rights in the South. But the movement generated immense excitement among ordinary blacks. The Exodus, as they called it, tapped deep religious convictions. The freedmen, a Montgomery black convention had declared shortly after the Democrats recaptured Alabama in 1874, might yet be compelled "to repeat the history of the Israelites" and "seek new homes . . . beyond the reign and rule of Pharaoh." To countless blacks, Kansas offered the prospect of political equality, freedom from violence, access to education, economic opportunity, and liberation from the presence of the old slaveholding class—in sum, the "*practical independence*" that Reconstruction had failed to secure.

Until Northern employers dismantled the color bar that restricted nearly all industrial jobs to whites, most blacks were destined to remain in the South. Yet the Kansas Exodus not only revealed the disillusionment that followed the end of Reconstruction, but testified to the fact that blacks' apparent quiescence did not imply consent to Redeemer hegemony. "We have no enemy in our front," commented Mississippi's Lucius Q. C. Lamar soon after Hayes's inauguration. "But the negroes are almost as well disciplined in their silence and inactivity as they were before in their aggressiveness." In black eyes, the entire system fashioned by the Redeemers bore the mark of illegitimacy. In 1879, on the final day of his nine-year Congressional career, Joseph H. Rainey offered a fitting commentary on Redeemer rule: "Doubtless [Reconstruction government] was more extravagant. . . . [But] can the saving of a few thousand or hundreds of thousands of dollars compensate for the loss of the political heritage of American citizens?" As under slavery, blacks in the Redeemers' New South never acknowledged the justice of the social order under which they were forced to live.

Epilogue

"The River Has Its Bend"

Thus, in the words of W. E. B. Du Bois, "the slave went free; stood a brief moment in the sun; then moved back again toward slavery." The magnitude of the Redeemer counterrevolution underscored both the scope of the transformation Reconstruction had assayed and the consequences of its failure. To be sure, the era of emancipation and Republican rule did not lack enduring accomplishments. The tide of change rose and then receded, but it left behind an altered landscape. The freedmen's political and civil equality proved transitory, but the autonomous black family and a network of religious and social institutions survived the end of Reconstruction. Nor could the seeds of educational progress planted then be entirely uprooted.

If blacks failed to achieve the economic independence envisioned in the aftermath of the Civil War, Reconstruction closed off even more oppressive alternatives than the Redeemers' New South. The post-Reconstruction labor system embodied neither a return to closely supervised gang labor nor the complete dispossession and immobilization of the black labor force and coercive apprenticeship systems envisioned by white Southerners in 1865 and 1866. Nor were blacks, as in twentieth-century South Africa, barred from citizenship, herded into labor reserves, or prohibited by law from moving from one part of the country to another. Without Reconstruction, it is difficult to imagine the establishment of a framework of legal rights enshrined in the Construction that, while flagrantly violated after 1877, created a vehicle for future federal intervention in Southern affairs.

Nonetheless, whether measured by the dreams inspired by emancipation or the more limited goals of securing blacks' rights as citizens and free laborers and establishing an enduring Republican presence in the South, Reconstruction must be judged a failure. Among the host of explanations for this outcome, a few seem especially significant. Conditions far beyond the control of Southern Republicans—such as the national credit and banking systems, the depression of the 1870s, and the stagnation of world demand for cotton—severely limited the prospects for far-reaching economic change. The early rejection of federally sponsored land reform left in place a planter class far weaker and less affluent than before the war, but still able to employ its prestige and experience against Reconstruction. Factionalism and corruption, although hardly confined to Southern Republicans, undermined their legitimacy and complicated their efforts to respond to attacks by resolute opponents. The failure to develop a lasting appeal to white voters made it nearly impossible for Republicans to combat the racial politics of the Redeemers. None of these factors, however, would have proved decisive without the campaign of violence that turned the electoral tide in many parts of the South and the weakening of Northern resolve, itself a consequence of social and political changes that undermined the free labor and egalitarian precepts at the heart of Reconstruction policy.

For historians, hindsight can be a treacherous ally. Enabling us to trace the hidden patterns of past events, it beguiles us with the mirage of inevitability, the assumption that different outcomes lay beyond the limits of the possible. Certainly, the history of other plantation societies offers little reason for optimism that emancipation could have given rise to a prosperous, egalitarian South, or even one that escaped a pattern of colonial underdevelopment. Nor do the prospects for the expansion of scalawag support—essential for Southern Republicanism's long-term survival—appear in retrospect to have been anything but bleak. And the nation lacked not simply the will but the modern bureaucratic machinery to oversee permanently Southern affairs. Perhaps the remarkable thing about Reconstruction was not its failure, but that it was attempted at all and survived as long as it did. Yet one can, I think, imagine alternative scenarios and modest successes: the Republican party establishing itself as a permanent fixture on the Southern landscape, the North summoning the resolve to enforce the Constitution.

Here, however, we enter the realm of the purely speculative. What remains certain is that Reconstruction failed, and that for blacks its failure was a disaster whose magnitude cannot be obscured by the accomplishments that endured. For the nation as a whole, the collapse of Reconstruction was a tragedy that deeply affected the course of its development. If racism contributed to the undoing of Reconstruction, so also Reconstruction's demise and the emergence of blacks as disenfranchised dependent laborers accelerated racism's spread, until by the early twentieth century it pervaded the nation's culture and politics. The removal of a significant portion of the laboring population from public life shifted American politics to the right, complicating for generations the efforts of reformers. Long into the twentieth century, the South remained a one-party region ruled by a reactionary elite that continued to employ violence and fraud to stifle internal dissent. An enduring consequence of Reconstruction's failure, the Solid South helped define the contours of American politics and weaken the prospects not simply of change in racial matters but of progressive legislation generally.

The men and women who fought to remake Southern society scattered down innumerable byways after Reconstruction's demise. Most carpetbaggers returned to the North, often finding there the financial success that had eluded them in the South. Former South Carolina Gov. Robert K. Scott returned to Napoleon, Ohio, where he became a successful real estate agent—"a most fitting occupation" in view of his involvement in land commission speculations.

Republican governors who had won reputations as moderates by courting white Democratic support and seeking to limit blacks' political influence found the Redeemer South remarkably forgiving. Daniel H. Chamberlain left South Carolina in 1877 to launch a successful New York City law practice, but was well received on his numerous visits to the state. In retrospect, Chamberlain altered his opinion of Reconstruction: a "frightful experiment" that tried to "lift a backward or inferior race" to equality, it had inevitably produced "shocking and unbearable misgovernment." "Governor Chamberlain," commented a Charleston newspaper in 1904, "has lived and learned."

Not all white Republicans, however, abandoned Reconstruction ideals. Adelbert Ames, who left Mississippi in 1875 to join his father's Minnesota flour-milling business and later settled in Massachusetts, continued to defend his Reconstruction record. Ames lived to his 98th year, never abandoning the conviction that "caste is the curse of the world." Another Mississippi carpetbagger, Massachusetts-born teacher and legislator Henry Warren, published his autobiography in 1914, still hoping that one day, "possibly in the present century," America would live up to the ideal of "equal political rights for all without regard to race." Louis F. Post, a New Jersey-born carpetbagger who took stenographic notes for South Carolina's legislature in the early 1870s, became a follower of Henry George, attended the founding meeting of the NAACP, and as Woodrow Wilson's Assistant Secretary of Labor attempted to mitigate the 1919 Red Scare and prevent the deportation of foreign-born radicals. Texas scalawag editor Albert Parsons became a nationally known Chicago labor reformer and anarchist, whose speeches drew comparisons between the plight of Southern blacks and Northern industrial workers. Having survived the perils of Texas Reconstruction, Parsons died on the Illinois gallows after being wrongfully convicted of complicity in the Haymarket bombing of 1886.

Many black veterans of Reconstruction survived on federal patronage after the coming of "home rule." P. B. S. Pinchback and Blanche K. Bruce held a series of such posts and later moved to Washington, D.C., where they entered the city's privileged black society. Other black leaders left the political arena entirely to devote themselves to religious and educational work, emigration projects, or personal advancement. Robert G. Fitzgerald continued to teach in North Carolina until his death in 1919. Others found, in the words of a black lawyer, that "the tallest tree . . . suffers most in a storm." Former South Carolina Congressman and Lieut. Gov. Alonzo J. Ransier died in poverty in 1882, having been employed during his last years as a night watchman at the Charleston Custom House and as a city street sweeper. Robert B. Elliott, the state's most brilliant political organizer, found himself "utterly unable to earn a living owing to the severe ostracism and mean prejudice of my political opponents." He died in 1884 after moving to New Orleans and struggling to survive as a lawyer. Most local leaders sank into obscurity, disappearing from the historical record. If their descendants moved ahead, it was through business, the arts, or the professions, not politics.

By the turn of the century, as soldiers from North and South joined to take up the "white man's burden" in the Spanish-American War, Reconstruction was widely viewed as little more than a regrettable detour on the road to reunion. To most white Southerners, it was axiomatic that Reconstruction had been a time of "savage tyranny" that "accomplished not one useful result, and left behind it, not one pleasant recollection." In more sober language, many Northerners, including surviving architects of Congressional policy, concurred in this judgment. "Years of thinking and observation" had convinced O. O. Howard "that the restoration of their lands to the planters provided for [a] future better for the negroes." John Sherman's recollections recorded a similar change of heart: "After this long lapse of time I am convinced that Mr. Johnson's scheme of reorganization was wise and judicious. . . . It is unfortunate that it had not the sanction of Congress."

This rewriting of Reconstruction's history was accorded scholarly legitimacy—to its everlasting shame—by the nation's fraternity of professional historians. Early in the twentieth century a group of young Southern scholars gathered at Columbia University to study the Reconstruction era under the guidance of Professors John W. Burgess and William A. Dunning. Blacks, their mentors taught, were "children" utterly incapable of appreciating the freedom that had been thrust upon them. The North did "a monstrous thing" in granting them the suffrage, for "a black skin means membership in a race of men which has never of itself succeeded in subjecting passion to reason, has never, therefore, created any civilization of any kind." The views of the Dunning School shaped historical writing for generations and achieved wide popularity through D. W. Griffith's film *Birth of a Nation* (which glorified the Ku Klux Klan and had its premiere at Woodrow Wilson's White House) and the national bestseller *The Tragic Era* by Claude G. Bowers. Southern whites, wrote Bowers, "literally were put to the torture" by "emissaries of hate" who inflamed "the negroes' egotism" and even inspired "lustful assaults" by blacks on white womanhood.

Few interpretations of history have had such far-reaching consequences as this image of Reconstruction. As Francis B. Simkins, a South Carolina–born historian, noted during the 1930s, "the alleged horrors of Reconstruction" did much to freeze the mind of the white South in unalterable opposition to outside pressures for social change and to any thought of breaching Democratic ascendancy, eliminating segregation, or restoring the suffrage to disenfranchised blacks. They also justified Northern indifference to the nullification of the Fourteenth and Fifteenth Amendments.

Only in the family traditions and collective folk memories of the black community did a different version of Reconstruction survive. Growing up in the 1920s, Pauli Murray was "never allowed to forget" that she walked in "proud shoes" because her grandfather, Robert G. Fitzgerald, had "fought for freedom" in the Union Army and then enlisted as a teacher in the "second war" against the powerlessness and ignorance inherited from slavery. When the Works Progress Administration sent agents into the black belt during the Great Depression to interview former slaves, they found Reconstruction remembered for its disappointments and betrayals, but also as a time of hope, possibility, and accomplishment. "The Yankees helped free us, so they say," declared eighty-one-year-old former slave Thomas Hall, "but they let us be put back in slavery again." Yet coupled with this disillusionment were proud, vivid recollections of a time when "the colored used to hold office." Some pulled from their shelves dusty scrapbooks of clippings from Reconstruction newspapers; other could still recount the names of local black leaders. "They made pretty fair officers," remarked one elderly freedman; "I thought them was good times in the country," said another. "I does believe that the negro ought to be given more privileges in voting," echoed Taby Jones, born a slave in South Carolina in 1850, "because they went through the reconstruction period with banners flying." Younger blacks spoke of being taught by their parents "about the old times, mostly about the Reconstruction, and the Ku Klux." "I know folks think the books tell the truth, but they shore don't," one eighty-eight-year-old former slave told the WPA.

Twenty more years elapsed before another generation of black Southerners launched the final challenge to the racial system of the New South. By this time the Reconstruction generation had passed from the scene, and even within the black community memories of the period had all but disappeared. Yet the institutions created or consolidated after the Civil War—the black family, school, and church—provided the base from which the modern civil rights revolution sprang. And for its legal strategy, the movement returned to the laws and amendments of Reconstruction.

"The river has its bend, and the longest road must terminate."

Rev. Peter Randolph, a former slave, wrote these words in 1893, as the dark night of injustice settled over the South. Nearly a century elapsed before the nation again attempted to come to terms with the implications of emancipation and Reconstruction's political and social agenda. In many ways, it has yet to do so.

Suggestions for Further Reading

A comprehensive bibliography of unpublished sources and historical works on Reconstruction as well as footnote citations for items in the text may be found in Eric Foner, *Reconstruction: America's Unfinished Revolution, 1863–1877* (New York, 1988). The following list focuses on those books that have been most influential in shaping historians' thinking on the Reconstruction era, with particular emphasis on important recent writing.

Preface

General accounts of Reconstruction by the "traditional" or Dunning school include William A. Dunning, *Reconstruction, Political and Economic 1865–1877* (New York, 1907), Claude G. Bowers, *The Tragic Era* (Cambridge, Mass., 1929), and E. Merton Coulter, *The South During Reconstruction 1865–1877* (Baton Rouge, 1947). Walter L. Fleming, *Civil War and Reconstruction in Alabama* (New York, 1905) and J. G. deRoulhac Hamilton, *Reconstruction in North Carolina* (New York, 1914) are among the state studies produced by the Dunning school. The reinterpretation of Andrew Johnson and the Radical Republicans in the 1920s is reflected in George F. Milton, *The Age of Hate: Andrew Johnson and the Radicals* (New York, 1930) and Howard K. Beale, *The Critical Year: A Study of Andrew Johnson and Reconstruction* (New York, 1930).

   W. E. B. Du Bois, *Black Reconstruction in America* (New York, 1935) poses a monumental challenge to the traditional point of view. See also James Allen, *Reconstruction: The Battle for Democracy* (New York, 1937). Kenneth M. Stampp, *The Era of Reconstruction 1865–1877* (New York, 1965), and John Hope Franklin, *Reconstruction After the Civil War* (Chicago, 1960) are influential summaries of the revisionist position, while Robert Cruden, *The Negro in Reconstruction* (Englewood Cliffs, N.J., 1969), is a useful revisionist survey. For a discussion of more recent trends in Reconstruction historiography, see Eric Foner, "Reconstruction Revisited," *Reviews in American History* 10 (December 1982): 82–100.

Many of the important public documents of the Reconstruction era are included in Edward McPherson, *The Political History of the United States of America During the Period of Reconstruction* (Washington, D.C., 1875). Dorothy Sterling, ed., *The Trouble They Seen* (New York, 1976) and LaWanda and John H. Cox, *Reconstruction, the Negro, and the New South* (Columbia, S.C., 1973) are excellent documentary records of the black experience in these years.

Chapter 1: The World the War Made

The best accounts of the destruction of slavery and the enrollment of black soldiers, together with extraordinary contemporary documents, may be found in Ira Berlin, ed., *Freedom: A Documentary History of Emancipation* (New York, 1982–). The political economy of the Southern upcountry is described in Steven Hahn, *The Roots of Southern Populism: Yeoman Farmers and the Transformation of the Georgia Upcountry, 1850–1890* (New York, 1983). On discontent within the Confederacy, see Paul D. Escott, *After Secession: Jefferson Davis and the Failure of Confederate Nationalism* (Baton Rouge, 1978). William T. Auman and David D. Scarboro, "The Heroes of America in Civil War North Carolina," *North Carolina Historical Review* 58 (Autumn 1981): 327–63 describes a particularly dramatic example of wartime Southern Unionism, while Philip S. Paludan, *Victims: A Civil War Story* (Knoxville, 1981) relates a bloody incident in the South's inner civil war.

For the wartime North, see Emerson D. Fite, *Social and Industrial Conditions in the North During the Civil War* (New York, 1910), Philip S. Paludan, *"A People's Contest": The Union and the Civil War, 1861–1865* (New York, 1988), and David T. Gilchrist and W. David Lewis, eds. *Economic Change in the Civil War Era* (Greenville, Del., 1965). George M. Fredrickson, *The Inner Civil War: Northern Intellectuals and the Crisis of the Union* (New York, 1965) discusses the war's effect on reformers, while Harold M. Hyman, *A More Perfect Union: The Impact of the Civil War and Reconstruction on the Constitution* (New York, 1973) describes the rise of a new attitude toward the national state. For changes in the status of Northern blacks, see Vincent Harding, *There Is a River: The Black Struggle for Freedom in America* (New York, 1981). Joel Silbey, *A Respectable Minority: The Democratic Party in the Civil War Era* (New York, 1977) discusses political opponents of the Lincoln administration. The most dramatic instance of resistance to the war effort is analyzed and placed in context in Iver Bernstein, *The New York City Draft Riots: Their Significance for American Society and Politics in the Age of the Civil War* (New York, 1989).

Chapter 2: Rehearsals for Reconstruction

Herman Belz, *Reconstructing the Union: Theory and Practice During the Civil War* (Ithaca, 1969) describes the evolution of wartime Reconstruction policy. For events in the loyal border states, see Richard O. Curry, ed., *Radicalism, Racism, and Party Realignment: The Border States During Reconstruction* (Baltimore, 1969), Victor B. Howard, *Black Liberation in Kentucky: Emancipation and Freedom, 1862–1884* (Lexington, Ky., 1983), Charles L. Wagandt, *The Mighty Revolution: Negro Emancipation in Maryland, 1862–1864* (Baltimore, 1964), and William E. Parrish, *Missouri Under Radical Rule 1865–1870* (Columbia, Mo., 1965). The process of wartime Reconstruction in the Confederate Upper South is described in Peter Maslowksi, *Treason Must Be Made Odious: Military Occupation and Wartime Reconstruction in Nashville, Tennessee, 1862–1865* (Millwood, N.Y., 1978). For the complex history of Louisiana's wartime Reconstruction, see Peyton McCrary, *Abraham Lincoln and Reconstruction: The Louisiana Experiment* (Princeton, 1978), Ted Tunnell, *Crucible of Reconstruction: War, Radicalism and Race in Louisiana 1862–1877* (Baton Rouge, 1981), and LaWanda Cox, *Lincoln and Black Freedom: A Study in Presidential Leadership* (Columbia, S.C., 1981).

Willie Lee Rose, *Rehearsal for Reconstruction: The Port Royal Experiment* (Indianapolis, 1964) is the best account of events on the wartime Sea Islands. Robert Engs, *Freedom's First Generation: Black Hampton, Virginia, 1861–1890* (Philadelphia, 1979) describes another "rehearsal." Wartime labor policies are analyzed and criticized in Louis S. Gerteis, *From Contraband to Freedman: Federal Policy Toward Southern Blacks, 1861–1865* (Westport, Conn., 1973), William F. Messner, *Freedmen and the Ideology of Free Labor: Louisiana 1862–1865* (Lafayette, La., 1978), and C. Peter Ripley, *Slaves and Freedmen in Civil War Louisiana* (Baton Rouge, 1976). For the Davis Bend experiment, see Janet S. Hermann, *The Pursuit of a Dream* (New York, 1981) and James T. Currie, *Enclave: Vicksburg and Her Plantations, 1863–1870* (Jackson, 1980).

James M. McPherson, *The Struggle for Equality: Abolitionists and the Negro in the Civil War and Reconstruction* (Princeton, 1964) and Herman Belz, *Emancipation and Equal Rights* (New York, 1978) describe the politics of emancipation in the final years of the war, and Harold M. Hyman and William M. Wiecek, *Equal Justice Under Law: Constitutional Development 1835–1875* (New York, 1982) stresses the constitutional significance of the Thirteenth Amendment.

Chapter 3: The Meaning of Freedom

Leon F. Litwack, *Been in the Storm So Long: The Aftermath of Slavery* (New York, 1979) vividly portrays blacks' actions in early Reconstruction. See also Peter Kolchin, *First Freedom: The Responses of Alabama's Blacks to Emancipation and Reconstruction* (Westport, Conn., 1972). The impact of the end of slavery on the black family is treated in Herbert G. Gutman, *The Black Family in Slavery and Freedom, 1750–1925* (New York, 1976) and Jacqueline Jones, *Labor of Love, Labor of Sorrow: Black Women, Work and the Family, from Slavery to the Present* (New York, 1985). For the rise of the black church, see Clarence E. Walker, *A Rock in a Weary Land: The African Methodist Episcopal Church During the Civil War and Reconstruction* (Baton Rouge, 1982) and James M. Washington, *Frustrated Fellowship: The Black Baptist Quest for Social Power* (Macon, Ga., 1986). For other institutions of the black community, see Armstead Robinson, "Plans Dat Comed from God: Institution Building and the Emergence of Black Leadership in Reconstruction Memphis," in *Towards a New South? Studies in Post–Civil War Southern Communities,* Orville V. Burton and Robert C. McMath, eds. (Westport, Conn., 1982).

The work of Northern missionaries and teachers is discussed in Joe M. Richardson, *Christian Reconstruction: The American Missionary Association and Southern Blacks, 1861–1890* (Athens, Ga., 1986) and Jacqueline Jones, *Soldiers of Light and Love: Northern Teachers and Georgia Blacks, 1865–1873* (Chapel Hill, 1980). Herbert G. Gutman, "Schools for Freedom: Post-Emancipation Origins of Afro-American Education," in *Power and Culture: Essays on the American Working Class,* Ira Berlin, ed. (New York, 1987) explores blacks' own efforts to establish schools. See also Robert C. Morris, *Reading, 'Riting, and Reconstruction: The Education of Freedmen in the South 1861–1870* (Chicago, 1981). Arnold H. Taylor, *Travail and Triumph: Black Life and Culture in the South Since the Civil War* (Westport, Conn., 1976) is a valuable general study.

Edward Magdol, *A Right to the Land: Essays on the Freedmen's Community* (Westport, Conn., 1977) explores the freedmen's economic aspirations. Eric Foner, *Nothing But Freedom: Emancipation and Its Legacy* (Baton Rouge, 1983) places the struggle over labor in a comparative perspective. The evolution of free black labor may be traced in the remarkable collection edited by Phillip S. Foner and Ronald L. Lewis, *The Black Worker: A Documentary History from Colonial Times to the Present,* 8 vols. (Philadelphia, 1978–84).

Proceedings of postwar black conventions are reprinted in two collections edited by Philip S. Foner and George E. Walker, *Proceedings of the Black National and State Conventions 1865–1900* (Philadelphia, 1986–) and *Proceedings of the Black State Conventions, 1840–1865,* 2 vols. (Philadelphia, 1979). Barry A. Crouch, "A Spirit of Lawlessness: White Violence, Texas Blacks, 1865–1868," *Journal of Social History* 18 (Winter 1984): 217–32 suggests the scope of postwar violence in one state.

Chapter 4: **Ambiguities of Free Labor**

Contemporary accounts of Southern conditions immediately after the war include J. T. Trowbridge, *The South: A Tour of Its Battle-Fields and Ruined Cities* (Hartford, Conn., 1866), Sidney Andrews, *The South Since the War* (Boston, 1866), John R. Dennett, *The South As It Is: 1865–1866*, Henry M. Christman, ed. (New York, 1965), and Whitelaw Reid, *After the War: A Southern Tour* (Cincinnati, 1866). Eugene Lerner, "Southern Output and Agricultural Income, 1860–1880," *Agricultural History*, 33 (July 1959): 117–25 makes clear the economic disaster the South suffered. Planters' reactions are explored in James L. Roark, *Masters Without Slaves: Southern Planters in the Civil War and Reconstruction* (New York, 1977). See also Roberta S. Alexander, *North Carolina Faces the Freedmen: Race Relations During Presidential Reconstruction, 1865–67* (Durham, 1985) and Michael Wayne, *The Reshaping of Plantation Society: The Natchez District, 1860–1880* (Baton Rouge, 1983). Lawrence N. Powell, *New Masters: Northern Planters During the Civil War and Reconstruction* (New Haven, 1980) studies Northerners who engaged in postwar cotton agriculture. The early emergence of sharecropping is traced in Roger L. Ransom and Richard Sutch, *One Kind of Freedom: The Economic Consequences of Emancipation* (New York, 1977) and Ronald F. Davis, *Good and Faithful Labor: From Slavery to Sharecropping in the Natchez District, 1860–1890* (Westport, Conn., 1982).

There is no adequate modern account of the Freedmen's Bureau, but see George R. Bentley, *A History of the Freedmen's Bureau* (Philadelphia, 1955) and William S. McFeely, *Yankee Stepfather: General O. O. Howard and the Freedmen* (New Haven, 1968). Aspects of the Bureau's history are treated in Donald G. Nieman, *To Set the Law in Motion: The Freedmen's Bureau and the Legal Rights of Blacks, 1865–1868* (Millwood, N.Y., 1979), Gaines M. Foster, "The Limitations of Federal Health Care for Freedmen, 1862–1868," *Journal of Southern History* 48 (August 1982): 349–72, and Claude F. Oubre, *Forty Acres and a Mule: The Freedmen's Bureau and Black Landownership* (Baton Rouge, 1978).

A valuable introduction to the South's economic reconstruction is Barbara J. Fields, "The Nineteenth-Century American South: History and Theory," *Plantation Society in the Americas* 2 (April 1983): 7–28. Gerald D. Jaynes, *Branches Without Roots: Genesis of the Black Working Class in the American South 1862–1882* (New York, 1986) is the best general account of the transition to free labor. Valuable studies of specific crop regions include J. Carlyle Sitterson, *Sugar Country* (Lexington, Ky., 1953), Crandall A. Shifflett, *Patronage and Poverty in the Tobacco South: Louisa County, Virginia, 1860–1900* (Knoxville, 1982), and John S. Strickland, "Traditional Culture and Moral Economy: Social and Economic Change in the South Carolina Low Country, 1865–1910," in *The Countryside in the Age of*

Capitalist Transformation, Steven Hahn and Jonathan Prude, eds. (Chapel Hill, 1985).

Chapter 5: The Failure of Presidential Reconstruction

The most recent assessments of Andrew Johnson's Presidency may be found in Hans L. Trefousse, *Andrew Johnson* (New York, 1989), James E. Sefton, *Andrew Johnson and the Uses of Constitutional Power* (Boston, 1980), and Albert Castel, *The Presidency of Andrew Johnson* (Lawrence, Kans., 1979). Eric L. McKitrick, *Andrew Johnson and Reconstruction* (Chicago, 1960) remains indispensable for understanding Johnson's personality and policies. Brooks D. Simpson et al., eds., *Advice After Appomattox: Letters to Andrew Johnson, 1865–1866* (Knoxville, 1987) reprints letters received by Johnson from Carl Schurz and others reporting on Southern conditions.

The best general account of Presidential Reconstruction is Dan T. Carter, *When the War Was Over: The Failure of Self-Reconstruction in the South, 1865–1867* (Baton Rouge, 1985). Events in one state are chronicled in William C. Harris, *Presidential Reconstruction in Mississippi* (Baton Rouge, 1967). Michael Perman, *Reunion Without Compromise: The South and Reconstruction 1865–1868* (New York, 1973) probes white Southern attitudes. Analyses of labor and lien laws may be found in Thomas Wagstaff, "Call Your Old Master—'Master'.": Southern Political Leaders and Negro Labor During Presidential Reconstruction," *Labor History* 10 (Summer 1969): 323–45 and Harold D. Woodman, "Post–Civil War Southern Agriculture and the Law," *Agricultural History* 56 (January 1982): 215–30. For the apprenticeship issue, see Rebecca Scott, "The Battle over the Child: Child Apprenticeship and the Freedmen's Bureau in North Carolina," *Prologue* 10 (Summer 1978): 101–13.

Northern responses to Johnson's policies are considered in Edward L. Gambill, *Conservative Ordeal: Northern Democrats and Reconstruction, 1865–1868* (Ames, Iowa, 1981), George R. Woolfolk, *The Cotton Regency: The Northern Merchants and Reconstruction, 1865–1880* (New York, 1958), J. Michael Quill, *Prelude to the Radicals: The North and Reconstruction During 1865* (Washington, D.C., 1980), and Eugene H. Berwanger, *The West and Reconstruction* (Urbana, Ill., 1981). Leslie H. Fishel, Jr., "Northern Prejudice and Negro Suffrage," *Journal of Negro History* 39 (January 1954): 8–26 discusses the politics of race in the North.

Chapter 6: The Making of Radical Reconstruction

Hans L. Trefousse, *The Radical Republicans: Lincoln's Vanguard for Racial Justice* (New York, 1969) is the best history of this influential group. Harold M. Hyman, ed., *The Radical Republicans and Reconstruction 1861–1870* (Indianapolis, 1967) is a valuable collection of Radical writings and speeches.

Biographies of leading Radicals include David Donald, *Charles Sumner and the Rights of Man* (New York, 1970), Hans L. Trefousse, *Benjamin Franklin Wade: Radical Republican from Ohio* (New York, 1963), Patrick W. Riddleberger, *George Washington Julian: Radical Republican* (Indianapolis, 1966), and Robert F. Horowitz, *The Great Impeacher: A Political Biography of James M. Ashley* (Brooklyn, 1979). For Stevens, see Eric Foner, *Politics and Ideology in the Age of the Civil War* (New York, 1980). Radicals' economic views are explored in Robert P. Sharkey, *Money, Class, and Party: An Economic Study of Civil War and Reconstruction* (Baltimore, 1967 ed.). See also Stanley Coben, "Northeastern Business and Radical Reconstruction: A Re-Examination," *Mississippi Valley Historical Review* 46 (June 1959): 67–90. Charles A. Jellison, *Fessenden of Maine* (Syracuse, 1962) and Mark M. Krug, *Lyman Trumbull: Conservative Radical* (New York, 1965) are lives of prominent moderate Republicans.

W. R. Brock, *An American Crisis* (London, 1963), Michael Les Benedict, *A Compromise of Principle: Congressional Republicans and Reconstruction 1863–1869* (New York, 1974), LaWanda Cox and John H. Cox, *Politics, Principle, and Prejudice 1865–1866* (New York, 1963), and David Donald, *The Politics of Reconstruction 1863–1867* (Baton Rouge, 1965) trace the evolution of Congressional policy. On civil rights and the Fourteenth Amendment, see Robert J. Kaczorowski, *The Politics of Judicial Interpretation: The Federal Courts, Department of Justice and Civil Rights, 1866–1876* (New York, 1985), Joseph B. James, *The Framing of the Fourteenth Amendment* (Urbana, Ill., 1956), Jacobus TenBroek, *Equal Under Law* (New York, 1965), William E. Nelson, *The Fourteenth Amendment: From Political Principle to Judicial Doctrine* (Cambridge, Mass., 1988), and Michael K. Curtis, "The Fourteenth Amendment and the Bill of Rights," *Connecticut Law Review* 14 (Winter 1982): 237–306. Charles Fairman, *Reconstruction and Reunion 1864–68: Part One* (New York, 1971) exhaustively discusses legal aspects of Reconstruction, while William M. Wiecek, "The Reconstruction of Federal Judicial Power, 1863–1875," *American Journal of Legal History* 13 (October 1969): 333–59 examines the expansion of the powers of the federal courts. Ellen C. DuBois, *Feminism and Suffrage: The Emergence of an Independent Women's Movement in America, 1848–1869* (Ithaca, N.Y., 1978) explores feminists' response to the postwar amendments.

Bobby L. Lovett, "Memphis Riots: White Reactions to Blacks in Memphis, May 1865–July 1866," *Tennessee Historical Quarterly* 38 (Spring 1979): 9–33 and Gilles Vandal, *The New Orleans Riot of 1866: Anatomy of a Tragedy* (Lafayette, La., 1983) offer accounts of political violence in 1866.

Chapter 7: Blueprints for a Republican South

Grass-roots black activism in 1867 is described in Peter J. Rachleff, *Black Labor in the South: Richmond, Virginia 1865–1890* (Philadelphia, 1984) and William C. Hine, "The 1867 Charleston Streetcar Sit-Ins: A Case of Successful Black Protest," *South Carolina Historical Magazine* 77 (April 1976): 110–14. See also Manuel Gottlieb, "The Land Question in Georgia During Reconstruction," *Science and Society* 3 (Summer 1939): 356–88. Michael W. Fitzgerald, *Union League Movement: Politics and Agricultural Change in the Deep South During Reconstruction* (Baton Rouge, 1989) is the best study of the Union Leagues. Richard N. Current, *Those Terrible Carpetbaggers: A Reinterpretation* (New York, 1988) traces the careers of prominent Northern-born Southern Republican leaders. See also Otto H. Olsen, *Carpetbagger's Crusade: The Life of Albion Winegar Tourgée* (Baltimore, 1965) and Lawrence N. Powell, "The Politics of Livelihood: Carpetbaggers in the Deep South," in *Region, Race, and Reconstruction: Essays in Honor of C. Vann Woodward*, J. Morgan Kousser and James M. McPherson, eds. (New York, 1982). A number of carpetbaggers published autobiographies, the most revealing of which is A. T. Morgan, *Yazoo: or, On the Picket Line of Freedom in the South* (Washington, D.C., 1884).

On scalawags see Sarah W. Wiggins, *The Scalawag in Alabama Politics, 1865–1881* (University, Ala., 1977), Gordon B. McKinney, *Southern Mountain Republicans: 1865–1900* (Chapel Hill, 1978), Allen W. Trelease, "Who Were the Scalawags?," *Journal of Southern History* 29 (November 1963): 456–63, James A. Baggett, "Origins of Upper South Scalawag Leadership," *Civil War History* 29 (March 1983): 53–73, David H. Donald, "The Scalawag in Mississippi Reconstruction," *Journal of Southern History* 10 (November 1944): 447–60, and Warren A. Ellem, "Who Were the Mississippi Scalawags?," *Journal of Southern History* 38 (May 1972): 217–40. E. Merton Coulter, *William G. Brownlow: Fighting Parson of the Southern Highlands* (Chapel Hill, 1937), Lillian A. Pereyra, *James Lusk Alcorn: Persistent Whig* (Baton Rouge, 1966), Joseph H. Parks, *Joseph E. Brown of Georgia* (Baton Rouge, 1976), and William C. Harris, *William Woods Holden: Firebrand of North Carolina Politics* (Baton Rouge, 1988) are biographies of Southern-born Republican governors.

Richard H. Abbott, *The Republican Party and the South, 1855–1877: The First Southern Strategy* (Chapel Hill, 1986) traces Northern efforts to construct and influence a Southern Republican party. The army's role in Reconstruction is explored in James E. Sefton, *The United States Army and Reconstruction 1865–1877* (Baton Rouge, 1967), Joseph G. Dawson III, *Army Generals and Reconstruction: Louisiana, 1862–1877* (Baton Rouge, 1982), and William L. Richter, *The Army in Texas During Reconstruction 1865–1870* (College Station, Tex., 1987). On the Southern constitutional conventions, see Malcolm C. McMillan, *Constitutional Development in Alabama 1798–1901: A Study in Politics, the Negro, and Sectionalism* (Chapel Hill, 1955) and Jack B. Scroggs, "Carpetbagger Constitutional Reform in the South Atlantic States, 1867–1868," *Journal of Southern History* 27 (November 1961): 475–93. Black participation in the conventions is discussed in Joseph M. St. Hilaire, "The Negro Delegates in the Arkansas Constitutional Convention," *Arkansas Historical Quarterly* 33 (Spring 1974): 38–69 and Leonard Bernstein, "The Participation of Negro Delegates in the Constitutional Convention of 1868 in North Carolina," *Journal of Negro History* 34 (October 1949): 391–409.

On Johnson's impeachment, see Hans L. Trefousse, *Impeachment of a President: Andrew Johnson, the Blacks, and Reconstruction* (Knoxville, 1975) and Michael Les Benedict, *The Impeachment and Trial of Andrew Johnson* (New York, 1973). Martin Mantell, *Johnson, Grant, and the Politics of Reconstruction* (New York, 1973) describes the election of 1868. Violence in the 1868 campaign is discussed in Lee W. Formwalt, "The Camilla Massacre of 1868: Racial Violence as Political Propaganda," *Georgia Historical Quarterly* 71 (Fall 1987): 399–426 and Melinda M. Hennessey, "Race and Violence in Reconstruction New Orleans: The 1868 Riot," *Louisiana History* 20 (Winter 1979): 77–91.

Chapter 8: Reconstruction: Political and Economic

Good introductions to Reconstruction in individual Southern states may be found in Otto H. Olsen, ed., *Reconstruction and Redemption in the South* (Baton Rouge, 1980). Among recent state studies are Jerrell H. Shofner, *Nor Is It Over Yet: Florida in the Era of Reconstruction, 1863–1877* (Gainesville, Fla., 1974), Joe Gray Taylor, *Louisiana Reconstructed, 1863–1877* (Baton Rouge, 1974), and William C. Harris, *The Day of the Carpetbagger: Republican Reconstruction in Mississippi* (Baton Rouge, 1979). There are still no modern, comprehensive histories for most of the Southern states, but see Elizabeth S. Nathans, *Losing the Peace: Georgia Republicans and Reconstruction, 1865–1871* (Baton Rouge, 1968), Richard Lowe, "Another Look at Reconstruction in Virginia," *Civil War History* 32 (March 1986): 56–76, and Carl Moneyhon, *Republicanism in Reconstruction Texas* (Austin, 1980). W. McKee Evans, *Ballots and Fence Rails: Reconstruction on the Lower Cape Fear* (Chapel Hill, 1967), William D. Henderson, *The Unredeemed City: Reconstruction in Petersburg, Virginia: 1865–1874* (Washington, D.C., 1977), Vernon Burton, "Race and Reconstruction: Edgefield County, South Carolina," *Journal of Social History* 12 (Fall 1978): 31–56, and Stephen V. Ash, *Middle Tennessee Society Transformed 1860–1870: War and Peace in the Upper South* (Baton Rouge, 1988) are valuable local studies.

Recent biographies of black Reconstruction leaders include Okon E. Uya, *From Slavery to Public Service: Robert Smalls 1839–1915* (New York, 1971), Victor Ullmann, *Martin Delany: The Beginnings of Black Nationalism* (Boston, 1971), Peggy Lamson, *The Glorious Failure: Black Congressman Robert Brown Elliott and the Reconstruction in South Carolina* (New York, 1973), James Haskins, *Pinckney Benton Stewart Pinchback* (New York, 1973), Peter

D. Klingman, *Josiah Walls* (Gainesville, Fla., 1976), Loren Schweninger, *James T. Rapier and Reconstruction* (Chicago, 1978), and Russell Duncan, *Freedom's Shore: Tunis Campbell and the Georgia Freedmen* (Athens, Ga., 1986). John R. Lynch, *Reminiscences of an Active Life: The Autobiography of John Roy Lynch*, John Hope Franklin, ed. (Chicago, 1970) is an important account by a Reconstruction black Congressman. See also two excellent collections of essays: Howard N. Rabinowitz, ed., *Southern Black Leaders of the Reconstruction Era* (Urbana, Ill., 1982) and Leon Litwack and August Meier, eds., *Black Leaders of the Nineteenth Century* (Urbana, Ill., 1988).

Among studies of black political leadership in individual states are Merline Pitrie, *Through Many Dangers, Toils and Snares: The Black Leadership of Texas 1868–1900* (Austin, 1985), Buford Satcher, *Blacks in Mississippi Politics 1865–1900* (Washington, D.C., 1978), Edmund L. Drago, *Black Politicians and Reconstruction in Georgia* (Baton Rouge, 1982), Charles Vincent, *Black Legislators in Louisiana During Reconstruction* (Baton Rouge, 1976), Elizabeth Balanoff, "Negro Leaders in the North Carolina General Assembly, July, 1868–February, 1872," *North Carolina Historical Review* 49 (Winter 1972): 22–55, Alwyn Barr, "Black Legislators of Reconstruction Texas," *Civil War History* 32 (December 1986): 340–52, David C. Rankin, "The Origins of Black Leadership in New Orleans During Reconstruction," *Journal of Southern History* 40 (August 1974): 417–40, Thomas Holt, *Black Over White: Negro Political Leadership in South Carolina During Reconstruction* (Urbana, Ill., 1977), and William C. Hine, "Black Politicians in Reconstruction Charleston, South Carolina: A Collective Study," *Journal of Southern History* 49 (November 1983): 555–84.

Works that concentrate on the black experience in individual states during Reconstruction include Joe M. Richardson, *The Negro in the Reconstruction of Florida, 1865–1877* (Tallahassee, 1965), Vernon L. Wharton, *The Negro in Mississippi 1865–1900* (Chapel Hill, 1947), Joel Williamson, *After Slavery: The Negro in South Carolina During Reconstruction, 1861–1877* (Chapel Hill, 1965), Alrutheus A. Taylor, *The Negro in Tennessee, 1865–1880* (Washington, D.C., 1941), and James W. Smallwood, *Time of Hope, Time of Despair: Black Texans During Reconstruction* (Port Washington, N.Y., 1981). On race relations, see Howard N. Rabinowitz, *Race Relations in the Urban South 1865–1890* (New York, 1978) and Roger A. Fischer, *The Segregation Struggle in Louisiana 1862–77* (Urbana, Ill., 1974). Aspects of Southern Republican social and economic policy are examined in Suzanne Lebsock, "Radical Reconstruction and the Property Rights of Southern Women," *Journal of Southern History* 43 (May 1977): 195–216, Carol R. Bleser, *The Promised Land: The History of the South Carolina Land Commission, 1869–1890* (Columbia, S.C., 1969), and Mark W. Summers, *Railroads, Reconstruction, and the Gospel of Prosperity: Aid Under the Radical Republicans, 1865–1877* (Princeton, 1984).

In addition to works cited above for Chapter 4, studies of the South's economic reconstruction include Barbara J. Fields, *Slavery and Freedom on the Middle Ground: Maryland During the Nineteenth Century* (New Haven, 1985), Jonathan M. Wiener, *Social Origins of the New South: Alabama 1860–1885* (Baton Rouge, 1978), Dwight B. Billings, Jr., *Planters and the Making of a "New South": Class, Politics, and Development in North Carolina, 1865–1900* (Chapel Hill, 1979), David L. Carlton, *Mill and Town in South Carolina, 1880–1920* (Baton Rouge, 1982), Lacy K. Ford, "Rednecks and Merchants: Economic Development and Social Tensions in the South Carolina Upcountry, 1865–1900," *Journal of American History* 71 (September 1984): 294–318, and James M. Clifton, "Twilight Comes to the Rice Kingdom: Postbellum Rice Culture on the South Atlantic Coast," *Georgia Historical Quarterly* 62 (Summer 1978): 146–54.

Chapter 9: The Challenge of Enforcement

Michael Perman, *The Road to Redemption: Southern Politics, 1869–1879* (Chapel Hill, 1984) traces the process by which Democrats regained control of Southern governments. For the "first Redemption" of 1869–71, see Jack P. Maddex, Jr., *The Virginia Conservatives 1867–1879* (Chapel Hill, 1970), Thomas B. Alexander, *Political Reconstruction in Tennessee* (Nashville, 1950), and Norma L. Peterson, *Freedom and Franchise: The Political Career of B. Gratz Brown* (Columbia, Mo., 1965).

The most comprehensive history of the Ku Klux Klan is Allen W. Trelease, *White Terror: The Ku Klux Klan Conspiracy and Southern Reconstruction* (New York, 1971). See also George C. Rable, *But There Was No Peace: The Role of Violence in the Politics of Reconstruction* (Athens, Ga., 1984). There is a wealth of firsthand testimony not simply about violence, but about every aspect of life during Reconstruction, in the hearings conducted by the Joint Congressional Committee that investigated the Klan; these are published as 42d Cong., 2d Sess., House Report 22. For specific instances of violence, see Melinda M. Hennessey, "Political Terrorism in the Black Belt: The Eutaw Riot," *Alabama Review* 33 (January 1980): 35–48, Gene L. Howard, *Death at Cross Plains: An Alabama Reconstruction Tragedy* (University, Ala., 1984), and J. C. A. Stagg, "The Problem of Klan Violence: The South Carolina Up-Country, 1868–1871," *Journal of American Studies* 8 (December 1974): 303–18. One state's effort to suppress violence is recounted in Ann P. Baenziger, "The Texas State Police During Reconstruction: A Reexamination," *Southwestern Historical Quarterly* 72 (April 1969): 470–91.

William S. McFeely, *Grant: A Biography* (New York, 1981) is the best life of the eighteenth President. William Gillette, *The Right to Vote* (Baltimore, 1969 ed.) examines the enactment of the Fifteenth Amendment. The role of Southern Republicans in national party affairs is discussed in Terry L. Seip, *The South Returns to Congress: Men, Economic Measures, and Intersectional Relationships, 1868–1879* (Baton Rouge, 1983). For the federal government's campaign against the Klan, see William S. McFeely, "Amos T. Akerman: The Lawyer and Racial Justice," in Kousser and McPherson, eds., *Region, Race, and Reconstruction,* and Ross A. Webb, "Benjamin H. Bristow: Civil Rights Champion, 1866–1872," *Civil War History* 15 (March 1969): 39–53.

Chapter 10: The Reconstruction of the North

Eric Hobsbawm, *The Age of Capital 1848–1875* (London, 1975) places the North's economic growth in an international context. A still useful general account of postwar economic change is Allan Nevins, *The Emergence of Modern America 1865–1878* (New York, 1927), while Alan Trachtenberg, *The Incorporation of America: Culture and Society in the Gilded Age* (New York, 1982) is a valuable modern survey. Alfred D. Chandler, *The Visible Hand: The Managerial Revolution in American Business* (Cambridge, Mass., 1977) explores the transformation of business management. The impact of business on Northern and national politics is revealed in Russell R. Elliott, *Servant of Power: A Political Biography of Senator William M. Stewart* (Reno, 1983) and Margaret S. Thompson, *The "Spider Web": Congress and Lobbying in the Age of Grant* (Ithaca, N.Y., 1985). Morton Keller, *Affairs of State: Public Life in Late Nineteenth Century America* (Cambridge, Mass., 1977) provides a comprehensive account of political change in these years, while C. K. Yearley, *The Money Machines: The Breakdown and Reform of Government and Party Finance in the North, 1860–1920* (Albany, 1970) suggests some of the problems of the new party politics.

James C. Mohr, ed. *Radical Republicans in the North: State Politics During Reconstruction* (Baltimore, 1976) examines political developments in several Northern states. Mohr's *The Radical Republicans and Reform in New York During Reconstruction* (Ithaca, N.Y., 1973) discusses one program of state-sponsored social change. For changes in Northern black life, see Emma L. Thornbrough, *The Negro in Indiana Before 1900* (Indianapolis, 1957), David A. Gerber, *Black Ohio and the Color Line 1860–1915* (Urbana, Ill., 1976), and Leslie H. Fishel, Jr., "Repercussions of Reconstruction: The Northern Negro, 1870–1883," *Civil War History* 14 (December 1968): 325–45. Phyllis F. Field, *The Politics of Race in New York: The Struggle for Black Suffrage in the Civil War Era* (Ithaca, N.Y., 1982) and Lawrence Grossman, *The Democratic Party and the Negro: Northern and National Politics 1868–92* (Urbana, Ill., 1976) examine the decline of racism as an explicit facet of party politics.

Steven M. Buechler, *The Transformation of the Woman Suffrage Movement: The Case of Illinois, 1850–1920* (New Brunswick, N.J., 1986) examines the evolution of the Northern women's movement. Other demands for state-sponsored social change are discussed in George H. Miller, *Railroads and the Granger Laws* (Madison, Wis., 1971) and Irwin Unger, *The Greenback Era: A Social and Political History of American Finance 1865–1879* (Princeton, 1964). For the labor movement, see David Montgomery, *Beyond Equality: Labor and the Radical Republicans 1862–1872* (New York, 1967) and Philip S. Foner, *Organized Labor and the Black Worker 1619–1973* (New York, 1974).

Studies of politics in individual Northern states include Frank B. Evans, *Pennsylvania Politics, 1872–1877: A Study in Political Leadership* (Harrisburg, Pa., 1966) and Dale Baum, *The Civil War Party System: The Case of Massachusetts, 1848–1876* (Chapel Hill, 1984), while lives of significant political leaders are recounted in David M. Jordan, *Roscoe Conkling of New York* (Ithaca, N.Y., 1971), Erwin S. Bradley, *Simon Cameron: Lincoln's Secretary of War* (Philadelphia, 1966), Leon B. Richardson, *William E. Chandler, Republican* (New York, 1940), and Allan Peskin, *Garfield* (Kent, Ohio, 1978). For the Liberal revolt, see John G. Sproat, *"The Best Men": Liberal Reformers in the Gilded Age* (New York, 1986), Ari Hoogenboom, *Outlawing the Spoils: A History of the Civil Service Reform Movement 1865–1883* (Urbana, Ill., 1961), and Joseph Logsdon, *Horace White: Nineteenth Century Liberal* (Westport, Conn., 1971). Hans L. Trefousse, *Ben Butler: The South Called Him BEAST!* (New York, 1957) is a life of the Liberals' bête noire.

Chapter 11: **The Politics of Depression**

The impact of the economic depression may be gauged from Samuel Rezneck, "Distress, Relief, and Discontent in the United States During the Depression of 1873–1878," *Journal of Political Economy* 58 (December 1950): 494–512, Samuel Bernstein, "American Labor in the Long Depression, 1873–1878," *Science and Society* 20 (Winter 1956): 60–82, and Herbert G. Gutman, "The Failure of the Movement by the Unemployed for Public Works in 1873," *Political Science Quarterly* 80 (June 1965): 254–76. Political responses are examined in Walter T. K. Nugent, *Money and American Society 1865–1880* (New York, 1968) and Richard Schneirov, "Class Conflict, Municipal Politics, and Governmental Reform in Gilded Age Chicago," in *German Workers in Industrial Chicago, 1850–1910: A Comparative Perspective*, Hartmut Keil and John B. Jentz, eds. (DeKalb, Ill., 1983).

William Gillette, *Retreat from Reconstruction 1869–1879* (Baton Rouge, 1979) traces the Grant administration's abandonment of Southern Republicans. For growing Northern disenchantment with Reconstruction, see also Robert S. Durden, *James Shepherd Pike: Republicanism and the American Negro, 1850–1882* (Durham, 1957). One particularly reprehensible episode in the retreat is related in Carl R. Osthaus, *Freedmen, Philanthropy, and*

Fraud: A History of the Freedman's Savings Bank (Urbana, Ill., 1976). For the Civil Rights Act of 1875, see S. G. F. Spackman, "American Federalism and the Civil Rights Act of 1875," *Journal of American Studies* 10 (December 1976): 313–28 and John Hope Franklin, "The Enforcement of the Civil Rights Act of 1875," *Prologue* 6 (Winter 1974): 225–35. Blanche B. Ames, ed., *Chronicles from the Nineteenth Century: Family Letters of Blanche Butler and Adelbert Ames*, 2 vols. (Clinton, Mass., 1957) contains graphic descriptions of the violent Mississippi election of 1875. See also Herbert Aptheker, "Mississippi Reconstruction and the Negro Leader, Charles Caldwell," *Science and Society* 11 (Fall 1947): 340–71.

Chapter 12: Redemption and After

Keith I. Polakoff, *The Politics of Inertia: The Election of 1876 and the End of Reconstruction* (Baton Rouge, 1973) is the best account of the Hayes-Tilden election. Works on the electoral controversy include Allan Nevins, *Abram S. Hewitt, With Some Account of Peter Cooper* (New York, 1935), C. Vann Woodward, *Reunion and Reaction: The Compromise of 1877 and the End of Reconstruction* (Garden City, N.Y., 1956 ed.), George C. Rable, "Southern Interests and the Election of 1876: A Reappraisal," *Civil War History* 26 (December 1980): 347–61, and Michael Les Benedict, "Southern Democrats in the Crisis of 1876–1877: A Reconsideration of *Reunion and Reaction*," *Journal of Southern History* 46 (November 1980): 489–524. For the railroad strike of 1877, see Philip S. Foner, *The Great Labor Uprising of 1877* (New York, 1977) and Robert V. Bruce, *1877: Year of Violence* (Indianapolis, 1959).

C. Vann Woodward, *Origins of the New South, 1877–1913* (Baton Rouge, 1951) remains the starting point for understanding the post-Reconstruction South, although some of its conclusions are challenged in J. Morgan Kousser, *The Shaping of Southern Politics* (New Haven, 1974). Studies of individual states include Allen J. Going, *Bourbon Democracy in Alabama 1874–1890* (University, Ala., 1951), George B. Tindall, *South Carolina Negroes 1887–1900* (Columbia, S.C., 1952), William Ivy Hair, *Bourbonism and Agrarian Protest: Louisiana Politics 1877–1900* (Baton Rouge, 1969), Paul D. Escott, *Many Excellent People: Power and Privilege in North Carolina, 1850–1900* (Chapel Hill, 1985), and Frenise A. Logan, *The Negro in North Carolina 1876–1894* (Chapel Hill, 1964). Charles L. Flynn, Jr., *White Land, Black Labor: Caste and Class in Late Nineteenth-Century Georgia* (Baton Rouge, 1983) focuses on one state's efforts to control labor, while Stanley B. Greenberg, *Race and State in Capitalist Development: Comparative Perspectives* (New Haven, 1980) and John W. Cell, *The Highest Stage of White Supremacy: The Origins of Segregation in South Africa and the American South* (New York, 1982) are suggestive comparative analyses of race and labor relations. Nell I. Painter, *Exodusters* (New

York, 1976) and Robert G. Athearn, *In Search of Canaan: Black Migration to Kansas, 1879–80* (Lawrence, Kans., 1978) explore the Kansas "Exodus." Vincent P. DeSantis, *Republicans Face the Southern Question* (Baltimore, 1959) traces the party's search for a post-Reconstruction Southern policy.

The enduring memory of Reconstruction among Southern blacks is explored in Mark D. Naison, "Black Agrarian Radicalism in the Great Depression: The Threads of a Lost Tradition," *Journal of Ethnic Studies* 1 (Fall 1973): 47–65. Theodore Rosengarten, *All God's Dangers: The Life of Nate Shaw* (New York, 1974) suggests some of the consequences of Reconstruction's failure.

Index

BOOKS BY ERIC FONER

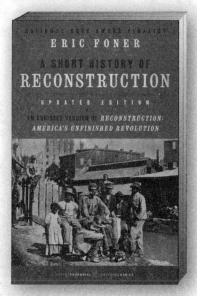

A SHORT HISTORY OF RECONSTRUCTION
Updated Edition

Available in Paperback and eBook

From the "preeminent historian of Reconstruction" (*New York Times Book Review*), comes a newly updated abridged edition of the prize-winning classic work on the post-Civil War period which shaped modern America.

"[A] smart book of enormous strengths."
—*Boston Globe*

"Foner's book traces in rich detail the bitter course of the history of the South's failure to adjust to the revolution that brought the Civil War. Only by tracing that history and understanding can the region fully disenthrall itself even today."
—*Atlanta Constitution*

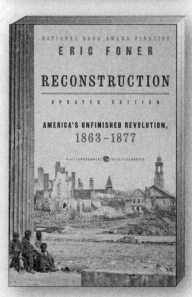

RECONSTRUCTION
America's Unfinished Revolution, 1863–1877
Updated Edition

Available in Paperback and eBook

Eric Foner's "masterful treatment of one of the most complex periods of American history" (*New Republic*) redefined how the post-Civil War period was viewed. *Reconstruction* chronicles the way in which Americans—black and white—responded to the unprecedented changes unleashed by the war and the end of slavery. It addresses the ways in which the emancipated slaves' quest for economic autonomy and equal citizenship shaped the political agenda of Reconstruction; the remodeling of Southern society and the place of planters, merchants, and small farmers within it; the evolution of racial attitudes and patterns of race relations; and the emergence of a national state possessing vastly expanded authority and committed, for a time, to the principle of equal rights for all Americans.